Pension Reform in Six Countries

What Can We Learn From Each Other?

Springer
Berlin
Heidelberg
New York
Barcelona
Hong Kong
London
Milan
Paris
Singapore
Tokyo

Axel H. Börsch-Supan
Meinhard Miegel
Editors

Pension Reform in Six Countries

What Can We Learn From Each Other?

With 36 Figures
and 35 Tables

Springer

Prof. Axel H. Börsch-Supan
University of Mannheim
Department of Macroeconomics
and Public Policy
Schloß L 9, 7
68163 Mannheim
Germany

Meinhard Miegel
Director of the Institute of
Economics und Society in Bonn
Ahrstraße 45
53175 Bonn
Germany

This publication is supported by
Deutsches Institut für Altersvorsorge (DIA)

ISBN 3-540-41714-1 Springer-Verlag Berlin Heidelberg
New York

Library of Congress Cataloging-in-Publication Data applied for
Die Deutsche Bibliothek – CIP-Einheitsaufnahme
Pension Reform in Six Countries: What Can We Learn From Each Other?; with 35 tables / Axel H. Börsch-Supan; Meinhard Miegel ed. – Berlin; Heidelberg; New York; Barcelona; Hong Kong; London; Milan; Paris; Singapore; Tokyo: Springer, 2001
ISBN 3-540-41714-1

Springer-Verlag Berlin Heidelberg New York
a member of BertelsmannSpringer Science+Business Media GmbH
http://www.springer.de

Printed in Germany

Cover-Design: Erich Kirchner, Heidelberg

SPIN 10799130 42/2202-5 4 3 2 1 0 – Printed on acid-free paper

Editors' Preface

Axel Börsch-Supan and Meinhard Miegel

The provision of retirement income is a dynamic system that needs to be adapted constantly to the ever changing economic and societal environment. Sometimes, incremental adaptations suffice; sometimes, however, larger reform steps are necessary. We see this evolutionary process both through history and across countries. Over and again societies are confronted with new challenges, not the least with respect to old age social security.

At this juncture of history, almost all industrialized countries face rapid population aging and need to adapt their pension systems to this historically unprecedented demographic change. The six countries in this study (Chile, Germany, Great Britain, the Netherlands, Switzerland, and the United States) have responded very differently to this new challenge. This is the point of departure for this book. Why did the countries respond so differently? What can we learn from each other?

It is not the point of this book to provide a universally optimal solution to the pension problems caused by population aging. The six countries are simply too different in terms of their demographic and cultural, and in particular in terms of their historical and economic backgrounds. However, since national discussions tend to be surprisingly narrowly focussed even in times of globalization, there is much to learn by looking over the neighbor's fence. And since some countries have reformed earlier than others, we even have the benefit of quite a few trials and errors in one country from which all other countries can learn.

The book is based on a German study that has been initiated by the German Institute on Old-Age Provision in Cologne (Deutsches Institut für Altersvorsorge, DIA, Köln). We are grateful for the generous financial support. DIA also published an edited and much abbreviated German translation of these country studies. Stefanie Wahl and Martina Börsch-Supan have edited earlier versions of the studies, and Stefanie Wahl has assisted this project at all stages. Melanie Lührmann has supervised the compilation of this English version, and Tom Kühner prepared the final manuscript. We owe them many thanks.

Axel Börsch-Supan, Meinhard Miegel

About the editors:

Axel Börsch-Supan is Professor for Macroeconomics and Public Policy at the Universitity of Mannheim, Director of the Institute of Economics and Statistics, and member of the Council of Advisors to the German Ministry of Economics and Technology.

Meinhard Miegel is Director of the Institute of Economics and Society in Bonn and was a member of the Commission for Pension Reform at the German Ministry of Labor and Social Affairs.

About the authors:

Lans Bovenberg and Lex Meijdam are Professors of Economics at Tilburg University. Lans Bovenberg was until 1998 Scientific Director of the Dutch Central Planning Bureau and Advisor of the Dutch government for tax, pension and labor market policy.

David Wise is Professor of Economics at the J.F.Kennedy School of Government of Harvard University and Director of the research area "Health and Retirement" at the National Bureau of Economic Research.

Klaus Schmidt-Hebbel is Senior Research Economist at the National Bank of Chile. He was Senior Researcher at the World Bank responsible for pension systems and their macroeconomik implications.

Richard Disney is Professor of Economics at the University of Nottingham, one of the Scientific Directors of the Institute for Fiscal Policy in London, and advisor of the Blair goverment for pension policy.

Maria Verena Brombacher-Steiner is Deputy at the Swiss Federal Ministry for Social Affairs responsible for pensions and international social security treaties.

Table of Contents

Six Countries–And No Pension System Alike

by Axel Börsch–Supan

Introduction to, and Synopsis of, a Comparison of Old Age Income Provision in Chile, Germany, Great Britain, the Netherlands, Switzerland and the United States

In most industrialized countries, people have become used to public old–age pension schemes as part of their social safety net, and there is a tendency to believe that there could hardly be another system of providing for the needs of the aged beyond our current tried and true one. All the more surprising, then, is a look over the fence at our neighbors. Even within the ever more closely connected countries in the European Union, a plethora of quite varied old–age pension systems coexist. Not only in the modalities of pension calculation and the collection of contributions, not just in the generosity of pension payments, but even basic conceptions of the role of the state compared with that of the individual in providing for the citizen's financial needs in old age differ among the systems of immediate neighbors. Examples are almost pure pay–as–you–go systems in France, Germany and Italy, but to a great extent funded systems in Great Britain, the Netherlands, and Switzerland. While Germany has an insurance–oriented approach, the first pillars in the Netherlands and Switzerland's provide largely flat pensions.

The purpose of this overview chapter is to compile these differences, explicate their consequences for the provision of income after retirement, and demonstrate that, as so often is the case, there is more than one way to meet a goal – in this case a stable and sufficient provision of income for the retired. Judging from one country, much in the current reform discussion is viewed as exotic, risky or even impossible – only to be standard practice in other countries. Conversely, many suggestions which seem to be quite original and new in one country are in actual fact simply re–inventions of a wheel that is long running in another country. Alongside to this main purpose, this introductory chapter will also hope in passing to explain a few of the central principles which recur in the six national studies and play an important part in the pension debate.

We proceed on an exemplary, not an inclusive basis, and investigate six countries. We start from Germany, the home country of the editors, and two immediate neighbors, the Netherlands and Switzerland. In these neighboring countries, the

old–age pension systems have long been in existence but are fundamentally different from that of Germany. Britain, the fourth country, is an example of another European country which has not shied away from experimenting with options for reform. We can learn much from their successes, but also, from their hopefully avoidable mistakes.
Two more distant countries, the United States and Chile, also serve as models forattempts at reform. To the surprise of many a reader, the United States has a public pension system quite similar in many ways to that of Germany. However, it has already been more reformed than the German system – which is rather ironic, as the problem of an aging population is much less dramatic in the United States than it is here in Germany. The far–reaching suggestions for reform currently being discussed should be instructive and idea producing for Germany as well. Chile is an exception, as no other country has so radically altered its public pension system until recently. This makes it an especially instructive experiment, particularly as it has been running for nearly 20 years now and sufficient long–term results are available to the researcher.

Before we go *medias in res*, let it be noted that all international comparisons have their limits because history and culture has put marks that cannot easily be ignored although much of this background is hard to capture particularly in quantifiable statistics. This is particularly so in the case of Chile, which cannot of course be compared directly with the European countries and the United States, as Chile is in a different stage of its economic development with completely different challenges by, and opportunities for, economic growth. The purpose of the comparative studies in this volume is in no way to find among these six countries an ideal model to be copied by all others; rather, we wish to understand which elements have resonated with the populace and which have not, and to what extent the many different elements in these countries' systems can be combined into a better one.

The six country studies are strictly organized according to the same template. Each has the same four sections, as does the following overview. Sections 1 provide a historically oriented introduction; Sections 2 provide an overview of the respective system; Sections 3 discuss how well the current pension system can meet the challenges of the future, and finally Sections 4 compile the most important proposals for pension reform in each country.

The Historical Development of Social Security Systems

In late 19th–century, Germany was a precursor with Bismarck's social laws. Britain, the Netherlands and Switzerland followed between 1911 and 1919. In the United States, a formal system of public old–age provision was first introduced in

1935 as part of F. D. Roosevelt's "New Deal", later, incidentally, than in Chile. All of these systems were extensively broadened during the 1960s and 70s. In the 1980s came the sobering up when the threatened explosion of expenditures became generally recognized. Social Security reforms followed, and are still subject of the political debate. Interestingly, and worthy of consideration, is the fact that Chile, Great Britain, the Netherlands, Switzerland, and the United States made earlier and more permanent attempts at reform than Germany, despite the fact that the German system is most immediately threatened by future demographic developments.

The Three Pillars: System Parameters, Interactions with the Social Safety Net, and Public Acceptance

The second sections in each country study describes the system of public and private old–age provision within the framework of the three pillar scheme. This three pillar scheme constantly gives rise to misunderstandings, as it is interpreted differently in the various countries. The most well–known definition comes from "Averting the Old–Age Crisis" (The World Bank, 1994). The World Bank defined the first pillar as the basic flat state insurance scheme. The second pillar is an earnings–related defined benefit plan which supplements the first pillar and is mandatory. This second pillar comprises public, individual and/or employer–based pension plans. The third pillar is defined by its voluntary nature. Again, these plans can be administered by the company or the individual household, and, at least in theory, also by the state.

In Germany, one has become accustomed to understanding the first pillar as the public so–called retirement insurance, while the second pillar consists of company–based pension plans and the third pillar of individual measures to provide for old–age, mainly life insurance and other forms of private saving.

In the Dutch system of old–age provision the two definitions are largely synonymous, but the case of Britain shows especially clearly how far apart they can be. (See Table 1.)

Table 1. The Three Pillars

	Germany	Netherlands	Switzerland	Great Britain	United States	Chile
First Pillar	Public Retirement Insurance (GRV)	Public base pension (AOW)	Public base pension (AHV/IV)	Public base pension (Part of NI)	Social Security	Public minimum pension
Second Pillar	Firm pensions (mostly reserve accounts)	Employer-related pensions (mostly DB-plans)	Employer-related pensions (BVG)	Public earnings-related scheme (SERPS"); Firm pensions; Private pensions; Stakeholder pensions	Firm pensions (DB- and DC-plans; 401(k)-plans)	Pension Funds (AFP)
Third Pillar	Own savings (mainly whole life insurance), other income.	Own savings (mainly pension funds and whole life insurance), other income.	Own savings (mainly whole life insurance and pension funds), other income.	Own savings (mainly pension funds, supplements to firm pensions), other income.	Own savings (mainly IRA- und Keogh), other income.	Own savings (mainly pension funds, supplements to firm pensions), other income.

The institutions in each pillar vary widely. This is especially the case for Britain. For this reason, a glossary and table of abbreviations in which the various institutions are briefly described is included at the end of this volume. Two dimensions of difference are especially important: Firstly, the method of financing, namely pay–as–you–go (PAYG) versus and fully funded; secondly, the form of contract, namely defined contributions (DC) versus defined benefits (DB).

As Table 1 shows, these two dimensions recur throughout all three pillars. In the first pillar, PAYG financing with DB–plans dominates (e.g., the German public retirement insurance, in which benefits are largely anchored to net wages, and contributions were adapted accordingly). The third pillar is characterized principally through fully–funded DC–plans (e.g., pension savings plans or whole life insurance) with premia paid in fixed monthly installments. Benefits then depend on contributions and the rate of return which could change in the future.

The relative size of the three pillars differs widely among the six nations under consideration. In Germany, the first pillar dominates and almost completely displaces the other two. In Britain, Switzerland and especially the Netherlands, the second pillar has a central importance. The third pillar is especially important in the USA. Besides the popularity of individual retirement accounts (IRAs) and similar instruments, this is largely due to income from work because the employment rate among people aged 65–69 is much higher in the US than in the European countries (Gruber and Wise, 1999).

Table 2. Share of Income from each Pillar (in %)

	Germany	Netherlands	Switzerland	Great Britain	United States
First Pillar	85%	50%	42%	65%	45%
Second Pillar	5%	40%	32%	25%	13%
Third Pillar	10%	10%	26%	10%	42% (of which 25% is earnings)

Note: Combined income from a two–person retiree household.

Source: Compiled from six country studies, Gruber and Wise (1999) and OECD (1998).

In spite of the differences visible in Table 2, Table 3 shows an astounding similarity in the overall replacement rates. If one adds up the payments from each of the three pillars, we find that households just after retirement receive approximately 85% of the income they enjoyed shortly before retirement. This replacement rate is nearly identical in Germany, the Netherlands, Switzerland and the United States; although it is lower in Great Britain.

Table 3. Replacement Rate of the Retirement Income

Germany	Netherlands	Great Britain	United States	Switzerland
85%	86%	72%	85%	80%

Note: Available household income of two–person retiree households between the ages of 65–69 divided by the available household income of two–person households aged 53–57.

Source: Compiled from the six national studies and from OECD (1998).

This finding suggests a strong substitution among the three pillars, that is, for a strong adaptation of the private individual and employer–based old–age provision to the public pension system. To what extent this adaptation works through microeconomic processes (i.e. the freedom of choice of the individual employee and/or employer), or on long–term institutional changes on a macroeconomic level, is described in detail in the country chapters. Of particular importance is the displacement effect of public pension systems on private savings.

Econometric studies based on time–series in Germany, the Netherlands and the USA confirm the impression given by Table 3 and show that the PAYG pension systems have in fact reduced the necessity for private savings, and thus the total stock of capital (with corresponding macroeconomic effects on growth) but the evidence needs more and longer–term studies to be fully convincing.

Along with these general and macroeconomic characteristics, the second sections of the six country studies also provide detailed descriptions of the most important system parameters of the public and employer–based old–age pension systems such as contribution rates and thresholds, replacement rates and pension levels, retirement ages and opportunities for taking early retirement.

With regards to contribution rates it bears noting that international comparisons are often misleading in this point. This is because the financing of the old age pension system varies from country to country, depending in varying degrees on contributions expressly devoted to the public pension system and on general tax revenues. A comparison between Germany and its immediate neighbors, Switzerland and the Netherlands, is instructive, as Table 4 shows.

Table 4. Contribution Rates (in % of Gross Earnings), 1999.

	Germany	Netherlands	Switzerland
Contributions to state pension insurance	19,5%	17,95%	9.8%
Taxes to finance the state pension insurance	8,2%	-	ca. 2.5%
Mandatory contributions to private pension funds	-	ca. 6%	9–10%
Total	27,7%	ca. 24%	ca. 22%

Source: Compiled from the country studies. Base year: 1999.

One discovers that, in Germany, the total contribution rate (almost 28% of gross earnings) is considerably higher than the direct contribution rate to the public pension system (19,5%) because another more than 8% of gross income is levied indirectly through general taxation. German employees pay especially high contribution rates despite receiving the same pension levels as their Dutch colleagues, see Table 3.

In examining Table 3, a further clarification of the term "replacement rate" is helpful. The concept of replacement rate is in some countries, notably Germany, understood as the relation between the pension income of current retirees and labor income of those currently employed. This is, thus, a comparison of the incomes of two different generations. We will call this "pension level" in a connotation to the German expression. The "replacement rate" in an economic context, by contrast, is defined as the relation of a specific person's pension income to the former labor income of the same person, usually using the income during the first year of retirement and that earned during the last year of employment. Depending on the increase of earnings with age, and on the adaptation of pensions to earnings over time, the (economic) replacement rate lies below or (less commonly) above the "pension level".

Along with the contribution rate and the level of benefits, the retirement age is the third main system parameter. In examining this, it is particularly noteworthy that employees in European countries can attain earlier retirement ages than in the United States, as the early retirement rules in Europe are especially generous and frequently present an explicit incentive to retire earlier than in an actuarial fair pension system. These incentive effects were thoroughly analyzed in the international comparisons of Gruber and Wise (1999). It will only be noted here that there is no evidence that early retirement has freed up jobs; on the contrary, a simple correlation shows that those countries with the most generous opportunities for early retirement are also those with the highest unemployment rates (see Layard, Nickell et al, 1985). While cause and effect cannot be inferred from such simple correlations, by the same toke, we do not have evidence for a causal effect from early retirement to low unemployment.

The systemic overview in the second sections of the country studies closes with an analysis of the extent to which the citizens of the six countries are satisfied with their system of old age provision. Even if survey results are taken with a grain of salt – for example, because one suspects responses may have been made to imprecise questions or merely represent general opinions not directly related to the question of old age provision – they show an astoundingly clear and unambiguous picture. The populace in Germany and the United States are most dissatisfied with their national systems, while the Swiss and the Dutch are quite content, and the British place further pension reform at the very bottom of the list of priorities for further policy actions. Thus, the two relatively large PAYG systems suffer from a shrinking popular support, while the workers in countries that have mixed PAYG-funded systems appear to me more content.

What Does the Future Hold?

The third sections of the country studies are devoted to the future developments to which the old age pension systems will need to respond. As is well known, all six countries whose old age provision is described in this study face a common problem: Their populations are aging, and they are aging especially quickly from the year 2010 on. Table 5 shows the development of the dependency ratios, the demographic parameter of most importance for the old age pension systems. The proportion of people of retirement age (here, 60 years and older) to those in their working years (20–59 years of age) climbs dramatically in all six countries:

Table 5. Population Aging: Demographic Dependency Ratios (in %)

	Germany	Switzerland	Netherlands	Great Britain	United States	Chile
1995	36,2%	33,4%	30,6%	38,0%	30,3%	18,3%
2010	46,5%	44,5%	40,3%	42,3%	34,6%	24,4%
2030	82,5%	78,3%	70,7%	62,1%	52,8%	40,9%
2050	101,7%	89,1%	85,3%	72,3%	52,9%	56,3%

Note: The population of aged 60 years and over is divided by the population aged 20 to 59.

Source: US–Bureau of the Census, International Data Base

The effects of population aging on the pay–as–you–go pension system have been the subject of much attention since the mid–1980s (OECD, 1988; The World Bank, 1994). One notices that this aging process is especially marked in Germany, particularly in comparison with the United States. According to all current demographic projections, until about the year 2040 Germany will have the highest proportion of older citizens, particularly in relation to the number of citizens of employment age. Later, about from the year 2050 on, will Japan have this dangerous distinction.

The crucial question is whether the six different systems of old–age provision are similarly well–equipped to deal with this problem – after all, despite many demographic and political differences between the countries, they present surprisingly similar pension incomes (Table 3) with roughly comparable contribution rates (Table 4).

This is not the case. In countries with a pronounced pay–as–you–go system (Germany being the main example), the expenditures financed by the contributions and taxes in Table 4 represent only expenditures for the current generation of retirees. In those countries in which a large portion of old age pensions is fully-funded, like in the Netherlands or in Switzerland, the current contributions measured in Table 4 include savings also for future pensions. In this regard, Table 4 compares apples and oranges – at least in the non–stationary case in which the relation between pensioners and contributors changes over time. However, this is precisely what population aging will do. In those countries where PAYG financing dominates, future expenditures will climb much more steeply than in those where pensions are partially funded because in the latter case savings have already been accumulated to finance the numerous members of the baby boom generation.

This brings us to the perennial discussion about the pros and cons of PAYG versus fully funded pensions. To understand why the pension reform discussion always returns to this point, it is important to keep in mind the central financing mechanism of a PAYG system. In PAYG, the contributions of those currently employed are used exclusively to finance the benefits of those currently drawing pensions. With PAYG, expenditures always equal income; neither is there a reserve built up from excess income, nor are debts incurred due to excess expenditure.

$$\text{Contributors} \times \text{Gross Earnings} \times \text{Contribution Rate} = \text{Retirees} \times \text{Pension Benefits}$$
$$\text{Receipts} = \text{Expenditures}$$

On the left hand side are the receipts of the PAYG system, where we combine direct and indirect contributions for simplicity in one contribution base (average gross income) and one resulting average contribution rate. To the right are the expenditures of the PAYG system, i.e. the average benefits per pensioner. As long as receipts equal expenditures, the contribution rate must thus be the product of the gross pension level and the dependency ratio:

$$\text{Contribution Rate} = (\text{Pensioners/Contributors}) \times (\text{Pension Benefits/Gross Earnings})$$
$$= \text{System Dependency Ratio} \times \text{Gross Pension Level}$$

In a PAYG system, the relationship between the contribution rate and the pension level can thus in no way be freely chosen by the political process; rather, it is dictated by the dependency ratio. This, in turn, has in the past been determined by two developments: by population aging, as made clear in Table 5, and by the decreasing employment rate. Particularly the decreasing retirement age has simultaneously decreased the proportion of the population that pays contributions to the PAYG system and increased the number of beneficiaries from the PAYG system, so that the system dependency ratio (pensioners by contributing workers) has risen more steeply than the demographic dependency ratio (persons aged 60+ by persons aged 20–59).

The increase in the demographic dependency ratios depicted in Table 5 therefore greatly restricts the possibilities for a political solution within the PAYG system. If one does not increase the contribution rate in proportion to the rise in the old age burden, either pension levels must drop or employment rates must increase. Both options are politically problematic. A reduction in benefits is very politically unpopular, while an increase in employment rates cannot be simply decreed. The only direct institutional lever is the raising of the retirement age, perhaps by raising the so–called "normal" retirement age and/or by restricting the various early retirement and pre–retirement rules. One cannot avoid noticing, however, that discussions in France and Germany are leading to a decrease, rather than an increase in the retirement age. Also note that raising the retirement age corresponds to paying longer and benefiting shorter, thus for all practical purposes a decrease in the value of pension benefits.

The greatly restricted possibilities for a solution within the PAYG system are also clearly expressed in the national comparisons of this study. Additional flexibility has been attained in several countries through pre–financing of pensions, i.e., by using the only mechanisms that can spread the demographic burden over a longer term. The five countries in this study demonstrate how diverse these funding mechanism can be. They range from an almost total state–regulated fully–funded system (Chile) to mixed systems, some in which the employer plays a central role (Netherlands, Switzerland) and others, in which private savings contracts have become rather important (United States).

Proposals for Pension Reform

Consequently, the fourth and last sections of the six country studies examine the reform discussions currently underway. None of the six systems of old age income provision are free of problems, but the problems differ widely.

In the United States and Germany, the main problem is the demographic burden threatening the first PAYG pillar. In the United States as in Germany, so–called "parametric" reforms (i.e. those that would entail retaining the PAYG system) are under discussion. In contrast to Germany, the official Social Security reform commission has also suggested blue prints for so–called "fundamental" reforms which would largely replace PAYG with fully–funded pensions – although without completely abandoning the PAYG pillar. The recommendations of the American pension reform commission have been simulated and thought through in great detail; thus, we will give them much attention in the American country chapter.

The problems of the other countries reflect design problem of funded pension schemes. We learn from the Dutch example that even fully–funded systems may be threatened by the aging process if they rest too firmly on the "defined benefits" principle. Pension funds without sufficient reserves may run into trouble in the case of an unexpectedly steep aging process or an unexpectedly low return on capital investments. The lesson from the Netherlands is, thus, that a stable and socially just old age pension system requires a reasonable division of risk between employees, employers and the state. Suggestions for reform of the British and Chilean systems are yet of another sort. They have to do with capital market risks and the intransparency of individually based pension systems. The experimenters in both countries had some pensioners pay a high price for their learning how to run a funded individual account system. Countries which are late in their reform efforts, notably Germany, thus have the chance to avoid mistakes of the kind these two countries made in shifting to a more fully–funded old age insurance system.

Conclusions

What do the six country studies teach us? For one, we have learned that there are a multitude of different methods to create a stable and sufficient old age insurance system. Much that has been rejected as "politically impossible" in the reformdebate of one country is everyday practice for the neighbors. By the same token, we see that pension reform discussion can take place in a somewhat more relaxed frame of mind as the sociopolitical problems are by no means unique, and we find a broad spectrum of solutions at our fingertips.

In particular, there exists a whole spectrum of mixed solutions between the PAYG and fully–funded own provisions. In this respect, the message of the third section is especially important: the higher the proportion of an old age pension system that is fully–funded, the greater the degree to which future pension expenditures have been prepaid, and thus the less expenditures will rise in future – as a matter of smoothing the burden of population aging. This author claims more – namely that funding to a certain extent also improves welfare – but this a long and subtle story and not subject of this book (Börsch–Supan, 1999). Interesting to note is that the survey respondents in those countries with about evenly shared mixed PAYG–funded pension systems express the greatest degree of satisfaction with it. Finally, an important and basic insight of this study is that no system of old age provision can exist without risks, as no young worker can predict precisely what the demographic, economic and political conditions will be at the time of his retirement in the distant future. PAYG systems have strong demographic and political risks, which are not non–existent but much smaller in funded private systems. In turn, funded systems have a large capital market risk. It is wrong to encourage the illusion that a pension system can insure completely against these risks; only a smart diversification in a mixed system can minimize the residual risks.

References

Börsch–Supan, A. (1999), "Zur deutschen Diskussion eines Übergangs vom Umlage – zum Kapitaldeckungsverfahren in der Rentenversicherung." *Finanzarchiv*. May 1999.

Gruber, J., and D. Wise (1997). eds., *Social Security and Retirement around the World,* Chicago: The University of Chicago Press.

OECD (1988). *Ageing Populations: The Social Policy Implications*, Paris: OECD.

OECD (1998). *Family Resources During Retirement,* AWP 4.3, Paris: OECD.

The World Bank (1994), *Averting the Old Age Crisis: Policies to Protect the Old and Promote Growth*, Oxford, Washington, D.C.: Oxford University Press.

1 The German Retirement Insurance System

by Axel Börsch–Supan

1.1 A Brief History of the German Public Pension System

The German public pension, or as it is called in German, “public retirement insurance”, was the first formal pension system in the world when it was installed over 100 years ago by Chancellor Bismarck. It has been very successful in providing a high and reliable level of retirement income and has become a model for many social security systems in the world. It has survived, although under severe modifications, through World Wars I and II, the Great Depression, and, more recently, the German unification.

The system started in 1889 as a disability insurance for blue collar workers, but was quickly expanded to a full–fledged retirement insurance (“Gesetzliche Rentenversicherung”, abbreviated GRV) that provided disability, retirement, and survivor benefits for essentially all workers in Germany. Main reason for its introduction was the perceived threat of social unrest by Bismarck. In a shrewd move, he preempted the social democratic movement in a large scale social security program that encompassed all branches of the modern welfare state from old age provisions and health insurance to a reform of the housing financing system. This social network was designed to encompass the entire work force and keep it from social democratic “mischief”.

From the beginning, the retirement insurance had the underlying philosophy that old age provision is a shared responsibility of workers, employers, and the state. This corporatist element is typical for German social policy. A second important element is the strong link of pensions to work. As opposed to other countries such as the United Kingdom and the Netherlands, which originally adopted a Beveridgian social security system that provided a fixed base pension for everyone, public pensions in Germany were from the start designed to extend the standard of living that was achieved during work life also to the time after retirement. Thus, people without formal work are not eligible for public pensions, while workers will receive pensions that are roughly proportional to their labor income averaged over their entire life course. Pensions are not a safety net –

however, as we will see later, means–tested social assistance benefits are particularly generous for elderly without sufficient other income sources. The few redistributive features of the German pension system are a main reason that it is called "retirement insurance" rather than "social security", the term used in the U.S.[1] Indeed, until recently, workers used to understand their contributions as "insurance premia" rather than "taxes" – although this is quickly changing as we will see later in Section 1.2. The insurance character is strengthened by institutional separation: Unlike to the U.S. Social Security Administration, the German retirement insurance system is not part of the government but a separate entity. Insurance surpluses cannot be used to decrease the government deficit like in the U.S. Three quarters of this entity's budget is financed by workers' and employers' contributions. The state has nevertheless an important role. In addition to a subsidy of the remaining quarter of the budget, the state sets the rules and determines benefits and contributions, unlike to the autonomy that is granted in many other affairs between workers and employers. Rationale for the state subsidy are non–insurance benefits such as benefits paid to German immigrants after opening the iron curtain.

The German retirement insurance started as a fully–funded system. However, during the Great Depression and after World War II, the capital stock of the retirement insurance was severely eroded. After a long and arduous debate, the German Bundestag decided in 1957 in a landmark reform to convert the system to a pay–as–you–go scheme. The remainder of the capital stock was spent down by 1967. Since then, the German system is purely pay–as–you–go with a small reserve that declined to only about 20 days of expenditures during 1997.

After 1957 and particularly in the 1970s, benefits were greatly expanded and the German system evolved to one of the most generous pension systems in the world both in terms of its replacement rate and its early retirement provisions. Most notably, the 1957 reform indexed pensions to gross wages, and the second landmark reform in 1972 introduced the opportunity to retire early without a direct adjustment of retirement benefits.

Contribution rates have been very low in the beginning, then gradually increased. There were many reasons for this increase. The system became more generous while the leftovers of the capital stock remaining after the war were exhausted; labor supply declined dramatically particularly among the elderly (from 75 percent in 1970 to 33 percent in 1995 for men aged 60–64); and unemployment started to erode the contribution base since 1980. Late in the 1980s, politicians began to realize that the increase will not stop in the foreseeable future – just the opposite, the demographic changes of population aging will add to the pressures. This precipitated the third landmark pension reform after World War II in 1992.

[1] Major redistributive features have been added in 1972 and during the last few years; this will be described below.

Indexation was changed to net wages and a schedule was introduced by which future retirees will receive lower pensions when they retire earlier than the normal retirement age, although the adjustments will remain less than actuarially fair. The 1992 reform proved insufficient to keep the contribution rate from rising. Since then, a flurry of small changes has continued. A reform attempt in 1998 intended to introduce a severe cut in future replacement rates by linking the replacement rate to the life expectancy at age 60; however, this central provision was revoked at the end of 1998 and the political fate of this reform is still uncertain.

1.2
The Pillars Providing Retirement Income in Germany

Although Germany has a three pillar retirement system – public pensions which are financed pay–as–you–go, firm pensions (most of which are funded), and own provision (savings, earnings, and family transfers) – the omnipresent social insurance system in Germany makes for a monolithic retirement income composition dominated by public pensions. Among households aged 65 and over, the income share of public pensions is about 85 percent. Public pensions were 10.3 percent of GDP in 1997, more than 2.5 times larger than in the U.S.[2] Adding other public retirement income (mostly means–tested social assistance) raises this share to 12.3 percent of GDP. Firm pensions, on the other side, are less than 1 percent of GDP in Germany and make up less than 5 percent of retirement income. Their assets have declined in recent years. Savings, earnings, and family transfers provide the remaining 10 percent of retirement income.[3] Thus, Germany has a huge first pillar while the others are much smaller than in the other countries described in this book.

Table 1.1. gives a more detailed picture for the younger elderly (aged 65–69 years). The income share of public pensions is 82 percent for single elderly, about 70 percent for married couples. This share rises with age. The share exceeds 90 percent in the lowest quintile of the income distribution. Funded asset income provides about 10 percent of retirement income and is about equally divided between firm pensions and private savings. Even in the upper quintile of the income distribution, asset income does not exceed a sixth of total income, very different from the Anglo–Saxon countries. Private transfers are important for lower income households, while earnings are still a major part of income for the married, high income elderly around 67 years.

---

[2] If civil servants are included, this share increases to almost 13% (Börsch–Supan and Schnabel, 1999).

[3] See Börsch–Supan and Reil–Held, 1998.

Table 1.1. Composition of Retirement Income

	Public Pensions	Asset Income	Private Transfers	Earnings
Single	81,9%	8,8%	4,9%	4,5%
Married	70,5%	11,8%	5,7%	12,1%

Public Pensions	All	Lowest Quintile	Median	Highest Quintile
Single	81,9%	92,7%	87,1%	71,2%
Married	70,5%	90,3%	84,6%	49,1%

Asset Income	All	Lowest Quintile	Median	Highest Quintile
Single	8,8%	2,4%	5,5%	15,0%
Married	11,8%	5,7%	8,2%	18,3%

Note: Income sources as a percentage of gross income of families with a head around 67 years of age.

Source: Börsch–Supan and Reil–Held (1998) based on the OECD Data on Family Resources in Retirement.

1.2.1 Main Features of the German Public Pension System

Financing. The German retirement insurance system[4] is financed by contributions that correspond to a 19.5 percent pay roll tax, and a government subsidy of almost 30 percent that would add around 8 percent to the contribution rate if it were levied as a payroll tax. Contributions are mandatory for all dependent workers – thus, coverage exceeds 90 percent of the work force. Contributions are (technically) shared equally between workers and employers, and are levied proportionally on earnings up to DM 8500 (4400 Euro) per month. This earnings ceiling effectively provides a maximum public pension since pension benefits are essentially proportional to contributions.

Both contribution rates and subsidy have increased considerably, see Figure 1.1. In the sixties, contributions were 14 percent of gross wages. However, the state subsidy had to be increased steadily. From 1968 to 1973 the direct contribution rate was increased and the state subsidy reduced. Since 1990, the policy has been reversed. At the end of 1997, a projected increase of the contribution rate beyond 20.3 percent was only avoided by increasing the value added tax by one percentage

[4] The system has several branches, for instance, blue–collar workers, white–collar workers, and miners have separate systems. However, the rules are essentially the same (miners may retire earlier but their contribution limit is higher). Civil servants are formally excluded but in effect have their own pay–as–you–go system via the government budgets. Truly excluded are only self–employed and workers with very low earnings (below 320 Euro per month). They may voluntarily join the public system.

point in order to finance a higher government subsidy. In 1999 the contribution rate was even lowered to 19.5 percent in spite of higher expenditures. The resulting gap was financed by a new tax on gasoline which raised the state subsidy to 29.5 percent. If one would convert the taxes used to finance the subsidy to contributions, the total contribution rate would be 27.7 percent. This total contribution rate has increased steadily since 1995.

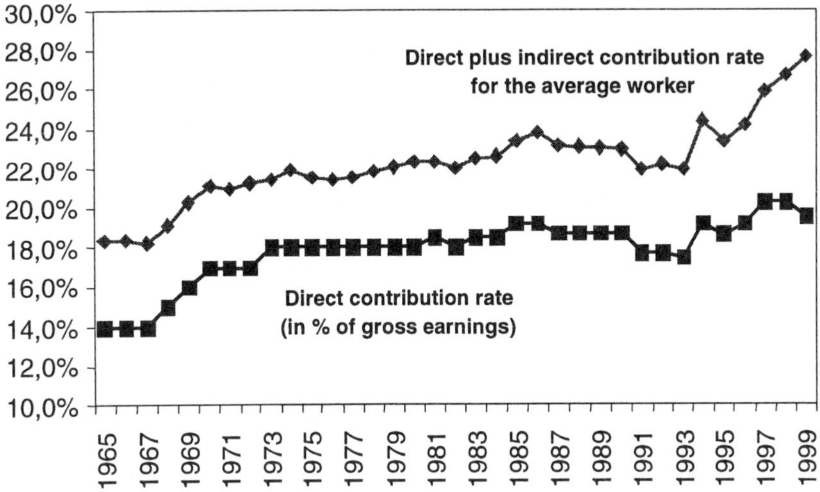

Fig. 1.1. Contribution Rates to the German Public Pension System, 1965–1999

Source: VDR

Benefit computation. Benefits are computed on a life–time contribution basis. They are the product of four elements: (1) the employee's contributions as a percentage of the average contributions, averaged over the entire earnings history, multiplied by (2) the number of years of service life (including not only years of employment, but also higher education, unemployment spells, and child raising), and (3) adjustment factors for pension type (old–age and two disability pension types) and retirement age (since the 1992 reform). These three individual elements are then multiplied by (4) the average pension level that is indexed "dynamically" (i.e., during the entire retirement period) to the current average net wage of the working population. The first three factors make up the "personal pension base" while the fourth factor determines the income distribution between workers and pensioners in general:

$$\text{Benefits} = \begin{matrix}\text{Individual}\\\text{Contribution}\\\text{Level}\end{matrix} \cdot \begin{matrix}\text{Individual}\\\text{Years of}\\\text{Service}\end{matrix} \cdot \begin{matrix}\text{Individual}\\\text{Adjustment}\\\text{Factors}\end{matrix} \cdot \begin{matrix}\text{Aggregate}\\\text{Pension}\\\text{Level}\end{matrix}$$

The relatively transparent benefit formula is one of the most helpful microeconomic features of the German retirement insurance. First, benefits and contributions are linked almost one–to–one, thus in theory avoiding the distortions (deadweight losses) that are associated with a tax–financed pension. In practice, this is not completely true because early retirement, effective minimum pension provisions, and, as we will see later, insufficient implicit rates of return generate intra– and intergenerational redistributions that give part of the contributions a tax character. An important second positive feature is to base the benefit level on the entire life earnings history. This avoids the distortions created in many pension systems by basing benefits on only a few years of recent earnings. The shorter the earnings base, the more room is given to employees and employers to engage in strategic wage setting briefly before retirement on the expense of the contribution payers, and the larger is the incentive to evade payment of contributions in early phases of work life. All this is avoided in the German system. Third, wage indexation has kept the income distribution between workers and pensioners constant as it has automatically transferred productivity gains also to pensioners. This is often seen as one of the most important reasons for social stability. In addition, it adds to the transparency of the link between contributions and benefits, because the formula leaves little room for pork–barrel politics on the one side, and the erosion of benefits through inflation on the other side. In turn, however, future productivity gains will not provide a "deus ex machina" that will generate additional income to finance the increasing pension load when population aging will set in.

Replacement rate. The German retirement insurance system has a high level of pension benefits. The after–tax pension for a current retirees who have had a 45–year earnings history and average life–time earnings is about 70 percent of average net earnings by current workers.[5] This ratio is substantially higher than in the U.S. where it is about 53 percent. The replacement rate with respect to a worker's last earnings (after–tax pension divided by net earnings immediately before retirement) is even higher and ranges from almost 97 percent in the lowest income quintile, 83.5 percent on average, to 70 percent in the top quintile. In addition, the German retirement insurance system provides generous survivor benefits that constitute a substantial proportion of total unfunded pension wealth, and disability benefits at similar and frequently even higher replacement levels than old–age pensions. As pointed out before, this high replacement rate has made public pensions by

[5] A 45 year earnings history defines the official German standard pensioner ("Eckrentner"). In fact, the average earnings history is about 38 years for a male employee.

far the largest pillar of retirement income and has made funded retirement income, such as asset income or firm pensions, largely unnecessary.

Early retirement provision. Until 1972, the German public pension system was very inflexible and permitted retirement only at age 65.[6] The only exception were disabled workers which, however, made up for roughly 50 percent of new retirement entries. We will discuss the disability provision further below. The 1972 pension reform changed this dramatically by introducing the opportunity to retire at different ages ("flexible retirement") during a "window of retirement". This window began at age 60 for women, unemployed, and workers who could not appropriately be employed for health or labor market reasons, and at age 63 for workers with a long service history (35 years, including higher education, military service, and a certain number of years for rising children). Normal retirement age was (and still is) age 65. The 1972 reform did not introduce actuarial adjustments. The 1972 pension rules were effective until very recently because the reforms in the 1990s are only slowly phasing in and will fully be in effect not until the year 2004. At that time, the window of retirement will begin for all workers at age 62 and will include an adjustment of benefits, although this adjustment will still be less than actuarially fair, see below. There is no earnings test after age 65, unlike to the U.S., but early retirees may (essentially) not work during the window of early retirement

The introduction of flexible retirement in 1972 had a huge impact on retirement age. Within a few years, retirement age among men dropped by about 3 years, see Figure 1.2., and average retirement age fell below age 60.[7] The resulting distribution of retirement ages became marked by distinct "spikes" at ages 60, 63 and 65. The retirement age of 65 now mostly applies to women with a very short earnings history, while the most popular retirement age among men became age 60. Since average life expectancy of a male worker at age 60 is about 18 years, the earlier retirement age amounts to an increase in pension expenditures of about 15 percent.

---

[6] We use "retirement" in this section to refer to the receipt of a public pension for the first time unless we also discuss labor force exit in the same context. However, there is substantial "pre-retirement" Introducing a wedge between receipt of public pension income and labor force exit.

[7] Averaged over new recipients of old–age and disability pensions. Results for women are similar.

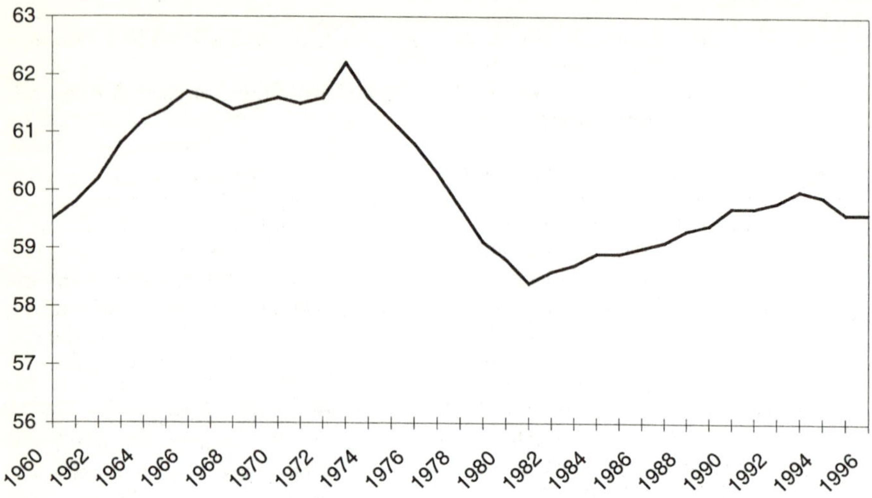

Fig. 1.2 Change in Average Retirement Age, Men, 1960–1996

Source: Börsch–Supan and Schnabel (1998), based on VDR Rentenzugangsstatistik.

Actuarial adjustments. Until the 1992 reform, there was no adjustment of benefits to retirement age.[8] Only because benefits are proportional to the years of service, a worker with fewer years of service would get about 2.5 percent lower benefits for each year of early retirement.[9] Thus, workers retiring at age 62 received 92.5 percent of the full pension for those retiring at age 65. This is much more generous than a pension that is adjusted in an actuarially fair way because such a pension would amount to only 77 percent of the full pension.[10] The 1992 reform is phasing in retirement age–specific adjustment factors. When fully enacted, they imply for retirees at age 62 a pension that is 82 percent of the full pension, still more generous than an actuarially fair pension. Table 1.2. shows a summary of pension benefits as a function of retirement age, comparing the 1972 legislation that was relevant essentially up to now with the 1992 legislation that will be fully phased in by the year 2004, and an actuarially fair adjustment system. The actual systems pay early retirees too much and late retirees too little.

---

[8] The German system before 1992 provided a large increase in retirement benefits for postponing work at ages 65 and 66. However, this incentive was ineffective because the inducements to early retirement by far offset it.

[9] For a worker with a service history of 40 years, one additional year represents 2.5%.

[10] These figures are computed at a 3% discount rate and 1992/94 male mortality rates. See Börsch–Supan, 1992.

Table 1.2. Effective Adjustment Factors to Pension for Retirement Ages 60 through 70

Retirement age	60	61	62	63	64	65	66	67	68	69	70
1972 Legislation	87,5	90,0	92,5	95,0	97,5	100	109,9	120,1	123,0	125,8	128,7
1992 Legislation	69,5	75,6	81,7	87,8	93,9	100	108,5	117,0	125,5	134,0	142,5
Actuarially Fair	66,0	71,5	77,6	84,3	91,7	100	109,2	119,6	131,2	144,4	159,4

Source: Börsch–Supan (1999b).

Note: Pension when retiring at given age in percent of pension when retiring at age 65, assuming 40 years of service. Actuarially fair pension computed at 3% discount rate and 1992/94 male mortality rates.

Because the German public pension system is not actuarially fair, the German social security system tilts the retirement decision heavily towards the earliest retirement age applicable. The system before the 1992 reform was particularly distortive in rewarding early retirement. The 1992 pension reform in Germany will diminish but by no means abolish this incentive effect. The failure to adjust benefits in an actuarially fair manner creates a loss in unfunded social security wealth when a worker postpones retirement because the shorter period during which a worker receives pension benefits is not made up by a sufficiently higher pension. This loss is large relative to the labor income that could be earned when working longer. It exceeded 50 percent of the earnings before the 1992 pension reform and will still be in excess of 20 percent when the 1992 reform will have been fully phased in. This corresponds to a huge additional tax on old–age labor.

Disability. Disability status is granted for medical reasons. In this case, no actuarial adjustments apply, even after the 1992 reform. Disability status is also given for economic reasons, for instance, when a worker could not find a job at all, or could not find an appropriate job. In the latter case, a lower replacement rate applies. Because the definition of disability in the law is vague, actual requirements have been loosened and tightened frequently, and the courts have played a major role in determining benefits.

The negative incentive effects on labor supply that we have identified for old-age pensions are even stronger if one manages to claim full disability status. In this case, implicit tax rates on work are similar to the pre–1992 regime and exceed 60 percent for workers retiring before age 60. It therefore does not surprise that disability became an important pathway to retirement, see Figure 1.3. Introduction of flexible retirement only briefly cut into disability shares. The tightening of disability eligibility from the mid 1980s on reduced the share, reaching a minimum in 1995. However, even in 1995, more workers entered retirement through the disability insurance (41%) than through old–age pensions (35%).[11]

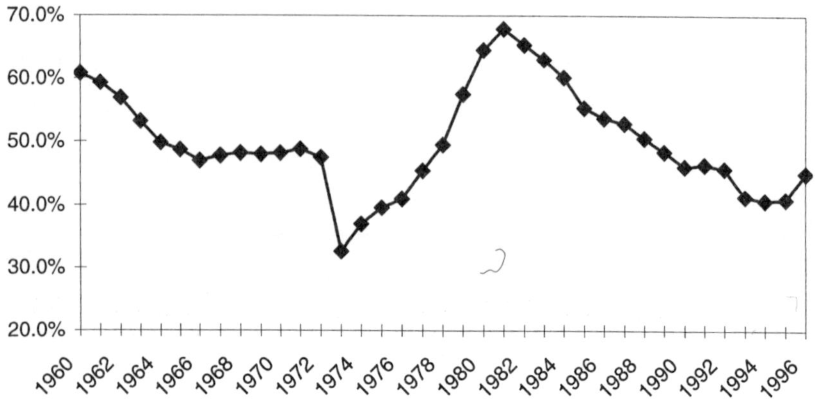

Fig. 1.3. Share of Entrants into Public Pension System that Receive Disability Benefits

Source: VDR, Rentenzugangsstatistik

Minimum retirement income. The German public pension system provides two floors for retirement income. First, contributions below a certain minimum have ex post been topped to lie between 50 and 75 percent of average contributions.[12] Although not an entitlement by the law, the Bundestag has regularly enacted such ex post adjustments to poor workers earnings histories, and has thereby effectively introduced a minimum pension. Second, means–tested social assistance provides a minimum income to which all Germans are entitled. Older households receive a higher minimum income than younger households (about 600 Euro for single elderly, 900 Euro for an elderly couple, including housing assistance).

This topping up mechanism has introduced a redistributive element along the income scale into the German retirement insurance. However, quantitatively this intragenerational redistribution is small relative to the other intragenerational redistribution through early retirement. Social assistance is quantitatively more important, and has shielded the elderly from poverty.

[11] The remaining 24% used the unemployment pathway.

[12] More precisely: in 1972 and 1992, the Bundestag established this retrospect topping up mechanism for all contributions made before 1972 and between 1973 and 1992, respectively.

Other redistributive elements are the inclusion of child raising and higher education years into the service history, and the payment of pensions to German-stock immigrants in particular after opening of the iron curtain. Their quantitative importance has been studied by Börsch–Supan and Reil–Held (1999).

1.2.2 Interaction of Public Pensions with Other Social Programs

The function of the entitlement to social assistance as a universal base income is a first example of a strong link between the public pension system and other social programs. It generates some interesting side effects in terms of fiscal federalism because social assistance is paid by the local governments while pensions are paid by the retirement insurance system. A reduction in the replacement rate of the retirement insurance therefore automatically creates an implicit transfer from local governments to the public pension system. This will become quite hurting to the local governments should the 1999 reform be enacted because it will reduce the replacement rate to a level below the social assistance threshold for all workers which have lifetime earnings below 79 percent of average lifetime earnings (assuming an earnings history of 40 years).

A second set of interactions between the public pension system and other social programs comes through the unemployment insurance. First, unemployed workers do not contribute to the retirement system; however, the unemployment insurance makes payments on their behalf. These payments are lower than what these workers had paid when they still were employed. High unemployment therefore implicitly raises the part of the budget that is financed by general taxes.[13]

In addition, the unemployment insurance system is an important mechanism that permits "pre–retirement" Figure 1.4. shows this pre–retirement (lower graph) as the difference between self–reported "out of labor force" (upper graph) and "receipt of a public pension" (middle graph). Labor force exit before age 60 is frequent: about 45 percent of all men call themselves "retired" at age 59 although they do not receive an old–age public pension. Only about half of them retire because of disability; the other 50 percent make use of one of the many official and unofficial pre–retirement schemes which mostly combine some sort of severance pay with unemployment benefits.

[13] It also raises contributions because there are fewer active contributors.

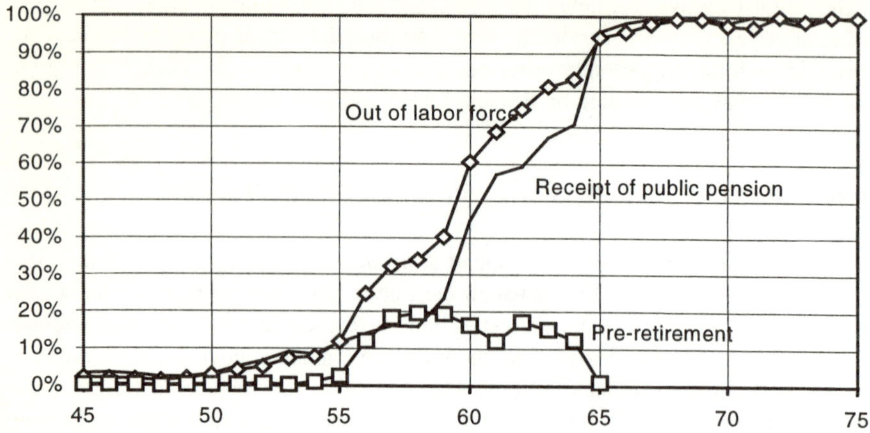

Fig 1.4. Pre–Retirement

Source: Börsch–Supan and Schnabel (1999)

These pre–retirement schemes induce very early retirement and are essentially a collusion of workers and employers on the expense of the contributors and taxpayers. According to the rules established after the 1972 reform, workers can enter the public pension system at age 60. When a firm wants to restructure and retire older workers, these workers are paid a negotiable combination of unemployment compensation and a severance pay. At age 60, they then receive a public pension. The effective retirement ages changed as frequently as the rules for pensions and the duration of unemployment benefits changed. Age 57 was particularly frequent in West Germany because unemployment compensation is paid up to 32 months for elderly workers; it is then followed by the lower unemployment aid. Earlier retirement ages could be induced by paying the worker the difference between the last salary and unemployment compensation for 32 months; and for further years the difference between the last salary and unemployment aid – it all depended on the so–called “social plan” which a firm would negotiate with the workers before restructuring the work force.

In addition, early retirement at age 58 was made possible in an official pre-retirement scheme (“Vorruhestand”), in which the employer received a subsidy from the unemployment insurance if a younger employee was hired. While the first (and unofficial) pre–retirement scheme was very popular and a convenient way to overcome the strict German labor laws, few employers used the official second scheme.

There is some interaction between the health insurance system and the pension system because retirees do not pay the full health insurance premium. However, since persons of all ages are covered by health insurance in Germany, there is not such a strong interaction in terms of retirement age and Medicare eligibility as for instance in the U.S.

1.2.3 Public Acceptance of the Current German Public Pension System

Public acceptance of the German Retirement Insurance has declined considerably. A number of formal and informal polls show particularly among younger persons a serious lack of confidence into the pension system. The results are very consistent. According to a poll by Allensbach (1996), 48 percent of all workers expect that they will experience a lower standard of living than current retirees. Emnid (1997) reports that 34 percent of the persons interviewed voiced a similar belief. More specifically, only 15 percent believed that the public pension system will provide a sufficient retirement income. Younger and better educated persons are more pessimistic than older persons and those with little education, see Table 1.3.

Table 1.3. "Do you believe that the public pension system will provide you with a retirement income that is sufficient for your standard of living?"

	All	Gender		Age			Education			
		Male	Fem.	18-29	30-39	40-50	Volks.	Lehre	MittR.	Abi-tur
"yes"	15,0	16,8	13,3	13,7	11,7	20,0	22,9	17,5	11,5	14,2
"no"	77,6	75,2	80,0	78,0	80,7	74,0	66,3	73,6	83,8	78,0
Don't know	7,3	8,0	6,7	8,3	7,6	6,0	10,8	9,0	4,7	7,9
Sample	2.195	1.075	1.119	745	747	702	152	788	770	485

Source: Emnid (1997)

A more recent broad based poll by the Wirtschaftsjunioren (1998) shows a very similar picture, see Table 1.4. Here, the question asked was "Do you have confidence in the German retirement insurance? " Less than a quarter had, and the lack of confidence was strongest among the young, female, least educated and persons living in the Eastern part of Germany.

Table 1.4. "Do you have confidence in the German retirement insurance?"

	All	Gender		Age					
	(weigh-ted)	Male	Fem.	< 18	18-29	30-39	40-49	50-59	> 64
"yes"	23,5%	20,1	12,2	9,0	5,2	9,0	16,5	35,0	57,2
"no"	64,5	71,9	75,8	58,7	82,7	84,8	74,1	56,0	35,5
Don't know	12,0	8,0	12,2	34,3	12,1	6,2	9,4	9,0	7,2
Sample	10.334	6.795	3.539	270	2.252	3.200	2.073	1.904	637

Source: Wirtschaftsjunioren (1998)

And also recently, in January 1999, after the change in the government, 68 percent believed that additional private retirement income will be necessary to maintain a reasonable standard of living, while only 13 percent thought that the public pension will suffice (Bundesverband, 1999).

1.2.4 Interaction of the Pillars

As pointed out earlier, it is somewhat asymmetric to call the German way of retirement income provision a "three pillars system". The huge public pension system (paying 85 percent of retirement income) which works pay–as–you–go completely dominates the other two funded pillars, namely firm pensions (5 percent) and private savings and other income (10 percent).

Unlike to the U.K., it is not possible for a German worker to change the absolute size of the first pillar. There is no mechanism to "opt out" unless a worker decides to become self–employed or uses other (often illegal) combinations of exempted and black market work. The size of the second pillar is also in most cases fixed for the individual worker as a matter of industry affiliation. Firm pensions are frequently set by collective bargaining agreements, and only very few companies give their workers a set of pension plans to choose from. Most firm pensions are based on book reserves in the workers' own company. They have declined in recent years when the favorable corporate tax treatment was reduced. Since the amounts are small, there is little discussion about the obvious accumulation of risks and the lack of governance in the book reserve system.

Only the third pillar, private savings, can be chosen freely. However, because the size of the other pillars is essentially a given, a worker cannot separately choose the total volume of retirement benefits from all three pillars and its composition at the same time. Thus, there is only little degree of freedom for substitution among the pillars on an individual basis. Of those workers who state that they systematically save for their retirement (about 55 percent), more than 70 percent have whole life insurance, only 15 percent have pension funds (Emnid, 1997). 40 percent of workers have no third–pillar old–age provision.

While there is little room for individual substitution, there are clear indications of substitution among the three pillars on a macroeconomic scale. The three pillars interact naturally as firm pensions are in most cases conditioned on topping up public pensions to some replacement level, say 90 or 100 percent of the most recent wage. In addition, the industry has provided private saving plans that fill any remaining expected "pension gap". The announcement of the 1999 pension reform with severe cuts in benefits has provided another indication that substitution from the first to the other pillars is likely. The announcement sparked a wave of advertisements by banks and pension funds for private pension savings, and cohort–corrected saving estimates show indeed an increase in savings of the younger generation. Moreover, both unions and employers' associations ponder whether the (small–sized and declining) firm pensions system should be reformed and possibly enlarged as part of future collective bargaining agreements.

This substitution on an aggregate level shows up comparisons over time. As will be discussed below, reductions or increases in the replacement rate of the first pillar have been compensated by opposite–directional changes in saving (Kim, 1992).

1.2.5 Implications of the Public Pension System on the German Economy

The macroeconomic impact of the retirement system stems from its sheer size. About 25 percent of all households in Germany have a head aged 65 or older. Thus, the manner in which income is provided to the elderly has an immediate impact on consumption and savings in Germany. In a pay–as–you–go system, retirement income is a transfer from the young to the old, raising the purchasing power of the old but lowering it for the young. The overall effect is determined mainly by the distortions that are caused by the transfer.

The discussion in Section 1.2.1 identified two main sources for distortions on the labor market: the classical wedge of a payroll tax and early retirement incentives. According to the polls quoted earlier and the low (or even negative) implicit rates of return discussed later, contributions to the retirement system have increasingly the character of a tax rather than that of an insurance premium. Taxes on labor decrease labor supply in proportion to the tax wedge. This wedge is large: total labor compensation in Germany is among the highest in the world, and almost 30 percent are pension contributions, see Figure 1.1. Although there is too little econometric evidence on labor supply elasticities in Germany to reliably compute the actual welfare loss on the supply side, the recent increase in the number of workers who manage to escape the otherwise mandatory retirement insurance system is an indication that these are important mechanisms. Between 1985 and 1995, the share of self–employed who voluntarily contributed more than the minimum amount to keep disability pension rights declined from 62 to 23 percent (Schnabel, 1998). At the same time, about 580,000 workers shifted from dependent to self–employed work (DIW, 1998). Finally, in 1997 were between 3.5 and 5.6 million jobs below the exemption threshold for social security contributions. Table 1.5. shows the estimated loss in contributions. It amounted to between DM 21 and 24 billion (11–13 bio. Euro) in 1997, about 7.5–8.5 percent of total contributions. On popular demand, regulations on self–employment were made substantially more stringent in 1999. At the same time, social security contributions were levied even on jobs with very low earnings. Whether these changes will achieve their aim – increase the contribution base – remains to be seen. More likely, this will result in added unemployment/non–employment and black market activities.

Table 1.5. Estimated Losses Due to "Evasion"

	Cases [000's]	Loss per Case [DM p.a.]	Total Loss [Mio DM]
Transitions to self-employment	560	10,625	5.950
Decline in voluntary contributions	1.080	9,115	9.845
Exempt low income jobs	3.500 – 5.600	1,510	5.285 – 8.458
			21.080 – 24.253

Note: The number of exempt low income jobs is under dispute. The lower number is a lower bound which excludes students and pensioners.

On the demand side of the labor market, the increase of the contribution rate has precipitated a vivid discussion about the competitiveness of German labor and the relocation of industries to countries with cheaper labor. This holds for manufacturing industries and increasingly also for the service sector. In the construction industry, temporary foreign workers make up for a considerable share of the work force. Little empirical work has been done to estimate the actual impact on German GDP.

A second important labor market distortion is generated by the more subtle impact of specific rules of the German retirement insurance, notably the incentives to early retirement which amplify the negative labor supply reaction of younger workers. Figure 1.1. has shown that retirement age declined by about 3 years due to the introduction of early retirement without actuarially fair adjustments. Average work life in Germany is 37 years. Thus, the decline corresponds to a 8 percent decline in labor supply.

The size of the German pay–as–you–system has also a large macroeconomic impacts through the capital market, first and foremost by supposedly crowding out savings. With a superficial view on Germany's relatively high saving rate, one might conclude from the cross–national evidence that this point cannot be supported. However, in a careful analysis Kim (1992) links time–series changes in the retirement system to the savings rate and shows that the German pay–as–you–go system has indeed crowded out saving and investment that could have led to higher growth. While there are many confounding factors in either analysis, an while no single econometric analysis can be the ultimate conclusive evidence, Kim's results appear much more convincing than aggregate cross–national evidence. The study is also in line with Feldstein's results in the U.S., see Feldstein and Pellechio (1979) and Feldstein (1996).

The other and more subtle channel of macroeconomic impact works through capital productivity. Pension funds are largely unknown in Germany, although an increasing number of workers, in particular young ones, have bought whole life insurance. Total pension fund assets held by Germans were 5.6 percent of GDP in 1997, as opposed to 90 percent in the U.K. As a result, Germany has few institutional investors and stock market capitalization is very low in international standards. The low capitalization is strengthened because life insurance companies are legally barred from investing more than a small part of their portfolios in stocks. Germany also provides less venture capital than other countries, in particular the U.S. and the UK, where pension funds provide most venture capital.

Low stock market capitalization and fewer institutional investors have strong implications for corporate governance. Capital productivity and rates of return to capital are lower in Germany relative to the U.S. As shown elsewhere (Börsch–Supan, 1999a), this lower capital productivity can only partially be explained by higher capital intensity. The remainder is an indication for weaker corporate governance that drives down total factor productivity and thus GDP per capita.

1.3 Future Developments

The main future threat to the German retirement system is the imminent demographic change. While all industrialized countries are aging, the aging process in Germany is particularly dramatic. Virtually all projections show that Germany will have the oldest population (measured as the share of persons aged 60 and older) in the world in the year 2035, the peak of German population aging.[14] According to Bos et al. (1994), the proportion of German elderly will increase from 21 percent in 1995 to 36 percent in the year 2035. The severity of the demographic transition has two causes: a quicker increase in life expectancy as elsewhere, partly due to a relatively low level still in the 1970s, and a more incisive baby boom/baby bust transition (e.g., relative to the U.S.) to a very low fertility rate of 1.3 children per women, only a bit higher than the rock–bottom fertility rate of 1.2 in Italy and Spain. Consequently, the ratio of elderly to working age persons – the old age dependency ratio – will increase steeply. While the OECD projects an increase from 20.6 percent in 1990 to 39.2 percent in 2030 for its European member countries, the German old age dependency ratio will far more than double from 21.7 percent in 1990 to 49.2 percent in 2030.[15]

Projections of the demographic dependency ratio vary by fertility, mortality and migration assumption. It is not particularly sensitive to fertility, since most workers around the year 2035 are already born. Migration is hard to predict and must be handled by scenarios that range from 50,000 to 300,000 net immigrants per year, see below. Mortality assumptions also vary from a complete stop of the current very quick improvement in life expectancy to a continuation of the current trend, adding one year of life every six years. In spite of the uncertainties about immigration and mortality, estimates of the dependency ratio agree on a serious increase in the order of 100 percent. Table 1.6 shows that even the most "optimistic" projection by the German Census Bureau ("Achte koordinierte Bevölkerungsvorausschätzung") yields a steep 80 percent increase in the dependency ratio, while the demographers' projections are truly alarming, far more than doubling the number of elderly per young person.

---

[14] Similarly Austria and Switzerland. Japan ages faster (as most other Asian countries) and will have an even higher share of elderly than Germany later in the mid 21st century.

[15] OECD, based on World Bank projection by Bos et al. (1994). The OECD dependency ratio relates persons age 65 and older to persons between ages 15 and 64.

Table 1.6. Projected Old–Age Dependency Ratios

	Life Expectancy			Dependency Ratio (60+/20-59)	
	2010	2030	2050	2035	*Change to 1995*
8. koordinierte BevVSch. (1994)	78	78	78	66,7	*80,7%*
Prognos (1998)	78,3	80,2	81,2	71,4	*93,5%*
Interministerielle AG (1996)	78,9	81,2	83,2	73,8	*100,0%*
Birg (1998), medium variant	79,6	83,1	85,3	79,2	*114,6%*
Birg (1998), upper variant	80,2	84,3	87,3	81,5	*120,9%*

Source: Börsch–Supan (1999b). Because this ratio relates elderly aged 60+ to persons 20–59, it has a much higher level than the OECD dependency ratio quoted earlier. Computed to this definition, the OECD forecast is very close to the medium projection by the " Interministerielle Arbeitsgruppe" (BMI, 1996).

The increase in the dependency ratio has immediate consequences for a pay–as–you–go social insurance system because fewer younger persons mean fewer workers who have to finance the benefits of more elderly. Projections of this *economic dependency ratio* are more difficult because they require forecasts of labor force participation. To a first approximation, one can assume constant labor force participation rates and compute the contribution rate that would be necessary to keep the current pension level in place. In this case, the German social security contribution rate, now at 20.3 percent of gross income, would exceed 30 percent of gross income at the peak of population aging in 2035 (Börsch–Supan, 1998). Official estimates range between 26 and 29 percent, assuming some adaptation of the retirement age, the replacement rate, female labor force participation, an optimistic view about future employment, and a pessimistic view about the development of life expectancy (Prognos, 1998).

This puts the limelight on future employment trends. Potential threats from the labor market on the German retirement insurance system are unemployment rates that stay as high as they are currently (or even increase further) and a continuation of the still ongoing trend of a declining old age labor force participation. These trends may be self–enforcing when the labor supply disincentives described in Section 1.2.1 become even stronger with a higher contribution rate. On the other hand, population aging maybe working in the opposite direction since less workers may drive wages up and make work more attractive in all age ranges. German labor supply has ample room for increase in female and old age labor force participation. An increase in female labor force participation may strengthen the contribution base before an offsetting increase in the number of beneficiaries will take place. Concerning old–age labor force participation, there are no signs that morbidity will be a problem – just the opposite, age–specific morbidity rates appear to have shifted in line with mortality (Cutler and Sheiner, 1998). Whether productivity declines significantly during the age range 55 to 65, which is the most relevant range for a realistic shift in the average retirement age, is a debated issue with little empirical guidance so far.[16]

Simulation exercises can shed some light on the sensitivity of future contribution rates to these labor force parameters. Börsch–Supan (1998) provides simulations with a detailed demographic and employment projection model and shows that in order to fully compensate for the effects of population aging, the average retirement age has to increase by about 9.5 years to age 69. This is a huge shift that makes counterarguments such as decreasing productivity with age much more relevant. An increase in female labor force participation reduces the retirement burden with a lag of about thirty years, assuming that take–up of employment comes relatively late in life due to child raising. This temporary relief helps considerably to bridge the problem period around the year 2035 and eliminates some of the current transfer payments in form of survivor benefits by pension benefits out of own earnings. However, the effect is small. Even if female labor force participation would reach the level of male labor force participation within the next decade, the increase of the social security contribution rate would be dampened by only about 6 percentage points. Finally, migration could theoretically offset the entire population aging problem if migrants are sufficiently younger than the native population. Again, the numbers required put doubt on this mechanism: at the current age differential of about 10 years between immigrants and natives, Germany needs a steady inflow of 800.000 immigrants per year for the next 25 years to offset the demographic transition, about three times as much as the historical long–run average.

Other important future trends that are likely to influence the working of the German retirement system are changes in the distribution of saving and wealth, and changes in the family composition. Elderly in Germany have relatively high saving rates, and there is no indication that financial assets decline in old age. Thus, the younger generation can expect a steep wealth increase caused by future inheritances. The estimated volume of this "inheritance wave" is huge and would provide an elegant way to finance a higher share of the third pillar (individual savings) which also has the attractive property of sharing the transition burden between two generations without much consumption distortions.

---

[16] See Lehr (1987).

Changes in family composition and kinship relations are hard to forecast. The declining number of younger to older persons naturally implies a higher burden of personal care for the younger generation which may be in conflict with higher labor force participation, particular among women. This implies that a lower retirement income cannot easily be substituted by family care. Cohabitation of multigenerational households, an important form of intergenerational transfers, has declined dramatically over the recent decades and may decline further, putting more strain on the retirement resources of the elderly when they have to purchase care on the "market" rather than obtain it through the family. Only a small part of these expenses are covered by the newly introduced long–term–care insurance, a fact that is not well known in Germany. All this puts a serious limit on potential benefit reductions.

1.4 Current Reform Options

The policy debate in Germany has focused on adding patches to the current system, a piecemeal approach that is exemplified by the 1992 reform and the many small modifications after. These fixes included downsizing the system by decreasing benefits through subtle and indirect mechanisms, increasing the retirement age, tightening the eligibility for disability pensions, and hoping for an increase in female labor force participation and some help from migration. As pointed out, these fixes require considerable additional absorption in the labor market and are nevertheless unlikely to stabilize the contribution rate to the German public pension system if the current generosity of benefits were maintained.

The current debate centers around three options. The first option is a continuation of this policy augmented by a more severe reduction in benefits. This option was the approach of the reform attempt in 1998 that was promptly revoked after the 1998 elections because the new government deemed the benefit reductions unpalatable. The other two options imply formal transitions to radically different retirement systems, either a fully funded mandatory retirement system that links benefits strictly to contributions, or a Beveridgian system of a base pension financed by general taxes. All three options can be combined, and indeed, the likely outcome of the current debate appears to be a considerably smaller and more redistributive pay–as–you–go pillar augmented by more private provision based on funded firm pensions and individual savings.

The first option combined decreasing benefits, increasing the retirement age, tightening eligibility for disability benefits, and increasing the state subsidy financed by a value–added tax hike. The main survivor of this so–called "Reform 1999" is a partial shift from contribution to tax financing, now augmented by a new tax on fossil fuel, while the benefit cuts were revoked. The original reform had planned to link the replacement rate to life expectancy at age 60 by a complicated mechanism.[17] The mechanism was tailored to a very conservative forecast of life–expectancy to generate a reduction of the average net replacement rate by about 10 percent. It used life expectancy lagged by eight years and had a built–in floor of the net replacement rate at 64 percent for a worker with 45 years of average earnings (the "official" length of work life), and at 53 percent for a worker with 37 years of average earnings (the average length of work life) which would just be hit at the peak of population aging. If one applies the projected life expectancy implied by the middle projection in Table 1.5. (BMI, 1996) rather than the actually used one, the replacement rate would hit the built–in floor much earlier; without the floor, the replacement rate would decline to about 55 percent for the "standard worker" with a 45–year history of average earnings in the year 2030.[18] This is still slightly higher than the current replacement rate of an average worker in the U.S. Social Security system.

The "Reform 1999" would have massively reduced the implicit rate of return of the pay–as–you–go system. Benefits would be reduced by more than 10 percent while contributions would increase to about 25 percent of gross wages (Prognos, 1998). The resulting implicit rates of return have been extensively documented in DIA (1998) and decline from about 3.5 percent in real terms for current retirees to about 0.3 percent if age–specific employment rates remain constant and life expectancy follows the official German forecast. If instead life expectancy will increase at the same pace as it has during the previous decade, real returns will become significantly negative. Low or negative rates of return generated by lowering benefits at increasing contributions will make the pay–as–you–go system less attractive, thereby increasing the incentives to evade from the system. The stabilizing patches thus in itself are potentially destabilizing by decreasing the contribution base.

These very low rates of return contrast with the rate of return in a funded system, the second reform option debated in Germany. Estimates for real returns under funding range from 4 to 8 percent, depending on the portfolio share of bonds and equities. Using an intermediate estimate of 5.5 percent, we can compute the costs of a funded pension that will pay an annuity at equals the average public pension at the generous 72–percent replacement rate that prevailed in 1995.[19] Such an annuity would require accumulating a capital stock of DM 276.000 (141.000

[17] A further reduction in the replacement rate that was well hidden from the political discussion occurs because higher education will count much less as part of the earnings history (down from a maximum of seven years to a maximum of three years), effectively reducing the replacement rate for person with a college degree by 10 percent.

[18] Remember that the "standard worker" is an artifact. For a worker with a 38–year history, the replacement rate is 54%.

[19] For similar and alternative computations, see Börsch–Supan, 1999b.

Euro). In order to do this, a worker needs to save about DM 170 (87 Euro) monthly during a 40 year service life. This saving is less than 20 percent of the average contribution to the current German retirement insurance (DM 886 in 1998, 452 Euro). This huge difference makes the transition burden quite palatable and led to a number of concrete transition proposals to a fully or partially funded retirement system in Germany, for instance by the Wissenschaftlicher Beirat (1998). Börsch–Supan (1999b) details that, even if the transition burden were imposed on only one generation, it would require additional savings of less than 4 percent of disposable income.

While this second option has many supporters among economists, it is not popular because of the perceived capital market risks. In particular, most workers find the thought of putting a major part of retirement savings on the stock market rather frightening. This reflects the underdeveloped capital market in Germany where stock market capitalization is low and pension funds are underdeveloped, as pointed out in Section 1.2.5.

The third option explicitly acknowledges the increasing redistributive nature of the current system when the statutory replacement rate declines. It radically departs from the one–to–one link between benefits and contributions that almost defines the original idea of the German retirement "insurance" Rather, it proposes a fixed base pension for everybody, financed from general taxes, similarly to, e.g., the Dutch and Swiss base pensions. The most well–know proposal of this kind was presented in Biedenkopf und Miegel (1997). This option is relatively popular: According to a recent poll (Wirtschaftsjunioren, 1998), 47 percent of workers favor a transition to this option, 37 are against it.[20] It is particularly popular among the well–to–do, self–employed, and among workers in East Germany.

Most such proposals entail levels of the base pension that are lower than the current average public pension. If the base pension level is low, it has the character of social assistance and the proposal comes close to a transition to a fully funded system because most worker would like to top up this low base pension. If the base pension level were high, the volume to be financed by general taxes would also be high. This would imply considerable distortions because these taxes are not linked to retirement benefits.

Although the new German government has renounced the reductions in the pension benefit level envisaged by the 1999 reform, it is likely that the demographic facts will sooner or later force the government to revive some version of benefit reductions. Indeed, "new" reform proposals are much in the spirit of a compromise consisting of elements of each of the three reform alternatives. The core of such a package is a reduction in the benefit level that amounts to a partial default on benefit promises made to workers who have paid contributions in the expectation to receive current replacement rates. Since retirees probably will not

[20] This poll, however, might be misleading because it did not specify a level of the base pension.

be content with a significantly lower retirement income and make up the resulting "pension gap" by their own savings, such a reduction will either formally or in a disguised fashion precipitate a step in direction of more funding. Finally, since many more workers will end up with a pension below the threshold level of social assistance, either a formal base pension will be introduced or local governments, who are responsible for social assistance in Germany, will increasingly have to top–up pensions. In any case, as it looks like, the future German pension system will become more redistributive, and it will include a higher share of funded retirement income.

References

Allensbach, Institut für Demoskopie (1996), Wachsende Bedeutung der Lebensversicherung als Säule der Alterssicherung. Allensbacher Archiv 4657, 5009, 5088, 6029.

Biedenkopf, K., Miegel, M.: Von der Arbeitnehmer – zur Bürgerrente: das Konzept der Grundsicherung im Alter, Bonn: IWG, (1997)

Bos, E., Vu, M.T., Massiah, E., und Bulatao, R. (1994), *World Population Projections, 1994–95*, The International Bank for Reconstruction and Development/The World Bank.

Börsch–Supan, A. (1992), Population Aging, Social Security Design, and Early Retirement, *Journal of Institutional and Theoretical Economics 148.*

Börsch–Supan, A. (1998), Germany: A Social Security System on the Verge of Collapse, in: H. Siebert (ed.) *Redesigning Social Security* , J.C.B. Mohr (Paul Siebeck): Tübingen.

Börsch–Supan, A. (1999a), Capital Productivity and the Nature of Competition, *Brookings Papers on Economic Activity, Microeconomics*, forthcoming in June 1999.

Börsch–Supan, A. (1999b), Zur Diskussion eines Übergangs vom Umlage– zum Kapitaldeckungsverfahren in der Gesetzlichen Rentenversicherung, *Finanzarchiv*, in Druck.

Börsch–Supan, A. und A. Reil–Held (1998), Retirement Income: Level, Risk, and Substitution among Income Components, in: OECD, *Maintaining Prosperity in an Ageing Society*. Paris: OECD, AWP 3.7, 1–21.

Börsch–Supan, A. und A. Reil–Held (1998), How Much Is Transfer And How Much Insurance In A Pay–As–You–Go System? The German Case. Working Paper, University of Mannheim.

Börsch–Supan, A., und R. Schnabel (1998), Social Security and Declining Labor Force Participation in Germany, *American Economic Review 88.2*, 173–178.

Börsch–Supan, A., und R. Schnabel (1999), Social Security and Retirement in Germany, in: J. Gruber and D. Wise, *Social Security and Retirement Around the World*, University of Chicago Press.

Bundesministerium des Inneren (BMI, 1996), Modellrechnungen zur Bevölkerungsentwicklung in der Bundesrepublik Deutschland bis zum Jahre 2040, Bonn.

Bundesverband deutscher Banken (1999), Deutschland nach dem Regierungswechsel, Demoskopie 3, 19–22.

Cutler, D., und L.M. Sheiner (1998), Demographics and Medical Care Spending: Standard and Non–Standard Effects, mimeo, Harvard University.

Deutsches Institut für Altersvorsorge (DIA, 1998), *Renditen der gesetzlichen Rentenversicherung im Vergleich zu alternativen Anlageformen*, Frankfurt.

Deutsches Institut für Wirtschaftsforschung (DIW, 1998), Zunehmende Selbständigkeit in Deutschland von 1990 bis 1996, *DIW–Wochenbericht 38/1998.*

Emnid–Institut (1997), *Lebensplanung – Altersvorsorge zwischen Wunsch und Wirklichkeit,* Studie im Auftrag von Allianz Leben, Bielefeld: Emnid.

Feldstein, M. (1996), Social Security and Saving: New Time Series Evidence, *National Tax Journal 49*, 151–164.

Feldstein, M., and A. Pellechio (1997), Social Security and Household Wealth Accumulation: New Microeconomic Evidence, *Review of Economics and Statistics 61(3),* 361–68.

Kim, S., (1992), Gesetzliche Rentenversicherung und Ersparnisbildung der privaten Haushalte in der Bundesrepublik Deutschland von 1962 bis 1988, *Zeitschrift für die gesamte Versicherungswirtschaft 81*, 555–.

Lehr, U. (1987), *Psychologie des Alterns*, Heidelberg: Quelle und Meyer.

Prognos (1998), Auswirkung veränderter ökonomischer und rechtlicher Rahmenbedingungen auf die gesetzliche Rentenversicherung in Deutschland, Basel: Prognos.

Schnabel, R. (1998), Intergenerational Distribution and Pension Reform in Germany. Working paper, University of Mannheim.

Schnabel, R. (1999), *Ersparnisbildung und Rentenversicherung*, Habilitationsschrift, Universität Mannheim.

Wirtschaftsjunioren Deutschland (1998), *Bevölkerungsbefragung 1998*, Bonn.

Wissenschaftlicher Beirat beim Bundesministerium für Wirtschaft (1998), *Grundlegende Reform der Gesetzlichen Rentenversicherung*, Gutachten vom Februar 1998, Bonn.

2 The Dutch Pension System

by A. Lans Bovenberg and Lex Meijdam

2.1 A Brief History of the Dutch Pension System

Public pensions were first established in 1919. In this funded scheme, the insurance view dominated as individual pension rights were closely linked to contributions. However, also elements of a state pension crept into this law. Workers older than 65 years were entitled to a state–financed benefit if their income was below a certain level. The real value of benefits quickly eroded as pensions were not indexed. This led to calls for reform. After parliament had taken temporary measures in 1947, it established a more definitive public pension scheme in 1956 in the General Old–age Act (Algemene Ouderdoms Wet). The law introduced compulsory pay–as–you–go old–age insurance for all residents. In contrast to the previous public system, employers did not contribute to the system. Pension benefits were payable at age 65 and not means tested, did not depend on premiums paid, and were indexed to contractual wages. The public pension benefit was increased several times on top of the indexation incorporated in the law. In the early 1970s the after–tax public pension for a couple was set equal to the after–tax minimum wage.[1]

Occupational pension schemes grew rapidly after World War II. The wage policy during the first decades after 1945 contributed to this growth. This policy limited wage increases but allowed for improvements in secondary conditions of employment, including occupational pensions. Other factors that stimulated growth were fiscal benefits for pension saving and the Occupational Pension Act (BPF), which was passed in 1949. This law made the negotiated supplementary pension provisions compulsory for all firms in a particular sector if requested by the employers' organizations and trade unions.

[1] In after–tax terms, the minimum wage was close to 80 percent of the modal wage during most of the seventies. Since then, it has declined to about 65 percent of the modal wage and about 55 percent of the average wage.

2.2 The Pillars Providing Retirement Income in the Netherlands

The Dutch pension system is close to a three pillar system. The third pillar, however, is relatively small because the aspiration level of the second pillar, namely collective, occupational pensions, is quite high and comes on top of a first pillar that provides already half of overall retirement income. The importance of occupational schemes reflects a strong Dutch corporatist tradition. According to this tradition, apart from the state providing a basic minimum pension, pension provision is primarily viewed as a collective responsibility of employees and employers.

Table 2.1. contains the income sources of the elderly. The income share of the basic public pension is about 50 percent for both single elderly and for (married) couples. Occupational pension schemes provide about 30 percent of the income of the elderly. Occupational benefits are less important for older cohorts. Annuities provide a relatively small share of the income of the elderly (about 7%), reflecting the relatively small third pillar in the Netherlands. However, if one includes other asset income and income from owner–occupied housing in the third pillar, income from the third pillar amounts to about half the average size of the two other pillars.

Table 2.1. Composition of retirement income

	Public pensions[a]	Occupational pensions	Asset income[b]	Other income[c]
Singles:				
65–69 years	48	30	18	4
70–74 years	49	28	19	4
75–79 years	51	27	18	4
80 years and over	50	26	20	4
Total	49	28	19	4
Couples:				
65–69 years	44	32	16	8
70–74 years	48	29	20	3
75–79 years	49	28	19	4
80 years and over	51	24	20	5
Total	48	29	19	4

Source: Besseling (1997)

[a] Excludes other public transfers.

[b] Includes income from owner occupied housing.

[c] Includes wages, profits and transfers.

[d] Both partners receive a public pension.

Figure. 2.1 to 2.3 provide macro–economic data on the three pillars of pension insurance. Figure 2.1 shows that assets in occupational pension schemes increased steadily.

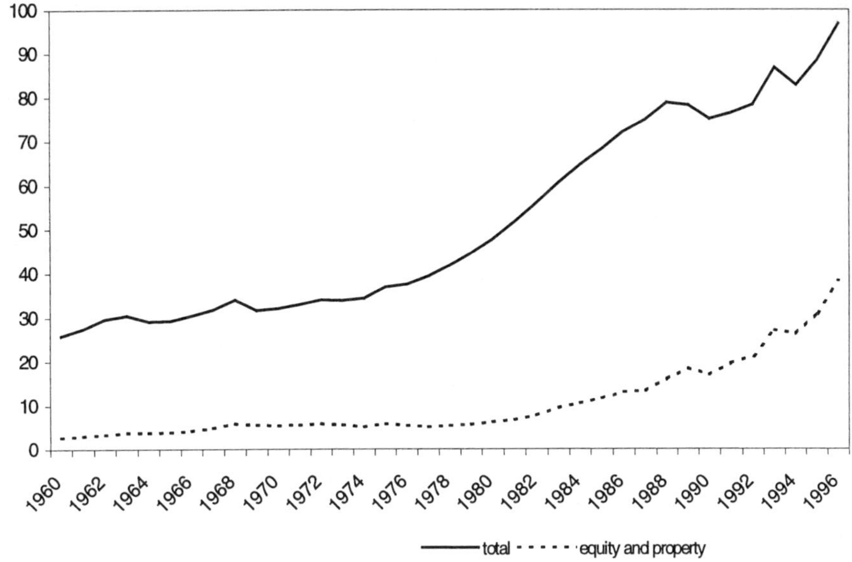

Fig. 2.1. The portfolio of the pension funds as a percentage of GDP, 1960–1996[a]

Source: Statistics Netherlands

[a] Excluding the contracts that have been reinsured by insurance companies.

Also rising occupational pension benefits (Figure 2.2) reflect the gradual maturing of these funded pension plans.

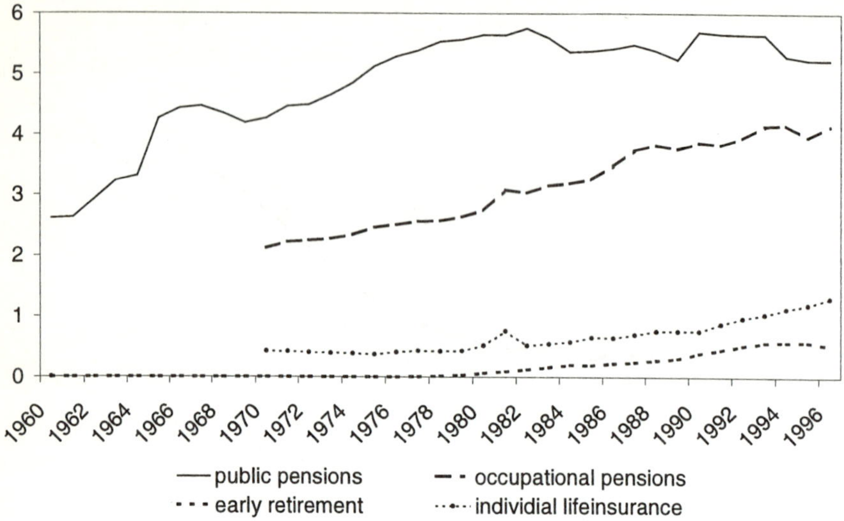

Fig. 2.2. Pension benefits as percentage of GDP, 1960–1996[a]

Source: CPB, Statistics Netherlands

[a] No data available on individual life insurance and occupational pensions before 1970.

Despite the increasing share of occupational benefits in retirement income, premiums for these pensions fell as a share of GDP during the eighties. This was due in part to high interest rates during this period which raised capital income collected by pension funds.

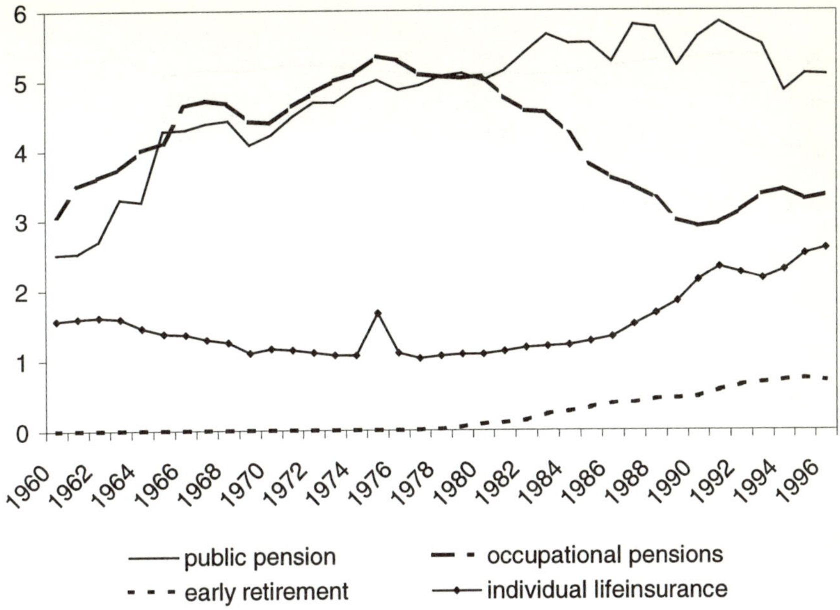

Fig. 2.3. Pension premiums as a percentage of GDP, 1960–1996[a]

Source: Statistics Netherlands

[a] Individual life insurance includes not only annuities but also other life insurance products.

2.2.1 The Public Pension System

Benefits. The Dutch public sector provides a minimum pension benefit to residents aged 65 or over. Neither early retirement nor opting out of the compulsory public scheme are possible.[2] The public benefit is flat; it does not depend on premiums paid during the working life and is not means tested. The entitlement to the public pension does not require retirement from the labour force. Hence, also housewives who have not participated in the formal labour market collect the public pension. The same holds true for groups with only a weak attachment to the labour market.

[2] Whereas the statutory retirement age has remained fixed at 65, the effective retirement age of male workers has declined from 66.4 years in 1950 to 58.8 years in 1995. Indeed, early retirement is facilitated by the public disability and unemployment schemes and by private early retirement schemes. See section 2.3.

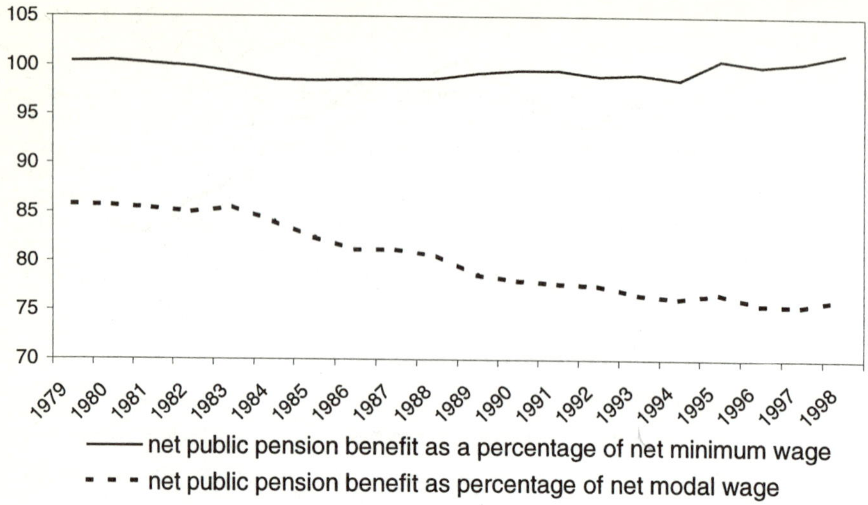

Fig 2.4. After–tax replacement rates[a] of the public pension benefit for couples, 1979–1998

Source: CPB/Ministry of Social Affairs and Employment

[a] The modal wage is approximated as 80% of the average wage.

Accordingly, with the public pension serving as an effective minimum pension, the elderly do not draw on welfare and thus do not burden social assistance.[3]

Single persons receive a higher benefit per individual than married persons do. Single persons collect a benefit that, in after–tax terms[4], amounts to 70% of the after–tax statutory minimum wage. For elderly persons living in a common household, each individual collects a benefit that (in after–tax terms) amounts to only 50% of the after–tax minimum wage.

The public pension is effectively indexed to contractual wages because of a statutory link between the minimum wage and contractual wages. Nevertheless, during the last two decades, the value of the public pension has declined compared to the average standard of living (see Figure 2.4.). The main reason for the public pension lagging actual wages is twofold. First, the minimum wage was frozen

[3] The social minimum provided by social assistance coincides with the public pension. In particular, in after–tax terms, it amounts to 70% of the minimum wage for single–person households and 100% of the minimum wage for two–person households.

[4] The fact that the link to the minimum wage is in after–tax terms moderates the increase in public pensions if ageing boosts spending on public pensions. The reason is that the higher costs of public pensions reduce the after–tax minimum wage by raising the burden of taxes and social security premiums. Since the public pension is linked to this after–tax wage, the elderly in effect share in the costs of financing their own benefits.

in nominal terms or indexed to prices rather than wages during most of the eighties in order to encourage wage moderation and reduce public spending on minimum social benefits, which are linked to the minimum wage. Second, contractual wages typically lag actual wages because these latter wages include promotions and other supplementary earnings that are not included in actual wage contracts. Moreover, average wages rise if the labour–force share of those earning higher wages increases. These changes in the composition of the labour force do not affect the index of contractual wages but do raise the average standard of living.[5]

Contributions. Whereas benefits are flat, contributions for the public pensions depend on taxable income. In particular, since a major tax reform in 1990, premiums are levied as part of the first bracket of the personal income tax.[6] Contributions are levied on all components of personal income, including capital income. The premium is paid only by those younger than 65 years of age. The resulting lower rate in the first tax bracket enjoyed by the elderly provides an incentive to defer labour income through occupational or personal pensions because pensions are taxed on a cash–flow basis: premiums are deductible from the personal income tax (including the premium for the old–age pension) while benefits are subject to the personal income tax. Accordingly, individuals can avoid the old–age pension premium by shifting their taxable income through pension saving toward retirement when they do not pay the premium for the public pension.

Funding. Current public pension benefits are traditionally paid out of current contributions according to the familiar pay–as–you–go system. The previous government modified the financing of public pensions in two major ways.

As a first modification, it intended to fix the pension premium in the first bracket of the personal income tax at its 1997 level. As the population ages, a fixed premium rate implies that revenues from premiums will increasingly fall short of expenditures on public pension benefits. This revenue shortfall will then have to be covered from general tax revenues. This implies that the elderly start to contribute to the financing of public pensions from their supplementary incomes because the elderly, who are exempted from paying public pension premiums on their

5 The gap between actual and contracted wages is the so–called incidental wage component. The law allows for once–off increases in the minimum wage and minimum public benefits if they are too much out of line with the average standard of living. Indeed, minimum benefits were increased substantially in the sixties and seventies. In the eighties, however, the link between benefits and contractual wages has been suspended several times. Indeed, according to a law instated in 1992, this link can be suspended if the ratio of the number of inactive persons claiming social benefits to the number of people having a job exceeds 0.826.

6 In 1999, the premium for the public old–age pension amounts to 17.95% of taxable income in the first bracket. The length of the first bracket is 48233 guilders (23441 Euro) while the tax free allowance is 8807 guilders (4280 Euro).

supplementary incomes, do pay taxes on these incomes. Despite these intentions of the previous government, however, both the previous and the current government have increased the public pension premium in order to shift the burden of financing the public pension away from the elderly who are a politically powerful group.

The second modification to the PAYG system is the accumulation of a so–called AOW fund to deal with temporarily high spending on public pensions when the babyboom generations retire. According to the definition used for computing fiscal balances for the purposes of the Stability and Growth Pact within EMU, the build–up of the AOW fund counts as a cut in the fiscal deficit. Indeed, the resources in the AOW fund are invested in government bonds. Accordingly, the AOW fund can be viewed as a cut in public debt that is earmarked for the public pensions of the babyboom generations. Figure 2.5 shows current projections for the AOW fund. At the end of 1998, the fund contained 4.337 mrd guilders (2.108 Euro) (i.e 0.55% of annual GDP).

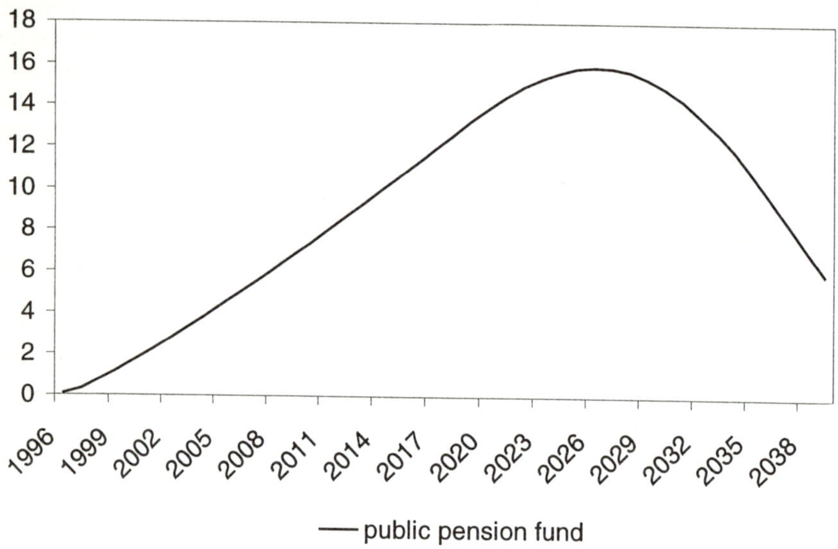

Fig 2.5. Projections of the public pension fund as a percentage of GDP, 1996–2040

Source: Ministry of Finance

2.2.2 Occupational Pensions

Occupational pensions are quite important in the Netherlands. Its provisions are set in collective bargaining by employers' organizations and trade unions in the private sector. At the same time, the government provides a legal framework and fiscal support. In particular, under the Pensions and Savings Funds Act (PSW), a pension fund must be established as a legal entity that is legally separate from the sponsoring firm. The Insurance Board, a private agency that supervises pension funds and insurance companies, formulates additional prudential rules involving the amount of funding and the valuation of assets. Pension funds are legally obliged to provide the Insurance Board with detailed information on benefit payments and investments of the fund.

Regulations that make the negotiated supplementary pension provisions compulsory for all firms in a particular sector if requested by the employers' organizations and trade unions in that sector play an important role in facilitating intergenerational risk–sharing in defined– benefit schemes.[7] Indeed, the compulsory participation of firms in sectoral pension funds allows these funds to keep the pension premiums relatively stable without endangering their pension promises. As a direct consequence of the compulsory participation of firms, most workers (91% in 1996) are covered by an occupational pension scheme. The government also provides fiscal benefits: pension contributions are tax exempt, capital income of pension funds is tax–exempt, and pension benefits are taxed. This regime is especially advantageous because the elderly aged 65 and over benefit from a low rate in the first tax bracket as they are exempted from paying public pension contributions (see section 2.1.1).[8]

Defined–benefit schemes. Occupational pension schemes are generally of the defined–benefit type. In particular, benefits are based on salary levels during the working life rather than on the discounted value of individual life–time contributions. The link between wages and benefits can take various forms. The final–pay

[7] A company can opt out of these industry pension funds and establish a company pension fund only if this company fund offers benefits that are at least as generous as those provided by the relevant industry–wide scheme.

[8] These tax benefits are available only if benefits are paid out in the form of annuities. The tax benefits are subject to certain limits. In particular, each individual can deduct up to about 6000 guilders (2916 Euro) per year in premiums for personal pensions (i.e. annuities). Those individuals who lack sufficient pension rights in occupational schemes, like the self employed, benefit from higher ceilings. Moreover, tax preferences used to be available only for collective pension benefits (including the public pension) not exceeding 70% of the final wage. Recently, however, the rules have been relaxed in order to facilitate more flexible pension arrangements in general and a more flexible retirement age in particular.

pension scheme is most common. In such a scheme, the pension benefit is linked to the wages at the end of the career.[9] Indeed, among the private sector employees covered by a supplementary pension scheme, about 73% participate in a final-pay scheme. Almost all other employees participate in so–called average–pay schemes. In these schemes, benefits are linked to the average rather than the final pay during the career. In recent years, the average–pay system has gained ground at the expense of the final–pay scheme.

In order to be able to pay wage–linked benefits, the occupational schemes rely not only on the accumulation of financial assets but also on an implicit contract between the firm, its workers, and retirees of different ages. If returns are low and wage increases are substantial, the firm and younger workers transfer resources to older generations.[10] If returns are high, in contrast, the former parties benefit from lower pension premiums.

The defined–benefit schemes thus back up the benefit promise not only by financial assets (as in defined–contribution schemes) but also by the market power of the firm and the commitment of future workers to the implicit contract. In particular, a firm can abide by this implicit contract only if it earns rents due to market power so that it can insure the elderly against low returns without being pushed out of the market by young firms that do not have to care for retired workers. Exit barriers for young workers ensure that defined–benefit schemes can transfer resources from younger workers to retirees and older workers. If young workers would be fully mobile across firms, they could not be forced to abide by the implicit contract with the retired and older workers in their firm; if a firm attempted to tax its younger workers to transfer resources to its retirees, these workers would move to young firms without retirees and older workers. Accordingly, firms can perform the intergenerational risk sharing associated with the benefit promise in defined–benefit schemes only in less than perfectly competitive product and labour markets.[11]

Another safety valve for firms operating in competitive product and labour markets is the conditional indexation of benefits. Whereas most current retirees benefit from indexation of occupational retirement benefits to inflation or even contractual wages, this indexation is generally not a regulatory requirement but rather conditional on the financial situation of the pension fund. The conditional

---

[9] Most final–pay plans include provisions that discourage strategic wage setting just before retirement. To illustrate, the increase in pension benefits due to wage increases immediately before retirement is usually constrained by a ceiling.

[10] In particular, wage increases result in considerable additional pension obligations with respect to older workers. The costs of these additional obligations are spread over all workers.

[11] Hence, in perfectly competitive markets, government regulations need to help occupational defined–benefit schemes to perform inter– and intragenerational redistribution by making collective labour agreements compulsory for particular sectors. Moreover, to prevent adverse selection, workers in a particular firm must be forced to participate in defined–benefit schemes.

indexation of pension benefits is not fully consistent with the defined-benefit character of the schemes. As competition on these markets intensifies, occupation schemes will acquire more of the features of the defined–contribution schemes.

Portability of pension rights. Vesting periods are typically shorter than one year. Moreover, since 1994 employees have the legal right to transfer the value of their accrued pension rights to another employer. Accordingly, the pension system does not inhibit the mobility of labour and insures the worker against job-mobility risk and firm–specific shocks. At the same time, the pension system does not tie the worker to the firm. Hence, employers can not employ occupational schemes as an instrument to alleviate imperfections in labour markets (see e.g. Lazear, 1986).

Contributions. Contributions to occupational pension schemes are typically shared between employers and employees. Premiums are usually levied on wage income above a certain franchise. Below this franchise, employees are covered by the public pension scheme (see section 2.2.2 below). Figure 2.6. contains the premiums as a percentage of gross wages since 1970. These rates are an average across pension funds. The decline in the average premium during the eighties was due to a combination of high interest rates and relatively low wage growth during this period.

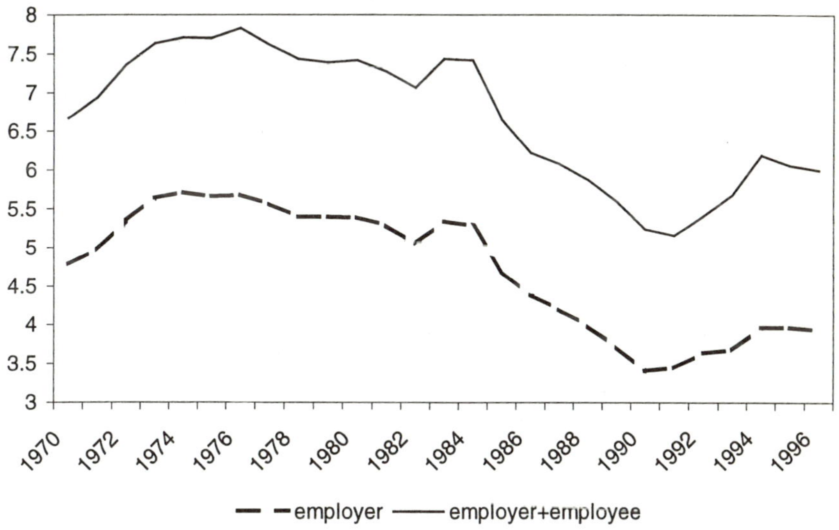

Fig. 2.6. Premium for occupational pensions as a percentage of gross wages[a], 1970– 1998

Source: CPB

[a] Averaged over all pension funds.

Funding. The flat minimum public pension together with compulsory participation in supplementary funded schemes and the fiscal benefits for pension saving has resulted in the accumulation of considerable capital in occupational pension funds (see Figure 2.1.). The legal requirement that at least 90% of these pension assets must be held outside the sponsoring firm yields several advantages for the allocation of capital. First, the pension funds diversify their investments and hence reduce investment risk. Second, they stimulate the development of capital markets, thereby facilitating the reallocation of capital away from older, mature firms towards younger, growing firms. Dutch pension funds traditionally invested mainly in low–risk government bonds, in part due to regulatory requirements of the Insurance Board. More recently, however, Dutch pension funds have significantly increased their holdings of domestic equities (see Figure 2.1.). Many pension funds contract out the management of the pension funds to competitive fund managers. Individuals cannot directly affect the way funds are managed as pension funds decide on fund management on a collective level. However, sponsoring firms, which face increasing competition, put more and more pressure on pension funds to improve their returns.

2.2.3 Individual Pensions

The third pillar of pension insurance includes voluntary pension insurance bought by individuals. Personal pensions are of the defined–contribution type and are typically supplied by life insurance companies. Figure 2.3 shows premiums for individual contracts with life insurance companies. These contracts include not only annuities but also other insurance products, including life insurance. Up to a ceiling, annuities benefit from the same preferential tax treatment as occupation pensions. Also life insurance products enjoy tax advantages. In particular, the capital income earned on these products is typically tax exempt.

2.2.4 Interaction Between Pillars

The first two pillars: aspiration levels of collective pensions. The first two pillars are closely related because the second pillar typically takes account of the first pillar in defining its aspiration level. In particular, many occupational pension schemes aim to achieve a collective pension (i.e. the sum of benefits from the first and the second pillars) of 70% of final earnings (before taxes) in case of a career of 40 years.

Most pension funds achieve this aspiration level by using a so–called franchise on which no occupational pension rights are accumulated because the government provides the pension on these earnings through the minimum public pension. In practice, many workers do not achieve the 70% final–wage aspiration level because of incomplete careers. Furthermore, even in the case of full careers, many two–earner families and single people collect a collective pension of less than 70% of the final wage (in before–tax terms) because the franchise is typically based on a public pension for a two–person family with a single earner (the so–called breadwinner) of 100% of the minimum wage. Two–earner families and singles, however, receive a public pension of only, respectively, 50% and 70% of the minimum wage.

Table 2.2 contains gross and after–tax replacement rates of collective pensions (i.e. public and occupational pensions) for the generation born in 1930. Notice that on average workers do not realize the gross pension level of 70% of the gross average wage that most occupational pension systems aim at. The high replacement rate for single woman is due to (on average) low final wages rather than high pension rights. The relatively high replacement rate for a one–earner family indicates that the Dutch pension system discourages partners of breadwinners from participating in the labour market.

Table 2.2. Pension benefit as a percent of final wage for cohort born in 1930

	One–earner family[a]	Single male	Single female	Two–earner family[b]
Gross public pension[c]	40	28	79	29
Gross overall pension[d]	60	48	88	46
After–tax overall pension[e]	76	65	104	61

Source: van Groezen et al. (1999), authors' calculations.

[a] Assuming a male breadwinner.

[b] Working couple (man and woman).

[c] Gross public pension as percent of average gross final wage.

[d] Gross overall pension (including public and occupational pension) as percent of average gross final wage.

[e] After–tax average overall pension (including public and occupational pension) as percent of after–tax average final wage.

Over the last two decades, the relative importance of the occupational schemes has grown compared to that of the public scheme. This is in part because the public benefits lagged actual wage growth (see subsection 2.1.1). Most private occupational schemes filled the gap left by the public scheme so as to ensure that collective pension benefits were maintained at 70% of the final wage (for a full career). By reducing the generosity of the public scheme, the government has thus in fact privatized part of pension provision.

The first and the third pillar. The first pillar interacts with the third pillar in at least two ways. First, uncertainty about the sustainability of the public pension in the face of the ageing population has encouraged the take up personal pensions. Second, the premium for the old–age pension (which is levied as part of the first bracket of the personal income tax, see subsection 2.1.1) provides a subsidy to personal pension saving in the form of annuities. This is because premiums for annuities are deductible from the personal income tax (including the premium for the public pension system that is levied as part of the first bracket of the personal income tax) while the pension benefits are not subject to the premium for the public pension. Accordingly, individuals can avoid paying the premium for the old–age pension by deferring their taxable income until retirement through pension saving in the form of annuities.

Table 2.3. Effective retirement age

	1950	1960	1970	1980	1990	1995
Males	66.4	66.1	63.8	61.4	59.3	58.8
Females	64.1	63.7	62.9	58.4	55.8	55.3

Source: OECD (1998)

2.2.5 Interaction Between Pensions and Social Programs

The programs providing income to the elderly imply a strong incentive to retire early. Employees who stop working can generally expect high replacement rates (see Kapteyn and de Vos (1997)). Indeed, the effective retirement age has declined to rather low levels over the past two decades (see Table 2.3.). This section describes the most important schemes facilitating early retirement (see Table 2.4.).

Table 2.4. Persons aged 55–64 by labour–market status, 1990[a]

	Men		Women	
	55-59	60-64	55-59	60-64
Employed	54.9	21.1	12.7	4.3
Disabled	31.3	37.7	10.5	10.8
Partly disabled/unemployed	1.8	1	0.4	0.3
Early retirement (VUT)	3.9	26.5	0.6	5.1
Social assistance	0.4	0.4	2.4	2
Unemployed	4.6	8.7	1.4	1.6

Source: OECD (1995)

[a] As a percentage of the population in that age category.

Early retirement benefits. Early retirement schemes (VUT) negotiated in collective bargaining between the social partners are an important route for early retirement. Indeed, about 27% of the men aged between 60 and 65 collect early retirement benefits at present. These schemes generally provide a benefit equal to 80% of previous earnings between the age of 60 up to the statutory retirement age of 65. In contrast to occupational pensions provided after the statutory retirement age, early retirement is generally financed on a pay–as–you–go basis. As another difference with regular occupational pensions, one must completely withdraw from the labour market in order to be eligible for the benefit. Moreover, the benefit does not typically depend on the number of years of service except that one should have been employed in the firm or industry for at least ten years.

The costs of early retirement have increased substantially (see Figure 2.3.). Moreover, the situation on the labour market has turned around since 1980 when the early retirement schemes were first introduced as a way to fight unemployment for younger workers. While at that time unemployment was rising rapidly, employers currently experience shortages on the labour market as the labour market is increasingly tight. Hence, many firms attempt to reduce entitlements and increase the age at which employees are eligible for early retirement. In a number of collective labour agreements, early retirement provisions for the elderly are gradually being phased out and replaced by individual saving schemes for younger workers that are more actuarially fair. In this way, early retirement can be expected to be increasingly financed through funded rather than pay–as–you–go schemes.

Disability benefits. In addition to private early retirement schemes, public schemes facilitate early retirement. The most popular public scheme for retiring from the labour force is the disability program, which does not distinguish between social and occupational risks. The percentage of males aged between 55 and 64 collecting a disability benefit increased from 12% in 1968 to 21% in 1975 to 37% in 1985. At present, about a third of the males between 55 and 64 receive a disability benefit (see Table 2.4).

Disability insurance has traditionally been an attractive route for early retirement. Disability benefits were typically more generous (before 1985 80% of the wage and since then 70% of the wage) and of longer duration than unemployment benefits. Moreover, while on disability benefits, one typically keeps accumulating pension rights. Furthermore, employers could get rid of elderly, less productive, employees without being constrained by the various legal obstacles that prevent employers from laying off these workers. In view of the rising costs of disability insurance, the government has tightened the eligibility criteria and the claim assessment procedure, reduced benefits[13], and introduced financial incentives for employers in the form of experience rating (see CPB (1997)).

Unemployment benefits. As a result of these measures involving the disability scheme, the unemployment scheme has become a more popular route for early retirement. Indeed, empirical research suggests that the various exit routes from the labour market are close substitutes (see e.g. Woittiez, Lindeboom and Theeuwes (1994)). The insurance character of unemployment benefits implies that elderly workers typically have accumulated substantial insurance rights. Indeed, most people aged 60 and over can expect to collect unemployment benefits equal to 70% of their previous earnings up to age 65 (in before–tax terms).[14] Another feature facilitating early retirement through the unemployment scheme is that unemployed workers older than 57 1/2 years do not have to apply for work in order to be eligible to unemployment benefits. Moreover, when laying off elderly workers, employers often provide supplementary severance payments to top up the unemployment benefits. In this way, by providing relatively small supplementary

[13] About 73% of the insured employees are in occupational schemes that aim for this aspiration level. In addition to these pension benefits, most occupational pension funds provide survivor benefits.

[14] However, additional supplementary benefits in collective labour contracts largely compensated for the cut in public benefits.

benefits, employers can assure that older laid–off workers can maintain their standard of living. Since the public sector pays for most of the benefits, the employer does not internalize the full costs of de facto early retirement.[15]

2.2.6 Public Support for Retirement Scheme

The first pillar. On the basis of a panel of almost thousand households, van der Heijden (1986) studied the public support for the public pension scheme. The results are reported in Table 2.5. Opinions concerning the contribution rate hardly differ among generations: between 55% and 65% of the respondents believe that the contribution rate is reasonable, while 20% to 25% believe it is high or very high. The results for the benefit levels are remarkably different. Only a small group of respondents believe that the public benefit is high or very high. In fact, about 60% of the middle–aged and the young think that the pension benefit for couples is low or very low, while 40% of the elderly persons think so.

Table 2.5. Opinion on the contribution rate and benefit level of public pensions[a]

	No opinion	Very low	Low	Normal	High	Very high
Contribution rate						
Old	17	0	6	56	20	1
Middle-age	7	0.5	6	63	21	0.5
Young	10	2	7	56	24	1.5
Pension for couples						
Old	7	5.5	33	54	0	0.5
Middle-age	2	6.5	52	37	2	0.5
Young	4	7	52	34	3	0
Pension for single–pension households						
Old	7	8	40	44	0.5	0.5
Middle-age	1	15	57	25	1	1
Young	3	18	54	23	1.5	0.5

Source: Van der Heijden (1996)

[a] As percentage of total number of participants per age group. The age group "old" is age 65 or over, the age group "middle–aged" is 45–65 years old and the "young" are under 45 years.

[15] Those earning low wages may face substantially higher replacement rates. In particular, social assistance benefits for breadwinners without other sources of income and wealth amount to 100% of the minimum wage.

Van der Heijden also asked the respondents for their opinion about the rates of return on contributions to the public pensions for the different generations. These were calculated to be 3.5 for the old, 2.4 for the middle–aged and 1.2 for the young, respectively. For all generations and all rates of return, the answer 'not too high or too low' is most frequent. Most respondents believe that the relatively high rate of return for the elderly is reasonable (about 80%). The same holds true for the average rate for return of the middle–aged (also about 80%). The relatively low rate of return for the young is judged reasonable by about 70% of the young and the middle–aged and 80% of the elderly.

Respondents also evaluated two scenarios that respond differently to ageing. In particular, the additional costs due to ageing are absorbed by either raising contribution rates and maintaining benefits (MB) or by maintaining contributions and reducing benefits (LB). These scenarios were evaluated by assigning a grade between 1 (worst) and 10 (best). Table 2.6. shows that all generations prefer to maintain public pension benefits (MB) rather than maintaining contribution rates (LB). The results are consistent with a panel survey by De Vos et al. (1997) who find that only 6% of the respondents favours a decrease in public pension benefits. These authors report also that 72% prefers partial funding of public pensions whereas 25% favours fixing the public pension premium and covering the revenue shortfall from general tax revenues.

Table 2.6. Evaluation of public pension scenarios[a]

	Old	Middle	Young
LB[b]	4.56	4.23	4.16
MB	5.93	6.03	5.39

Source: Van der Heijden (1996)

[a] Grades from 1.00 (worst) to 10.00 (best).

[b] LB= ageing, maintaining contributions;

MB= ageing, maintaining benefits.

Table 2.7. Preferences for supplementary pensions[a]

	Positive	Neutral	Negative
Level premium / benefit	59	10	31
Retirement age	36	13	51
Pension guaranteed	90	7	3
Participation compulsory	74	14	12
Free choice pension fund	26	17	57
More risk	23	27	50
Switch to average pay	29	42	29
Switch to defined contribution	8	51	41

Source: de Vos et al. (1997)

[a] As a percentage of total number of respondents.

The second pillar. De Vos et al. (1997) showed that the Dutch are quite satisfied with not only the public pensions but also occupational pension schemes (see Table 2.7.). In particular, a majority is satisfied with the premium level in relation to the expected pension benefit. Those who are not satisfied in most cases prefer a higher premium in order to accumulate more pension rights (24%). About half prefers a lower retirement age. However, when confronted with the rise in the premium rate that results if the retirement age falls by one year, only 19% still favours this decrease. The respondents tend to prefer defined–benefit schemes. Only 8% would like to see a transition to defined–contribution schemes. The transition to average pay systems attracts more support (30%) than a move towards defined–contribution schemes, but the group that opposes such a transition to average–pay schemes is equally large. Morever, the compulsory participation in the pension system is broadly supported (74%). About 25% of the participants prefer to have the discretion to select their own pension fund.

2.2.7 Macroeconomic Implications of Pension Schemes

Labour market. The pension system impacts the labour market through various channels, namely pension contributions affecting the marginal tax wedge on labour income, early retirement incentives reducing labour supply, and occupation pensions limiting labour mobility. This subsection discusses these three channels in turn.

Pension contributions and the marginal tax wedge. The flat benefit in the public scheme is financed through a proportional tax on income. Without an individual link between benefits and premiums, the public scheme does not rely much on the insurance principle and involves redistribution from those with higher life–time incomes to those with lower life–time incomes. On the one hand, this progressive pension system implies a substantial marginal tax wedge, which reduces the number of hours worked in the formal sector[16] and discourages partners of breadwinners to participate in the labour market.[17] At the same time, however, the progressive system contains the premium burden on low–skilled workers with low incomes. This helps to maintain the access to work for these vulnerable groups, thereby reducing the number of people on social benefits. Moreover, the focus of

[16] This is an example of public and supplementary private insurance yielding excessive insurance and moral hazard because the private insurer fails to internalize the adverse external effects of additional moral hazard on the public insurer (see Pauly (1974)).

[17] Estimates for the size of the informal sector show a wide range from 1% to almost 10% of GDP (Graafland and de Mooij (1998)).

the public scheme on poverty alleviation reduces the burden of social assistance in fighting old–age poverty.

Early retirement. Old–age provisions exert the most powerful impact on the labour market through the provisions affecting early retirement. Kapteyn and Vos (1997) survey the empirical literature in the Netherlands on the retirement decision. They find that incentives to retire early are very powerful. Moreover, the financial attractiveness of the three main alternative routes to exit the labour force (i.e. early retirement, disability, and unemployment) is an important determinant of the choice between these three alternatives. They conclude that 'the dramatic fall in labour force participation among the elderly in the Netherlands can probably explained largely by the introduction of additional incentives to retire over the last three decades.

Labour mobility. By facilitating the portability of pension rights, Dutch occupational pensions allow for external flexibility, thereby providing insurance against job mobility and firm–specific shocks. At the same time, however, the portability of pensions implies that firms cannot use the pension scheme to encourage commitment and firm–specific investments in human capital. This is in contrast to the situation in Germany, where occupation pensions generally tie workers to the firm. These institutional differences in occupational pensions between Germany and the Netherlands are consistent with the different character of the German and Dutch labour markets more generally. In particular, the German labour market focuses on commitment, whereas the Dutch institutional arrangements involve a mix between commitment and flexibility (see CPB 1997)). Table 2.8., which contains information on the share of jobs with a short tenure, confirms this picture. It suggests that the labour market has become more flexible during a time when pension rights have become more portable.[18]

Table 2.8. Jobs with a tenure of less than one year

	Netherlands	Germany
1985	12	9
1991	24	13

Source: CPB (1997)

[18] Also occupational schemes add to the marginal tax wedge because the link between individual contributions and benefits is quite weak in final–pay occupational schemes.

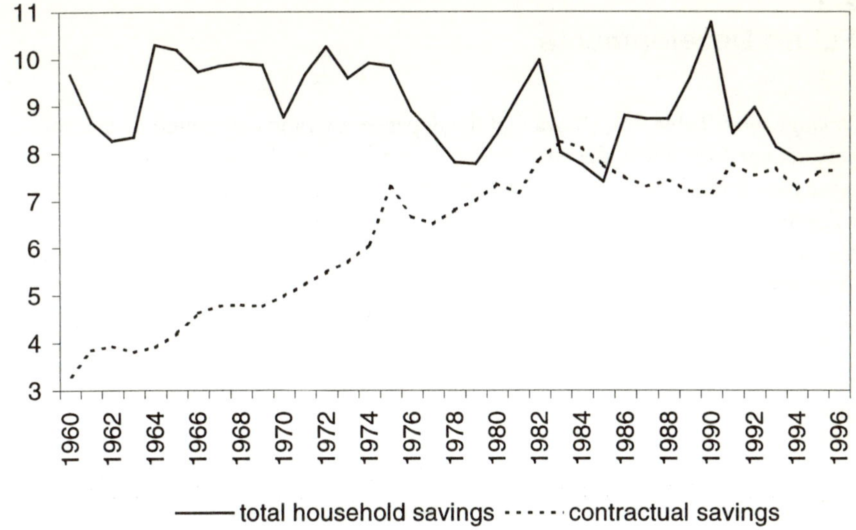

Fig. 2.7. Household savings as percentage of GDP, 1960–1996[a]

Source: Statistics Netherlands

[a] Contractual savings comprises savings trough occupational pensions and individual life insurances.

The capital market. Dutch pension funds are increasingly investing in equity. This facilitates the investment of pension saving in high–yielding projects in the corporate sector, enhances capital mobility within the corporate sector, allows a higher expected return over a long horizon, makes the return less sensitive to unexpected price inflation, and may help to improve corporate governance. Indeed, the Dutch pension system facilitates both capital and labour mobility.

Contractual saving through pension funds and life insurance companies has increased substantially since the second world war. At the same time, the overall level of private saving as a percentage of GDP has been quite stable (see Figure 2.7.). This does not necessarily imply, however, that contractual saving has crowded out other private saving because the expanding public pension (see Figure 2.2.) rather than the building up of private pensions may have reduced non–contractual private saving. Indeed, on the basis of micro–econometric research, Alessie, Kapteyn and Klijn (1997) find that social security wealth fully displaces private wealth. They do not find significant displacement of non pension wealth by pension wealth.[19]

[19] The decrease in average job tenure between 1985 and 1991 needs to be interpreted with caution because it also reflects the relatively rapid growth of employment in the Netherlands during this period and the increasing share of job–shopping young workers.

2.3 Future Developments

Demography. Table 2.9. shows that the dependency ratio (measured as the ratio of persons aged 65 and older and persons aged between 20 and 65) is expected to more than double from its current value of 21 percent[20]. Compared to other OECD countries, fertility in the Netherlands stayed at a high level (above 3) until 1965 but then dropped rapidly during the next decade to 1.66 in 1975. As a direct consequence, the Dutch population is relatively young at the moment but will age more rapidly than the population in most other OECD countries during the first half of the 21st century. The labour force is ageing fast at the moment as the baby-boom generation is entering the 50–64 age group. The rise in the population share of the elderly aged 65 and over will accelerate around 2010. This population share will peak around 2040.

Labour–force participation. The demographic factors that cause ageing provide some offsetting effects on the economic dependency ratio by raising labour supply. In particular, lower fertility tends to raise labour–force participation rate of women. At the same time, increased life expectancy should allow for a rise in the effective retirement age. Also market forces are likely to alleviate the negative effects of ageing on labour supply as higher wages induced by labour scarcity raise both labour productivity growth and labour supply.

[20] The authors caution, however, that measurement error in pension wealth may have biased their results toward finding no significant crowding out.

Table 2.9. Demographic projections

	Total population (million)	65+ population (million)	Dependency ratio (65+/20-64)
1995	15.5	2.0	21.2
2000	15.8	2.2	21.9
2010	16.5	2.5	24.3
2020	16.9	3.2	31.6
2030	17.2	3.9	40.1
2040	17.2	4.3	46.3
2050	16.9	4.0	43.3

Source: de Beer (1997)

Note: The numbers in the table refer to the so–called Medium variant. De Beer (1997) also contains projections for a High and a Low variant.

Various CPB scenarios project increasing labour–force particulation in the period up to 2020. In particular, the participation rate of women between 20 and 65 years, which has already risen rapidly during the past two decades, is expected to continue to rise further from about 50 percent in 1995 to about 70 percent in 2020. Indeed, whereas at present two–earner households are about as common as a household with a breadwinner and a non–participating partner, the two–earner family will become more important in the next century. At the same time, the share of single–person households will rise from 30% at the moment to about 40% in 2020. This boosts spending on public pensions as single elderly collect a higher public pension than elderly in two–person households do.

Public pensions. Various projections for the costs of public pensions are contained in Table 2.10. Reflecting the development of the dependency ratio, these costs start to rise rapidly in 2010 and reach a peak in 2040. However, the costs of the public pensions (in terms of GDP) do not double between 1995 and 2040 as could have been expected from the doubling of the dependency rate during this period. This is due to three main factors. First, the increase in labour–force participation mitigates the rise in the economic dependency ratio. Second, as explained in subsection 2.1.1, the public pension benefit lags the average standard of living because the pension benefit is linked to contractual rather than actual wages.[21] Third, the public pension is linked to the after–tax minimum wage. Accordingly, by cutting the after–tax wage, a higher pension premium decreases the costs of public pensions.

[21] This projection is based on the Medium variant in de Beer (1997). In the Low and the High variant the dependency rate rises to about 44 and 49, respectively.

Table 2.10. Costs of public pensions, projections[a]

	1995	2010	2020	2030	2040	2050
Base scenario	5.3	5.7	6.8	7.8	8.1	7.1
High participation[b]	5.3	5.5	6.4	7.2	7.4	6.3
No incidental wage increases[c]	5.3	5.9	7.2	8.4	8.9	8.0
Less ageing[d]	5.3	5.6	6.5	7.3	7.4	6.3

Source: CPB (1996b)

[a] As a percentage of GDP.

[b] Participation rate (in persons) increases to 66.3% instead of 56.3% in 2060.

[c] Incidental wage increase of 0% instead of 0.25% per year.

[d] Dependency ratio increases to 28.0% instead of 33.0% in 2060.

Occupational pensions. Ageing affects also funded occupational schemes, albeit more indirectly than public pay–as–you go schemes. In particular, ageing makes the premiums levied by funded defined–benefit systems more sensitive to changes in the rate of return because it reduces the premium base compared to the insured pension rights. Moreover, ageing may depress the rate of return and raise wage growth as it makes labour more scarce compared to capital. Table 2.11 shows that a permanent fall in the rate of return of 1 percentage point raises the required premium costs of the occupational pensions by about 4 percent of gross wages.[22]

Table 2.11. Costs of occupational pensions, projections[a]

	2010	2030	2050
Real rate of return 4.3%	9.4	9.7	9.4
Real rate of return 3.3%	13.0	14.7	13.7
Real rate of return 2.3%	15.9	18.5	18.1

Source: Tamerus (1997)

[a] As a percentage of total gross wages

[22] As a result, projections for the costs of public pensions are rather sensitive to assumptions about incidental wage growth. At present, CPB expects this growth to be 0.25% a year.

2.4 Current Reform Options

This section elaborates on various reform options discussed in the Netherlands. We discuss public pensions, occupational pensions, and early retirement schemes in turn.

2.4.1 Public Pension

The impact of ageing on the public pension system can be addressed either by strengthening the financing of the public pension through broadening the contribution base or by reducing the generosity of the benefit through the adoption a less generous indexation method, a rise in the statutory retirement age, or a cut in benefits for single–person households.

Broadening the contribution base. To broaden the contribution base, also those older than 65 could be required to contribute to the public pension system by financing the public system entirely out of general tax revenues. Shifting the burden of financing the public pension system to the more affluent elderly[23] reduces the burden of the public pension system on workers, thereby alleviating labour–market distortions. In order to reduce the burden on existing retirees who have not been able to anticipate the contributions for the public pensions, the contributions by the elderly may have to be phased in gradually.

Indexation. The indexation mechanism promises to remain a controversial issue. Some have proposed to link public benefit to prices rather than contractual wages (Nyfer (1996)). This would gradually privatize pension provision as rising real wages would reduce the value of the public pension relative to the average standard of living. Others, in contrast, favour to raise benefits not only with contractual wages but also the incidental wage. This would maintain the relative standard of living of the elderly and contain the costs of supplementary pensions that have build in the public pension (Jansweijer (1996)).

[23] The growth of real wages is another important determinant of the costs of occupational defined–benefit pensions because benefits are directly linked to wages. In the Dutch institutional setting, the growth of incidental wages is a particularly important determinant of the costs of occupational pensions because incidental wage growth causes the public pension to lag average wages. This raises the costs of these latter scheme to the extent that the public pension is build into the occupation pension schemes. Hence, high incidental wage growth contains the costs of the public pension but boosts the costs of the private pensions.

Statutory retirement age. A higher statutory retirement age is generally not seen as an attractive option in the short run. Before raising the statutory retirement age, the excessive retirement incentives in early retirement schemes (see section 2.3) should be addressed. In the longer run, however, a higher statutory retirement age may be called for, especially if the ageing of the labour force causes labour to become increasingly scarce. Some have argued in favour of the government early announcing an increase in the statutory retirement age so that current workers can anticipate this by investing more in either human or financial capital (see e.g., Don (1996)).

Supplement for single–person households. In order to reduce the possibilities for fraud in an increasingly individualized society, it has been proposed to abolish the differentiation of the pension benefit across different household sizes (see, e.g., de Vries (1997)). This proposal, would either raise the costs of public pensions (if the public benefit was set close to the current level for single–person households) or reduce the living standard of single–person households who are often in greatest need of the public pension (if the public benefit was set close to the current level for two–persons households).[24]

2.4.2 Occupational Pensions

In addition to ageing, various developments demand an adaptation of occupational pension schemes. These trends include individualization, a more heterogeneous population with diverse tastes and needs, an increasingly competitive environment, a more flexible labour market, and higher labour–force participation of women.

Reducing ambition levels. The previous government favoured a move away from final–pay to average–pay schemes to cut labour costs by reducing the ambition level of collective pensions. Indeed, the mandatory, collective level of pension insurance is quite high in the Netherlands. As tastes have become more heterogeneous and the aspiration level has increased in after–tax terms, some workers may have become over–insured.[25] This calls for a reduction in the collective part of old–age insurance for the middle– and higher incomes. The earners of these

[24] The less affluent elderly who rely mainly on the public pension as a source of income would not be hurt by this measure because the public pension benefit is linked to the after–tax minimum wage.

[25] Of the social minimum for social assistance was not adjusted in the same way, many single-person households would call on social assistance.

incomes are typically better able to deal with old–age risks. In this connection, more possibilities for firms and individuals to opt out of industry–wide pension funds are sometimes discussed. However, a wholesale shift from occupational defined–benefit schemes to defined–contribution schemes does not attract much support in the Netherlands (see subsection 2.4.2).

The franchise. Most occupational schemes employ the franchise (discussed in subsection 2.1.2) to take into account the public pension in determining pension rights. More and more pension funds no longer directly link the franchise to the public pension, thereby shifting the political risk of lower public benefits to workers.

As documented in subsection 4.1.2, the franchise in most occupational pension plans is linked to a public pension for a two–person household. It implies that two–earner households and singles do not reach the aspiration level of 70% of the final wage. To do more justice to the increasing importance of two–earner households, many favour a lower franchise.[26]

2.4.3 Early Retirement

A major way to improve the sustainability of the pension system in the face of ageing is to boost labour–force participation of the elderly. Indeed, in an environment of an increasingly tight labour market, encouraging early retirement is more and more viewed as a more and more inappropriate policy. Hence, social partners in many sectors are presently studying the possibilities of gradually phasing out pay–as–you–go schemes that provide large incentives for early retirement and substituting these schemes by individual pension plans that are more actuarially fair. As regards public benefits facilitating early retirement, the government has tightened eligibility requirements (e.g., stricter evaluations of disability, making unemployment benefits conditional on retraining or accepting less desirable jobs), is intensifying checks on improper use of social benefits, and aims to enhance the efficiency of the organizations administering social benefits (see CPB (1997)).

[26] The fact that many elderly save substantial parts of their incomes provides evidence for over-insurance.

[27] Proposals for a lower franchise are often combined with cost cutting measures such as a lower rate of accumulation of pension rights or lower survivor benefits.

2.5 Conclusions

The current three–pillar structure in the Netherlands is generally viewed as a good framework for pension insurance. An important reason for adopting a mix of pension systems is to diversify macroeconomic risks. Indeed, workers should not put all their eggs in one basket to avoid excessive exposure to the substantial political, investment, and human capital risks over a long time horizon. The selected mix and the particular features of each of the pillars, however, should depend on political preferences, the functioning of capital and labour markets, and expected future trends. Indeed, various of these trends require modifying the current pension systems. To illustrate, the ageing of the population may require changes in the pay–as–you–go pensions provided by the public sector and demand a higher effective retirement age. The trends involving a more heterogeneous population, individualisation, and more flexible labour markets may result in less collective insurance through occupational defined–benefit schemes and collective early retirement schemes, leaving more discretion to the individual worker in personal pension plans of the defined–contribution type. Indeed, the third pillar of pension insurance, which is currently quite small in the Netherlands, is likely to gain in importance in the future.

References

Alessie, R.J.M., Kapteyn, A., Klijn, F.: Mandatory Pensions and Personal Savings in the Netherlands. De Economist, Vol. 145, pp. 291–324 1997

Beer, J. de: Population Forecasts 1996: less population growth, increased ageing. Maandstatistiek Bevolking 1997/1 1997

Besseling, P.J.: Het tweerichtingsverkeer tussen economie en pensioen. Paper prepared for conference on pensions at Tilburg University on June 10, 1997

CPB: Omgevingsscenario's Lange Termijn Verkenning 1995–2020, CPB Werkdocument No. 89 1996a

CPB: Macro Economische Verkenning 1997, The Hague: Sdu Publishers, 1996b

CPB: Challenging Neighbours: Rethinking German and Dutch Economic Institutions. Berlin: Springer Verlag, 1997

Don, H.: Pensioen, overheid en markt. Economisch Statistische Berichten, No. 4065, pp. 585–608 1996

Graafland, J.J., Mooij R.A. de: Analyzing Fiscal Policy in the Netherlands: Simulations with a Revised MIMIC. CPB Research Memorandum No. 140 (1998)

Groezen, B. van, Kraamwinkel, M., Meijdam, L., Nelissen, J., Verbon, H., Vermeulen, H.: Pensioenresultaten. CentER Applied Research, Tilburg University (1999)

Heijden, E. van der: Altruism, Fairness and Public pensions: An Investigation of Survey and Experimental Data. CentER Dissertation 15, Tilburg Universtity 1996

Jansweijer, R.M.A.: Gouden Bergen, Diepe Dalen: De inkomensgevolgen van een betaalbare oudedagsvoorziening. Scientific Council for Government Policy Study V92, The Hague: Sdu Publishers, 1996

Kapteyn, A., Vos, K. de: Social Security and Retirement in the Netherlands, NBER Working Paper No. 6135, Cambridge 1997

Lazear, E.P.: Retirement from the Labour Force. in: Ashenfelter, O., Layard, R.: Handbook of Labour Economics. Vol.1, North Holland, Amsterdam 1986

Nyfer: Lang Zullen We Leven! En wie zal dat betalen..., Special study No. 3, Sdu Publishers, The Hague 1996

OECD: The Labour Market and Older Workers. Social Policy Studies No. 17 1995

OECD: Beyond 2000: The new Social Policy Agenda. Paris: 1997

OECD: The Retirement Decision in OECD Countries. OECD Working Paper No. 202 1998

Pauly, M.V.: Overinsurance and Public Provision of Insurance; the Roles of Moral Hazard and Adverse Selection. Quarterly Journal of Economics, Vol. 88, pp. 44–62 1974

Tamerus, J.: De vermeende onbeheersbaarheid van de eindloonregeling, Pensioen Magazine, Nr. 6, pp. 12–17 1997

Vos, K. de, Alessie, R.J.M., Fontein, P.: Pensioenen: regelingen, percepties en preferenties, EIT, Tilburg University

Vries, B. de, R.A.J.: Dur Verzilverd Vergrijzen. OCFEB Discussion Paper, Erasmus University Rotterdam 1997

Woittiez, I., Lindeboom, M., Theeuwes, J.: Labour Force Exit Routes of the Dutch Elderly; A Discrete Choice Model. in: Bovenberg, L.: The Economics of Pensions: The Case of the Netherlands, OCFEB, Erasmus University Rotterdam 1994

3 The Swiss Three–Pillar Model

by Maria Verena Brombacher Steiner

3.1 A Brief Look at How the Swiss System of Old Age, Survivors and Disability Insurance Evolved

3.1.1 Gradual Development

The current Swiss social security system evolved over a number of decades, with the very first steps reaching back into the 19th century. Since the system is not based on an overall concept, we must look at its historical development to understand the complex structure.

At a federal level, health insurance was introduced in 1914 and accident insurance in 1918. This was followed after the Second World War by old age and survivors insurance (AHV), family allowances for farm owners, unemployment insurance and, finally, disability insurance (IV). A new phase of expansion began in the mid–sixties: apart from developing two further pillars for old age, survivors and disability insurance, accident and unemployment insurance was improved in 1984 (extended to cover all employees, admission of private insurance policies in accident insurance), and in 1996 health insurance was reorganized (including introduction of compulsory insurance for the entire population).

3.1.2 Focus on Old Age, Survivors and Disability Insurance

Personal saving ("a penny in time") is the earliest form of provision for unexpected circumstances. This was soon followed by company insurance schemes created by a few progressive employers. Soon after the turn of the century, the concept of a national insurance system for retirement, death and disability for the entire population emerged in Switzerland. The Swiss voted to lay the constitutional basis for this in 1925. But the transformation from a constitutional mandate to a federal law took some time. An initial draft presented by the Bundesrat (Swiss executive), which called for only modest contributions and pension benefits, was clearly rejected by the Swiss population in a referendum in 1931. It took another 17years until old age and survivors insurance (AHV) was finally realized. A referendum was also held on this new draft which was partly based on experience gained during the war in connection with payroll compensation for soldiers. An overwhelming majority voted in favour of the new law, which came into force on January 1, 1948. Twelve years later, i.e. 35 years after the constitutional mandate had been resolved, disability insurance (IV) was passed on January 1, 1960; it is closely linked to the AHV and its pension system.

Even at that early date, both the Bundesrat and parliament chose to pursue a three–pillar concept. In order to enhance the basic insurance coverage provided by AHV and IV to ensure the welfare of the population, a federal law on supplementary benefits (ELG) was passed on January 1, 1966. At the time, it was thought that these benefits would only be necessary temporarily until AHV and IV pension benefits managed to cover people's welfare needs.

The population voted in favour of the three–pillar concept in 1972, and it became part of the Federal Constitution. In 1973, a substantial rise in old age, survivors and disability benefits by 80% was resolved, followed by a further increase of 25% in 1975. At the same time, the contributions to this first pillar were raised to a rate that has remained unchanged up to the present.

The constitution also called for some form of occupational insurance. After much political debate, the Federal Act on Occupational Insurance (BVG) was drawn up, but it is basically only a compromise that has not fully reached the constitutional targets. Nevertheless, the draft was approved by the population, and the law enacted on January 1st, 1985.

With regard to the third pillar, i.e. making one's own provision for the future, the constitution is not as concrete. It only says that this pillar is to be supported by fiscal and ownership policy. Thus, at the same time the Act on Occupational Insurance was passed, the federal government also introduced regulations on the tax deductibility of contributions to recognized forms of insurance which formed the basis of the so-called tied self–insurance scheme. Somewhat later, a federal Act on the Promotion of (Owner–Occupied) Dwellings was passed. Besides this, there is also the wide segment of so–called voluntary self–insurance, which includes personal savings and private insurance schemes.

This gradual development of Swiss law reflects the fact that Switzerland is a federation and that the member states (cantons) are sovereign entities. So the central government can only enact legislation if it has been empowered to do so by the constitution, which is only done within very strict limits. In addition, Switzerland is a direct democracy, where the population participates in the legislative process by its right to (compulsory or facultative) referendums and on the basis of people's initiatives. This explains why it took nearly a century to lay the constitutional groundwork and establish a social security system.

3.2 The Three Pillars of Old Age, Survivors and Disability Insurance in Switzerland

3.2.1 The 1st Pillar: National Old Age, Survivors and Disability Insurance (AHV/IV) to Preserve the Welfare of the Population, with Cantonal Supplementary Benefits, if Needed

The first pillar called for by the constitution is a compulsory old age, survivors and disability insurance for the entire population. The pension benefits paid are to guarantee certain standards of well-being for the population. This insurance system is to be organized by public–law institutions that are to be set up by the federal government, the cantons and, on a voluntary basis, associations of employers and the self–employed.

The group of persons insured thereby automatically covers all natural persons whose civil–law place of residence is in Switzerland. All persons employed in Switzerland are also subject to compulsory insurance (this includes cross–border commuters, seasonal labourers, temporary workers).

The benefits provided by AHV are primarily pension benefits. Survivors pensions only make up about 5% of the total AHV pension payments; and because of this minor role, they will be largely disregarded in the following. In the case of disability insurance (IV), the principle of "integration before pension" applies, which is why the insurance system assumes the cost of (medical and occupational) integration measures before it extends pension payments, which are only given if the former do not produce the hoped–for effect. Helpless minors are entitled to special educational measures and care under disability insurance; children with birth defects are eligible for benefits from birth. Alongside pension benefits, both insurance systems also grant other monetary benefits (daily allowances during integration phase, benefits for the disadvantaged or helpless) and physical assistance (aid). The disability insurance scheme also gives substantial financial support to institutions that offer services for the insured parties (so–called collective benefits to promote disability assistance).

The pension benefits under AHV/IV are in principle a form of compensation income, and are therefore, with the exception of orphans benefits, only granted to persons over 18. Eligibility for ordinary pension benefits arises as soon as contributions have been credited for at least one full calendar year.

The calculation of AHV and IV pension benefits is based on the number of years the insured person has paid contributions and his/her average annual income over the entire insurance period.

The contribution period is considered complete if, in the event of an insurance claim, the person has made contributions for the same number of years as others born in the same year. A contribution year is defined as follows:

- period over which a person has made contributions;
- period over which the spouse of a non–employed person has paid at least twice theminimum contribution amount (these contributions are later split equally among the two);
- periods for which credits for child–raising or care for elderly or infirm family members have been awarded.

If full contributions have been paid, full pension benefits are awarded; for 1999, monthly pensions were between CHF 1,005 (so–called guaranteed minimum pension) and CHF 2,010 (maximum pension limit). If the contribution period is not complete, partial pensions are paid on the basis of the insured person's years of contribution compared with others born in the same year (pension scale 1–44).

For calculation purposes, average annual income consists of the following:

- earned income (i.e. income on which contributions are paid. In the case of unemployed persons, the contributions are transformed into earned income. Income earned by a spouse during the years of marriage are split, with each spouse receiving half.);
- child–raising credits (awarded for every year in which an insured person has exercised parental authority over one or more children up to the age of 16, a credit amounting to three times the minimum annual old age pension is calculated);
- infirmity care credits (awarded for every year in which infirm or incapacitated family members living in the joint household are looked after; credits are awarded along the same lines as child–raising credits);

Up to an imputable average annual income of CHF 12,060, minimum pension benefits will always be calculated (assuming a full contribution period). People with an imputable average annual income of CHF 72,360 or more are entitled to the maximum pension benefits, which, according to law, must be exactly twice the size of the minimum benefits.

The combined pension benefits of a married couple may not exceed 150% of the maximum amount of a single retirement pension, i.e. at most an annual CHF 3,015 (assuming contributions are fully paid in). In addition to these pension benefits, supplementary pension benefits are also paid for the wife (who is not, or not yet, entitled to a pension – this type of pension is due to be discontinued soon) and so-called children's pension benefits. This latter instrument replaces children's allowances, which in Switzerland are part of wages and salaries and can thus only be given to employed persons.

All pension benefits (both current and newly resolved) are adjusted to wage and price developments (arithmetic mean) every two years. However, if the consumer price index has risen by more than 4% in the course of one year, adjustments are made on an annual basis. Adjustments based on such a mixed index have proven to be effective: from 1986 to 1996, the level of pension benefits was raised by 34.7%, and during the same period the consumer price index rose by 31.3%, wages and salaries by 37.7%.

Men over the age of 65 and women over the age of 62 or 63 (from 2001) or 64 (from 2005) are entitled to old age pension benefits. Under various circumstances, men and women can receive these pensions up to two years earlier, in which case, however, the pension benefits will be reduced by 6.8% for each year of premature payment (this rate has been actuarily calculated on the basis of life expectancy). For women, the deduction rate is 3.4% up to 2008. Pension payments can be delayed by up to five years at most, which is rewarded with mark–ups of between 5.2% and 31.5%.

Widow's and widower's pension benefits amount to 80% of the respective old age pension benefits. Orphan's benefits are, as a rule, 40% of the corresponding old age benefits; full orphans receive two orphan's pensions. Disability pensions are calculated on the same basis as old age pensions. Depending on the degree of disability (at least 66 2/3% or 50% or 40% incapacitation), there are full, half or quarter pensions.

For both AHV and IV, financing is conducted on a pay–as–you–go basis combined with fluctuation reserves, which accounted for 90% of annual spending as late as 1997. Sources of income are contributions paid by the insured parties and employers, on the one hand, as well as subsidies from the federal and cantonal governments on the other hand. The latter are financed through general tax income, tobacco tax and excises on spirits. They are geared to the annual expenditure of the insurance system and total 20% of AHV or 50% in the case of disability insurance. To help finance the increasing costs of AHV/IV insurance, VAT tax was raised from 6.5% to 7.5% with effect from January 1, 1999. 17% of the additional VAT income goes to the federal government (not the cantons), which has pledged to use these funds to subsidize old age, survivors and disability insurance. Interest paid on the funds in the fluctuation reserve produce further income amounting to roughly 4% of expenditure (until one year ago, AHV was only allowed to invest its assets in fixed-income Swiss franc instruments – above all government paper; since 1997, limited equity investments are permitted).

As a rule, all insured persons must make compulsory social insurance contributions over the entire period of their gainful employment. Employees currently contribute 4.2% of their gross income to old age and survivors insurance and 0.7% to disability insurance; their employers pay the same rates. In the case of the self–employed, their contribution rate amounts to 9.2% of their income (contributions are graded, with a minimum of 4.2% for low annual incomes). It should be noted that there is no upper contribution limit. Non–employed persons' (this includes homemakers, students, recipients of full disability or survivors pensions, as well as unemployed persons) compulsory contributions begin at the age of 20 and end when they reach retirement age. Contributions are geared to the insured party's circumstances (assets and pension income) and, for AHV and IV together, amount to between CHF 390 and CHF 10,100 per year. Selected groups of insured persons are exempted from making compulsory contributions. Minors, for instance, pay no contributions. In addition, non–employed spouses of employed and insured persons will be considered to have paid their contributions if the employed spouse pays contributions amounting to at least twice the minimum contribution.

In 1997, average old age pension benefits for singles were CHF 1,675 and CHF 1,381 each for married persons. 33% of all unmarried pensioners and 53% of all married couples received the maximum pension benefits. Owing to the fact that AHV/IV pension benefits are at times not sufficient to guarantee the welfare of elderly or handicapped persons or survivors (e.g. in case of incomplete contribution payments owing to periods spent abroad or insufficient income), the cantons grant so–called supplementary benefits financed by the public budget. The federal government contributes subsidies of 10% to 35% – depending on the financial position of the canton involved – to help finance these benefits.

The supplementary benefits are non–contributory contingency benefits. Pensioners are entitled to these benefits if the payments they need to meet exceed their income, and if their imputable annual income does not reach the level of guaranteed minimum income. Naturally, this can only cover minimum welfare requirements, so not all expenses can be taken into account. The law therefore specifies which income and spending is applicable (e.g. general living necessities, rental payments, contributions to insurance, maintenance and support, etc.) and sets upper limits. Alongside these supplementary benefits, costs relating to illness or a handicap are also reimbursed.

The amount of the supplementary benefits depends on the additional spending needs, and in 1999 was between CHF 47,760 per year (for persons living at home) and CHF 28,512 (for persons living in an institution). In 1997, about 15% of all AHV and IV pensioners received supplementary benefits from their canton. About one–third of all recipients, who account for two–thirds of total spending, use these funds to pay the substantial cost of living permanently in a home or institution. So, in fact, the supplementary benefits cover the remaining costs of nursing care.

Despite a constant improvement in old age, survivors and disability benefits, the supplementary benefits are by no means losing in importance. On the contrary: the need for supplementary payments is rising owing to higher rental expenses and a rise in costs for nursing care and accommodation in nursing homes.

3.2.2 The 2nd Pillar: Occupational Insurance (BV), Based on Statutory Minimum Insurance and a Voluntary Additional Insurance

The second pillar is meant to rest on the first, and together the two are to allow recipients to continue their accustomed standard of living. But the Federal Act on Occupational Insurance only provides guaranteed minimum insurance. But under their legally guaranteed autonomy with regard to benefits, financing and organization, the various social insurance providers are free to offer higher benefits (known as benefits exceeding compulsory levels). Compulsory occupational insurance is interpreted as AHV/IV pension payments plus occupational pension benefits, which together are to make up roughly 60% of gross income, (for which there is a ceiling). The system will be in an introductory phase until 2025, which is why compulsory social insurance does not always reach this performance target at present.

Occupational insurance is handled by a number of individual social security institutions of various sizes and structures. In 1996, there were roughly 11,600 collective social security institutions at insurance companies, autonomous institutions with or without reinsurance, partially independent institutions, etc., with very divergent numbers of insured parties. Each of these institutions can organize itself at its own discretion in the legal form of a foundation, cooperative or public-law institution.

Each social security institution insures the risks of old age, death and disability according to its own benefit plan, administers the financing of these performance targets independently and is responsible for providing the benefits offered. Their income is obtained mainly from contributions from employers and employees, the proceeds of investing these funds and cancellation profits (premium reserves that are no longer needed). Basically the principle of full funding is applied. But in certain exceptional cases, such as benefits to offset inflation or for a new generation entering the system, a kind of pay–as–you–go scheme has also been chosen.

The social security institutions, which are often administered on a parity basis, invest their assets independently, taking into account considerations of security, earnings, proper risk distribution and liquidity. The act specifies which investments are permissible, and also sets investment limits. If a social security institution goes bankrupt, there is a back–up fund financed with contributions from all social security institutions which will step in and ensure that statutory minimum benefits are paid. The fund also subsidizes social security institutions that have a more unfavourable age structure than others.

Occupational insurance (BV) is compulsory for all employees who earn more than CHF 24,120 per year (so–called coordination deduction or lower wage limit, corresponds to twice the annual AHV minimum pension). This applies to over 80% of all employees. The self–employed can participate on a voluntary basis. Because compulsory BV payments supplement old age, survivors and disability insurance, they must also be subject have an upper limit. This ceiling is three times the minimum wage (1999: CHF 72,360), and thus the maximum pension–forming income under AHV. Therefore, the insured (or coordinated) income amounted to a maximum of CHF 48,240 in 1999.

Benefits are generally paid in the form of pensions, but for small benefits, or – if agreed otherwise in the regulations – a lump–sum compensation payment is also conceivable. In 1996, an annual occupational pension (on average for all types of pensions) amounted to CHF 19,819, and the average old age pension to CHF 25,027. In about 5% of all cases, monetary compensation averaging CHF 93,000 was paid. The calculation of benefits is based on so–called retirement credits, which are booked onto a personal old age account for each insured person. These credits consist of certain percentage of coordinated income, depending on the person's age (so–called conversion rate, between 7% and 18%), plus interest (4% minimum interest, unchanged since 1965). The occupational insurance benefits are calculated as apercentage of the retirement credits the insured person has acquired on reaching retirement age. The statutory minimum conversion rate is currently 7.2%, irrespective of gender or marital status, and is based on a retirement age of 65 for men and 62 for women.

Old age pension benefits are granted to men over 65 and women over 62. The regulations of the pension funds may, however, provide scope for early retirement benefits, starting at the earliest five years before this statutory retirement age, or may call for the same retirement age for men and women. In this case, the pension amount will be lower, owing to lower retirement credits and a reduced conversion rate. In case of death of the insured employee or pension recipient, survivors benefits are paid. In case of an incapacitation percentage of 50% or more, insured persons are entitled to disability benefits. For these premature benefits, fictitious retirement credits are calculated for the years missing up to retirement age.

Under the second pillar, only disability and survivors pension benefits are subject to a compulsory adjustment to price developments, and so they enjoy a certain degree of protection from inflation. However, once retirement age has been reached, it is at the discretion of each pension fund to conduct such adjustments. Numerous social security institutions have undertaken to do so on a voluntary basis in their regulations.

Employees cannot select the social insurance institution themselves. These are determined by the employer. If a staff member leaves a company and its social insurance institution before retirement age, he is entitled to a so–called termination payment. Depending on the social insurance provider, this payment corresponds either to the amount saved plus premium reserve or the cash value of benefits acquired. When the insured party joins a new company and a new social insurance provider, this amount will be credited to him as an entry benefit. If the termination payment is not used for switching into a new social insurance fund (e.g. owing to interruption of employment or unemployment), then the funds must be transferred to a blocked account or paid into a blocked insurance policy. Benefits can only be disbursed if the pension beneficiary leaves Switzerland permanently or becomes self-employed and is therefore no longer subject to compulsory insurance.

The size of contributions depends on the regulations of the social insurance provider which the employer has chosen to work with. The law itself only stipulates that contributions are to be paid by both employer and employee, and that the employer contribution must at least equal total employee contributions. Generally speaking, employee and employer contributions will be between 17% and 18% each of the coordinated (insured) wages. The average contribution rate is probably somewhere between 9% and 10%.

Second–pillar funds may also be used to expand the third pillar. If, for instance, the insured person would like to buy residential property for his own purposes, social security entitlement can be pledged or an advance payment up to the amount of the termination payment can be applied for. This will, however, lead to a cut in his/her future benefit entitlement.

3.2.3 The 3rd Pillar: Individual, Tied and/or Voluntary Self–Insurance

As incomes rise, it is becoming increasingly difficult for pillars 1 and 2 of state social insurance to guarantee a continuation of the accustomed standard of living. This is where the 3rd pillar comes in: people must take initiative and assume responsibility for setting their own targets and making appropriate financial arrangements.

In this respect, the Federal Constitution instructs the federal government to take fiscal and ownership policy measures to promote this pension–building component. In the fiscal sector, these measures consist of tax alleviations attached to certain conditions (so–called tied self–insurance or pillar 3a).

Tied self–insurance is geared primarily to employees and the self–employed who are not covered by the second pillar. These persons can make contributions to certain recognized pension providers (retirement policy with an insurance company or retirement account with a bank foundation) which can be deducted from their taxable income up to an annual maximum amount. This annual maximum amount accounts for 20% of their earned income, or at most 40% of the ceiling for coordinated income (1999: CHF 28,944). Persons who have an occupational pension scheme can only deduct a maximum of 8% of the coordinated income ceiling (1999: CHF 5,789). Non–employed persons are not eligible for tied self–insurance.

The amounts paid in (and deducted from tax) remain blocked until an insurance claim is lodged. They can be paid at the earliest five years before the AHV retirement age is reached, but in that case are liable to taxation. The person who made the pension arrangements is entitled to receive benefits; in case of death, his/her direct heirs are eligible claimants. If there are no heirs, the entitlement goes to any person designated by the insured person.

This tax deduction facility for tied self–insurance has led to a ninefold increase in such capital investment over a 10 year period. In 1995, assets accumulated in this form of insurance accounted for about 4.8% of second–pillar assets, or about 5.8% of GDP. It is thought to correspond to about 10% of the estimated national saving volume.

In the case of voluntary self–insurance, numerous alternatives are available, which of course depend on the amount of income available for this purpose. These include above all life insurance policies, bank savings schemes, securities or real estate. Although the focus here is not on tax alleviations, certain deductions can be made on direct federal taxes and cantonal income tax (e.g. for insurance premiums and savings interest).

There is no way of reliably determining how much capital has been saved in personal pension arrangements. No figures or estimates are available. It is assumed, however, that it is a multiple of the average of the second pillar and tied self-insurance together. Estimates lie somewhere between CHF 1,000 and 2000 billion. So this type of provision is very significant in a social and economic policy respect.

3.2.4 The Coordination of the Three Pillars

The constitution calls for a coordination of the first and second pillars. This is to ensure that compulsory occupational insurance sets in at an income level that corresponds to twice the AHV/IV minimum pension (so–called coordination deduction).

Consequently, up to an annual income of CHF 12,060 (= annual AHV/IV minimum pension) this produces a compensation rate of 100 % and more, (always assuming full contributions over the entire insurance period). For annual incomes between CHF 12,060 and CHF 24,120 (= lower income limit for the second pillar) an increasing AHV/IV pension is paid, but no pension under the occupational insurance scheme. The compensation rate drops to 60 %. For annual incomes between CHF 24,120 and CHF 72,360 (= income ceiling) the AHV/IV pension up to the maximum amount is complemented by (linear) compulsory occupational insurance benefits, so that the compensation rate remains more or less unchanged at 60 %. The compensation rate declines further for annual incomes above CHF 72,360, so insured persons depend increasingly on benefits which exceed compulsory levels and/or (tied or voluntary) self–insurance.

The (latest) survey conducted in 1990 revealed the following income structure for pensioners' households: single households: 46 % old age and survivors' insurance (AHV), 22.2 % occupational insurance (BV), 9.8 % investment income, 6.2 % income from gainful employment and 16 % other forms of income; two–person households: 41.5 % AHV, 31.7 % BV, 7.1 5% investment income, 11.3 %

income from gainful employment and 8.4 % other sources of income.

3.2.5 Coordination with Other Social Insurance Schemes

Welfare/public assistance is the responsibility of the 26 cantons and in some cases also of communities in Switzerland and it is designed to fill any gaps not covered by the social insurance scheme. It is not related to any specific risk and is given to those in financial need. The size of benefit payments is not regulated by law; payments are made according to need on a case–by–case basis. Recipients of retirement pensions will only require welfare in exceptional cases – for instance if they need round–the-clock care – since AHV pensions and supplementary benefits will cover their needs as a rule.

A question that repeatedly arises is why not revert to other branches of social security insurance in the difficult labour market situation. An analysis conducted in the field of disability insurance has shown that a rise in pension spending for disability insurance by roughly 50 % is attributable largely to the increase of pension recipients, but that this increase stems primarily from changes in the structure in the population and higher life expectancy of disabled persons. In 1993 for instance only 3 % of new pension recipients were directly related to unemployment.

In the case of unemployment it was discovered that the unemployment rate of elderly persons was below average. In addition, it was found that when companiesconduct reorganization measures they tend to recommend that older staff members go into early retirement and receive occupational insurance pensions instead of having them apply for unemployment benefits.

3.2.6 Acceptance of the Three Pillar System by the Population

The question of political acceptance does not arise in Switzerland because each new extension of the social security system has been the subject of far–reaching, democratic debate and acknowledges a broad political consensus, often confirmed by a referendum.

With regard to social acceptance there is only little empirical data. Inasmuch as surveys are to believed, the general attitude has not changed much despite growing social burdens. Surveys point to a continued feeling of solidarity (e.g. between the younger and older generations). However, given the continued economic stagnation and a globalization of markets there are increasing political discussions as to how much social security Switzerland wants and can afford.

A survey conducted when the old age and survivors insurance scheme turned 50 showed that employed persons are well acquainted with the three pillar system and also rely fully on both the first and the second pillar when it comes to their old age pensions. It was gratifying to find that a large percentage of respondents made their own provisions for old age as part of the tied self–insurance programme. Generally speaking this system was thought to be safe and flexible.

3.2.7 Effects on the National Economy

At present no statistical data or specific studies are available on how the various extensions of the social insurance system affected the Swiss economy. This is probably attributable to the fact that it was a slow process and each new law was simply a confirmation of what already existed on a voluntary basis. In addition there is also widespread political and social acceptance of the system as shown by the fact that only very insignificant attempts are made to circumvent it.

The old age and survivors insurance system and the disability insurance system are an example for solidarity between lower and higher wage earners. The maximum pension is only twice the size of the minimum pension, but contributions for the maximum pension are six times as high as for the minimum pension. This redistribution effect is also promoted by the fact that the contributions to AHV/IV are calculated on a basis of the entire income even though the size of the pension is only influenced by income up to a certain ceiling. Despite the strong social redistribution component the old age, survivors and disability insurance systems are considered to be fair by most. A parity–based financing using fixed wage percentages is well established among the social partners; moonlighting or unrecorded employment is not a major problem. What's more, the percentage people who leave gainful employment to take up leisure time activities or work outside gainful employment is only very insignificant.

The income situation and development of income in certain categories of population (e.g. pensioners) has not been analysed systematically to date. In 1990 it was established that the average monthly income of gainfully employed households amounted to CHF 7,587,that of pensioners households to CHF 4,123 and that the average monthly spending of gainfully employed households amounted to CHF 6,989 and for pensioners households to CHF 4,053. But these rough averages must be treated with caution and should not lead us to forget that there are also elderly people with very low incomes. Their economic need is partly attributable to the fact that they had no second pillar (a situation that should improve gradually) and that the costs for health insurance have risen more strongly than the wage and price index. In Switzerland there is a general obligation to conclude individual nursing care insurance, but premiums must be paid exclusively by the insured parties themselves.

3.3 Future Developments

Is the Swiss three pillar concept really the optimal system? Overall it can be said that on international comparison the Swiss social insurance system is characterized by high performance stability and flexibility even after several years of economic stagnation. The concept can be considered exemplary for a social market economy and the redistribution component of the first pillar serves as an example of practically applied solidarity.

But how will the present system – 25 years after its inclusion in the constitution - stand up to expected social and economic changes in the future? This question was analysed critically a few years ago. Five experts, working independently, came to the unanimous conclusion that the concept had proved its worth because the combination of pay–as–you–go and fully funded systems in the first two pillars achieved an optimal risk spread (population growing older, inflation). They came to the conclusion that the constitutional mandate had not been completely met but that in view of economic and social developments the three pillar concept as a whole was well equipped to prevent poverty. Their conclusion was that the system should be upheld in future without any major shifts in weighting between the two pillars.

Another study commissioned by the department of the interior confirmed this outcome and also concluded that an adjustment of the system to the exact wording of the constitutional mandate (preservation of welfare through insurance benefits) was not necessary. Instead they recommended reformulating the constitutional target so that welfare preservation takes priority over all other targets, including the continuation of an accustomed standard of living and any more far–reaching needs. And finally supplementary benefits should also be laid down in the constitution so that they assume a permanent function in the system. It was also pointed out that there were still numerous gaps that needed to be filled.

New challenges. After dynamic developments in the years of economic upswing and a phase of consolidation in the eighties, the entire Swiss social security system is undergoing a phase of reorientation.

One reason for this are demographic developments. Growing life expectancy – basically a positive development – and the resulting shift in the relationship between pensioners and the employed population not only affect the first pillar where benefit payments have risen by 15 % over the last few years. The second pillar is also affected because the same amount of accumulated capital is needed to finance additional years of pension income. For 65 year old men the expected length of pension payments rose from 12.4 (1950) to 16 years (1995) and for women of the same age from 14 (1959) to 20.5 years with an increasing trend. So for old age and survivors insurance that means that by the year 2010 five additional pension years are to be expected for men and nine more for women. The age quotient is also expected to rise accordingly from 23.5 % (1990) to 29.1 % (2010) and 34 % (2020):

At the end of the eighties the AHV system was in a very favourable position. The gainfully employed population was growing just as strongly as the number of pensioners and the contributions paid by foreign workers were higher than the benefits this group received. But the overall conditions changed very rapidly. The financial surpluses of foreign labourers have gradually fallen, while the number of pensioners in Switzerland is growing and employment figures are stagnating, so that the gulf between income and spending is growing steadily. As late as 1995 AHV spending was largely financed (55.8 %) by current contributions. Even based on a conservative estimate, this figure should be down to 90.9 % by 2010 and to no more than 76.7 % by 2025 unless the legislation is changed.

As concerns the second pillar there is also the additional problem that these compulsory insurance benefits are still in a build–up phase and are thus relatively low compared with contributions. The end of the transitional phase and a shift in the age structure will lead quite quickly to higher retirement credits. The idea was that growing life expectancy should lead to a drop in the conversion rate owing to the growing average length of pension payments. This reduction could be postponed through higher interest income, but in that case interest income could not be used for other purposes – such as for an inflation adjustment and retirement pensions – as they are today.

The financial consequences of aging cannot be solved on the benefits side: Switzerland does not want to reduce benefit levels nor increase the age of pension entitlement to 75. So a solution to the problems must be found on the income side. How can revenue be increased to ensure that both pillars are financially stable in a long term?

The demographic problems have been exacerbated over the last few years through economic developments. The low wage increases since 1992 have had an unfavourable effect on the income situation for pension insurance schemes whose contributions are based on a fixed income percentage. In addition unemployment has also increased rapidly: from 1990 to 1994 alone, the unemployment figure has increased almost tenfold and so spending for unemployment insurance (whose contributions are also based on a fixed income percentages) have virtually exploded. The higher spending for health care and disability insurance in turn has had a strong effect on overall social spending. Consequently in the three years 1990 to 1993 the percentage increased from 20.7 % to 27.0 % while the nominal overall social insurance revenues only increased by 9 % per year on average. During the same period the gross domestic product only showed a slight increase, even falling in real terms.

Naturally economic growth would make additional funds available for the pension system but only to the extent that taxes and administrative costs are kept within bounds. But an economic upswing is slow to get under way and lasting growth is not in sight. Based on historic comparisons, modest growth estimates (constant employment rates and average unemployment of 2.5 %, which corresponds roughly to current estimates for basic unemployment) call for productivity growth and growth in real wages of an annual 1.0 % as well as a constant wage ratio (share of growth income from dependent employment to national income). These assumptions produce an averag annual GDP growth of 1.3 % until 2010 and 0.5 % from 2010 to 2025.

Although the financial position of pensioners is not affected as strongly by economic fluctuations as the rest of the population it is considered absolutely essential in Switzerland that the purchasing power of AHV/IV pensions remain at the level currently achieved. So to finance this category of pensions alone a 2 % increase would be needed by 2010 and 5 % by 2025.

The question is how to procure additional sources of financing without placing too strong a burden on economic growth and labour and doing so in a way that is acceptable for the Swiss population (referendum). Two alternatives under consideration for financing the AHV/IV system are a further increase in VAT tax or the introduction of a consumption tax (e.g. an energy levy), but not an increase in contribution rates.

Adjustments are also required in line with social changes that have occurred. The tenth AHV amendment marked a major milestone, taking into account to the increased role of women. But further amendments are still required to ensure equal treatment of men and women. The three pillar concept was originally established for a society built on stable family and labour structures. But today an ever growing part of the population is experiencing interruptions in employment, flexible working hours, an increase in part–time work, continuing professional development and gradual retirement schemes. The social insurance systems on the other hand are still largely based on an outdated model of a family head in permanent full–time employment and are intended primarily to cover income losses or burdens resulting from certain specified events. So they are not well suited to cover structural risks and more complex living and working arrangements.

Further shifts result from the rise in the employment rate for women which has risen over the last 15 years from 33.3 % to 42 %, whereas the rate for men only increased from 61.9 % to 63.1 %. However this increase in the employment rate was linked with an expansion of part–time work which is why the overall labour volume rose at a smaller rate. On the other hand old age insurance is facing the challenge of increasing numbers of older employees who want to go into retirement earlier.

The entire pension system is thus faced by the problem of early retirement schemes which have hardly been taken into account in legislation to date. The lower income brackets are affected above all – their already low pensions cannot be reduced further (despite early retirement). On the other hand early retirement schemes should not be a disincentive or an obstacle to continued employment.

3.4 Amendments under Discussion

Against the background of the above developments and growing public deficits, extensive discussion has ensued on the financing of social security. In this connection much attention is being given to the redistribution effects and the efficiency of the existing systems as well as an examination of far–reaching reform proposals, a step considered necessary to ensure that Switzerland remains an attractive location.

In this connection a cross–departmental working group (IDA FiSo) drew up two reports on behalf of the Bundesrat. The first report came up with possible solutions for the medium to long term financing for all branches of social insurance. The report covered specific assumptions on the development of spending up to the year 2010, and also carried estimates forward into 2025 as a rough indication of expected developments. Whereas demographic trends are quite easy to estimate, economic forecasts and the development of other factors (e.g. employment rates) are difficult to pin down in the long term.

The first report reached the conclusion that additional demands for old age and survivors benefits would increase steadily up to 2010 but that benefits would be just barely covered until 2005. In the years between 2005 and 2010 increased demand would arise which would have to be covered either by increasing the percentage of income to be paid for contributions or through government subsidies.

The second report examined the benefits paid by the social insurance institutions and analysed possible amendments based on three financing scenarios up to 2010: continuation of current benefits (status quo) / expanding benefits / reducing benefits.

Based on these reports the Bundesrat presented amendment proposals for the next (11th) AHV amendment and a simultaneous first amendment of the BV scheme, which are aimed at securing long time stability of both pillars. The Bundesrat is well aware that a departure from the status quo no matter in which direction is politically very risky and solutions with no effects on costs are the better alternative. At the same time gaps in the system are to be filled and selective cuts carried out where they are socially compatible. The proposals made by the Bundesrat are currently being reviewed by all interested parties. It remains to be seen whether they become part of the formal legislative procedure in future and have a chance of being passed by a referendum.

References

Federal Office for Social Insurance (BSV):
AHV and IV Pensions January 1997/98
Swiss Social Insurance Statistics for 1998
Statistics on AHV Income, 1993
Facts and Figures on Social Security, 1995

Federal Office for Statistics (BFS):
Pension Fund Statistics 1996
Statistical Yearbook of Switzerland 1999

Bundesrat (1988):
The Influence of Demographic Developments on the Financing of AHV.

Swiss Department of the Interior:
5 Expert Reports on the three pillar concept of Swiss old age, survivors and disability insurance, 1991.
Report on current structure and development of the Swiss three pillar concept of old age, survivors and disability insurance, 1995

Swiss Commission (1995):New Retirement Report, Aging in Switzerland.

Cross–departmental working group IDA FiSo:
Report on the Financing Outlook of Social Insurance Systems, 1996
Analysis of Social Insurance Benefits, 1997

Federal Administrative Committee (1996): Challenges of populations shifts – Prospects for Switzerland

4 The UK System Of Pension Provision

by Richard Disney

4.1 The Evolution of the UK Pension System

The UK has a multi–pillar scheme of pension provision: The first pillar, the floor, provides a flat pension, financed largely out of payroll taxes ("National Insurance contributions") on a pay–as–you–go basis. This pillar has its origins in the Beveridge scheme of social insurance. Membership is mandatory for all employed and self–employed people.

The second pillar, which is also mandatory, allows individuals a wide range of choice of pension scheme to which to contribute. The dominant "route" is to be a member of one of a variety of types of private pension schemes. If individuals choose to make a private pension arrangement, they become contracted–out of the second pillar of the state scheme and pay a lower level of National Insurance (NI) or even have NI contribution rebates credited to their pension account. If they choose not to utilise a private pension plan, then by default they are contracted–in to a supplementary state pension scheme known as the State Earnings Related Pension Scheme (SERPS), shortly to be reformed and known simply as the State Second Pension (SSP). Contracted–in individuals pay a higher rate of NI contribution.

The third pillar is voluntary retirement saving in a variety of private pension plans offering varying degrees of tax privileged saving.

The UK system of pension provision grew up gradually, and some of the key features of its development are now briefly described.

4.1.1 The Genesis of the UK System: The Beveridge Scheme

The basis of UK pension provision is the Beveridge scheme of social insurance, known as National Insurance in the UK. The scheme was first introduced in 1911, extended gradually in the inter–war period, and completed in 1946. The basic principles of the Beveridge scheme were that the scheme was contributory with flat benefits and contributions. Benefit levels were to be related to the minimum standard of living required to subsist, measured by household nutrition studies, and increases in benefits to changes in that minimum standard, although there was some real increase in benefits, especially in the 1960s and 1970s. The scheme was supplemented by a universal means–tested scheme of national social assistance, financed from general tax revenues.

Beveridge's "vision" grew out of the activities of friendly societies and other workers organisations in the late C19th and early C20th, in which workers engaged in voluntary saving to provide various forms of social insurance and mutual aid (other products of that era included the co–operative movement). It sought to incorporate the principles of these societies into a social scheme of state provision. It was therefore a "bottom up" not a "top down" pension reform.

Additional features of the Beveridge scheme were that men could first receive the state pension at age 65, and women at age 60. There were no opportunities for earlier receipt of the state pension at a reduced rate, although the pension could be deferred until age 70/65 with an actuarial adjustment. Working after 65/60, unless pension benefits were explicitly deferred, was subject to an "earnings test" at up to a 100% marginal tax rate on the pension. The "earnings test" was abolished in 1989. Furthermore, under 1995 legislation, the normal pension age for men and women will be equalised at 65 between the years 2010 and 2020.

The public pension scheme has operated largely on a PAYG (unfunded) basis. Contributions are notionally levied on employees and employers. There was, initially, a supplementary contribution from general tax revenue, designed in part to finance the incorporation of existing old people into the system after 1946 who had not made sufficient contributions in the pre–war period. This contribution from other taxes was largely phased out in the 1980s for contributory benefits.

4.1.2 The Erosion of Beveridge's "Vision"

By the early 1960s, there was a clear political divide over the future of the pension programme in the UK. Critics of the Beveridge scheme pointed to the low level of benefits (especially relative to the more comprehensive systems of public provision in continental Europe). They argued that more privileged individuals had access to separate private pensions provided by companies and that the "social cohesion" of the Beveridge scheme was being eroded by the existence of "two nations" of pensioners: those with only the low, flat, state pension and those with access to more generous private pensions. Finally, the first implications of demographic ageing for the flat rates of payroll tax (which was deemed to be "regressive") were just being understood.

Throughout the 1960s and 1970s, a fierce political debate took place between the Labour Party and the Conservative Party, which alternated in power, over the future of state pension provision in the UK. Broadly speaking, the Labour Party wanted to introduce comprehensive earnings replacement by a public programme much closer in spirit to the Bismarckian model, possibly retaining private provision as an alternative where individual employees were already covered. The problem with this solution was simply its cost. The Conservative Party on the other hand wanted to impose mandatory private second tier coverage while retaining the essentially flat nature of state pension benefits. The problem with the latter solution in the late 1960s and early 1970s was that, while employers were perceived as the natural providers of private pensions, the economic problems of that period (growing unemployment, high inflation and low real returns on assets) made private employers reluctant to extend coverage. Indeed employer–provided coverage peaked in the 1970s.

4.2 The Development of a Multi–Pillar Pension System from 1975 to 1999

4.2.1 The Reform Process

As a result of this ongoing debate, there have been several attempts to reform pension provision in the UK, with major legislation in 1975, 1986, 1995 and a Green Paper introduced in December 1998 that seems likely to presage further legislation in 1999. The outcome of this process is a scheme dominated by private funded coverage of the workforce – suggesting that the Conservative solution dominated. This is partly correct; after all the Conservatives were in power for the bulk of the period – from 1970–74 and from 1979–97 – but this "transition" to a largely funded, privatised, scheme of pension provision was far from smooth. Indeed the 1975 legislation saw a major extension in the generosity of state pension provision by a Labour government, which was subsequently reversed when the costs of provision arising from the reform at maturity became apparent. Furthermore, some of the key extensions of private coverage, notably the development of the market for "Personal Pensions" seems to have occurred by accident rather than design, with consequent problems of administrative complexity.

The pillars in 1980. As a result of 1975 legislation in 1975, the government introduced a second tier earnings–related pension known as "SERPS" (the State Earnings–Related Pension Scheme). Benefits were based on '20 years best revalued lifetime earnings', integrated with the basic flat pension, and involved generous treatment of widows (full transfer of spouses' benefits). Contributions were to be earnings–related between a floor (equal to the value of the flat pension) and a ceiling of around seven times the "floor" (this cap also applies to SERPS benefits). The basic Beveridge pension was also improved, with procedures by which years spent out of the labour force due to sickness, unemployment and caring duties were "credited" with contributions towards the flat pension, and the basic pension in retirement at this time was indexed to either price or earnings growth (whichever was the larger).

Contracting–out of the public programme: a key element. By the early 1970s, around half of the workforce belonged to some form of private pension scheme in addition to the mandatory Beveridge scheme. These private schemes (known as "occupational pensions") exhibited varying degrees of generosity and included schemes of both the "defined benefit" and "defined contribution" types. The 1975 reform integrated private (occupational) pension plans into the mandatory second pillar by permitting them to "contract out" of SERPS, subject to gaining approval from the state. The criterion for approval in 1975 was that the plan should be a funded scheme of the "defined benefit" form, and should guarantee to pay a pension at least as generous as SERPS: this was known as the "Guaranteed Minimum Pension" (GMP). The state and the private sector shared responsibility for indexing this GMP in retirement.

Contributors to a "contracted–out" scheme, both the employee and the employer, pay a lower rate of National Insurance contribution. The difference between the full and reduced rate is the contracted–out rebate (COR) which is a key parameter of the UK scheme of pension provision. It was set by the government, on the advice of the Government Actuary, such that the rebate, for projected real return, was sufficient to pay the GMP – in fact, the COR has typically been more generous, as an incentive to persuade the majority of plans to gain approved status to contract–out. By 1980s, roughly half the workforce were in approved private plans, roughly 40%+ in SERPS, and the rest had earnings below the "floor" and might ultimately be entitled to the flat benefit or to social assistance. This period, from 1978 (when the 1975 legislation was introduced) to 1986, is the high water mark of generosity of public provision in the UK pension scheme. The scheme as it looked around 1980 is illustrated in the next Box.

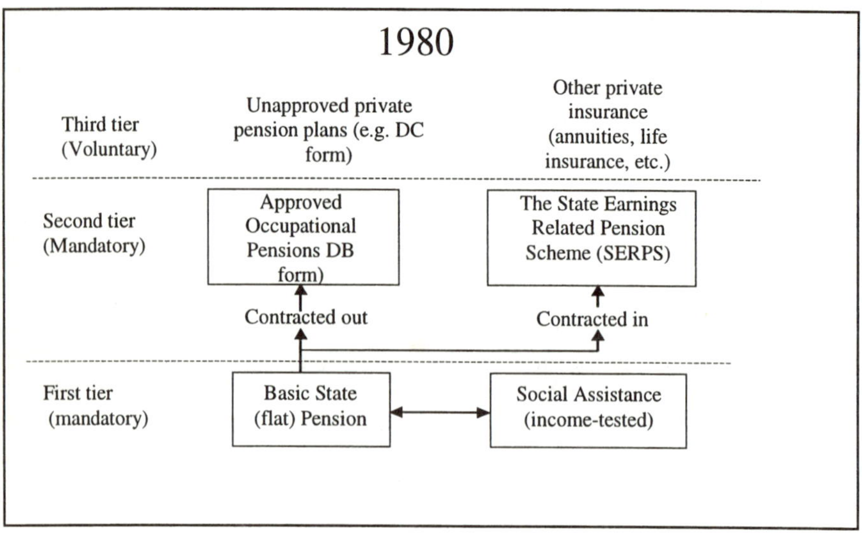

The pillars in 1990. By now, the Thatcher administration had been in power for over a decade. During this period, several radical changes in the pension system took place. In the case of public benefits, there were two key changes in the 1980s. First, the flat pension benefit in retirement, as well as the "floor" and "ceiling" to contributions and SERPS entitlements, were indexed to price increases since 1982, rather than the faster of price or earnings increases. It should be noted that real earnings growth throughout the 1980s averaged 1½–2% per annum. Second, after simulations by the Institute for Fiscal Studies and the Department of Social Security (DSS) as to the high projected costs of SERPS when the "baby boom" generation start retiring, future SERPS generosity were cut back sharply under legislation enacted in 1986. Benefit accruals in SERPS were subsequently to be related to lifetime average earnings, the accrual factor was reduced, and widows' benefits halved in generosity. The reduction in SERPS benefits halved the scheme's costs by 2040, and the cutback in indexation of the flat benefit was projected to reduce the cost of the paying the basic benefit by 2040 by some 40% (although social assistance payments may rise).

An even more striking change took place on the private pension side. Whereas the 1975 legislation only allowed defined benefit plans approval to contract–out, the 1986 legislation now permitted "defined contribution" plans, whether group provided, or provided by individual insurance companies, to gain approved status. For various reasons, the explosion in private coverage that occurred from 1988 onwards (when the 1986 legislation came into force) took place among individual retirement saving accounts (provided by institutions such as insurance companies and banks) known as Personal Pensions. Here the contracting–out scheme works differently from the case of "occupational" or company plans: the DSS pays the contracted–out rebate directly into the individual's chosen Personal Pension account and the individual can choose to save additional amounts, with tax relief up to a fraction of earnings, in his or her account.

As before, coverage by some form of approved private plan or by SERPS is mandatory, but individuals can choose to switch between any type of provision. For example, unlike the decade before, coverage by a DB plan does not automatically mean that an individual is contracted–out; they can choose to remain in SERPS or leave their DB plan and buy a Personal Pension, taking advantage of the "free" rebate paid in by the government to the latter. Many young people left SERPS to buy a Personal Pension; others left a DB plan to do so. By 1990 the workforce is covered as follows: 45–50% in an occupational pension plan, some 20–25% in a Personal Pension, 17% in SERPS, and the remainder covered by social assistance or only earning credits towards the flat pension. A stylised description of the situation in1990 is given in the Box – note the choice of "contracting–out route" compared to 1980. Note that the third "pillar" encompasses a choice of additional voluntary retirement saving routes: for example an individual can "top up" their company pension plan by making additional contributions to that provider (these are known as Additional Voluntary Contributions – AVCs), or make a separate contract to top up their company pension plan through a different insurance company (FSAVCs or "Free standing" AVCs).

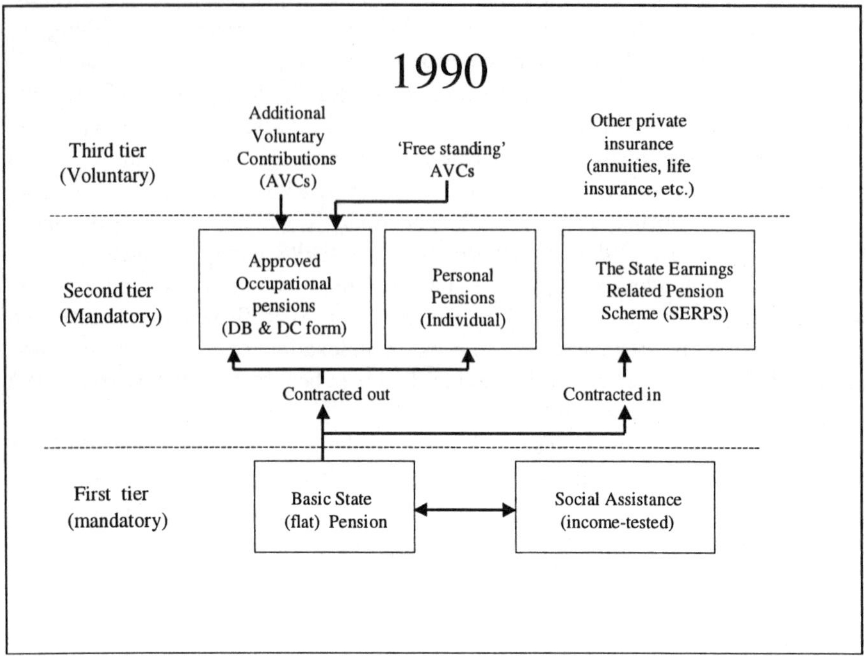

The pillars in 2000. The frequency of "fundamental" pension reforms accelerated in the 1990s. Legislation in 1995 made a number of changes. A key change was to equalise prospective pension ages for the state benefits (the Basic State pension and SERPS) at 65 for men and women between 2010 and 2020. Individuals could however receive private pensions from an earlier date. Second, future SERPS entitlements were again cut significantly further by a complicated change to the formula calculating benefits (described in Disney, 1996, 72–73). In addition, regulation of occupational pension schemes was tightened up in the light of the celebrated Maxwell scandal (see Blake, 1995, 261–279) and a scheme of age-related rebates for Personal Pensions was introduced.

In 1998, yet more changes have been proposed by the Labour government (HMSO, 1998). On the side of public benefits, the major change has been an attempt to arrest the decline, relative to earnings, of the value of the flat pension. However, this is not done by restoring the indexation to earnings of the National Insurance flat pension, but by introducing a Minimum Income Guarantee for all pensioners (this is not the same as the GMP described earlier, which was abandoned in 1995). The MIG provides a minimum income, at the social assistance level, for all pensioners, whether or not they have the requisite contributions. In effect this implies extending income–testing of the minimum, although the extent of asset–testing remains under review (currently social assistance asset tests above assets to a value of £8000 excluding home ownership). In December 1998, it was proposed that this new guaranteed "floor" should normally be indexed to earnings not prices, thus arresting the decline in the value of the "floor" relative to real earnings growth. However the basic contributory flat pension is still indexed to prices, so that there is a growing "wedge" between the contributory pension and the guaranteed minimum income. This change spells the end of Beveridge's vision of providing a flat pension through contributory "social insurance".

SERPS is also to be replaced, but in a more complex way. Despite the advocacy of some policy–makers (notably the Minister of Welfare Reform appointed in 1997, Frank Field, who resigned during 1998), private funded provision has not been made mandatory. SERPS is replaced by a State Second Pension, explicitly targeted at low earners. It restores some of the generosity of SERPS by raising the benefit accrual rate up to £9000 per annum or £175 a week (Euros 15300, and 295, respectively); this also has the effect of raising second tier pensions by a smaller amount above this level, tapering off at £18000 per annum (around 30600 Euros).

At the same time, a new contracted–out route is offered: the "stakeholder pension" which, it is assumed, will ultimately lead to the vast majority of individuals above £9000 per annum choosing to opt out of the State Second Pension, if they are not opted out already. The mechanics of the "stakeholder pension" are not clear at the time of writing, but seem likely to be based on group defined contribution providers, perhaps analogous to 401k plans in the United States, rather than contracts with individual insurance companies like Personal Pensions. However, the effect of these prospective reforms is that individuals are free to choose between four pension "routes" in this second pillar. These are the new State Second Pension, a traditional occupational pension plan, a Personal Pension, or a stakeholder pension.

As a result of these changes, which we assume will be enacted, the UK scheme of pension provision has become much more complicated, and is described in the next Box assuming that the scheme will be in place by the year 2000.

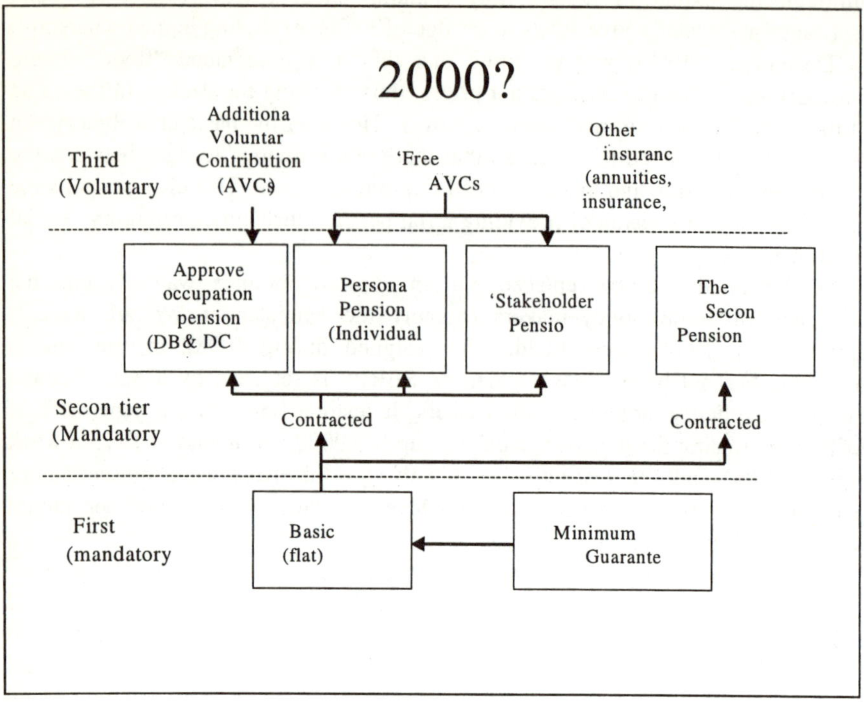

4.2.2 Description of Main Components

Total expenditure by the government on pensions. Contributions to the National Insurance scheme finance the basic state pension, SERPS, and other National Insurance benefits (which are now primarily disability benefits). Total contribution revenue in 1997–98 was around £45 billion (Euros 77 billion, and 5.3% of UK GDP of around £840 billion) of which some £37 billion (Euros 63 billion, and 4.4% of UK GDP) is spent explicitly on pension benefits. In addition, general tax revenues are used to finance income–tested benefits. The value of these various expenditures are given in Table 4.1. We can also include, at a different stage of the life cycle, the value of tax reliefs to private pension schemes and again Table 4.1 gives the details. The total cost of expenditure on pension benefits and pension tax reliefs therefore total some £64.2 billion (109.1 billion Euros), costing approximately 7.6% of UK GDP in 1998.

The public pillar. The structure of National Insurance contributions is broadly proportionate, between a floor and a ceiling. The floor is the value of the basic (flat) state pension, set at £64 per week in the fiscal year 1999–00 (Euros 109). Below this "floor" no contributions are paid, although individuals may acquire credits towards National Insurance benefits if they have earnings of less than this amount (including zero) if they are registered as sick, unemployed or in a caring role (known as Home Responsibility Protection). The contribution is levied on employees and employers. Until the 1999–00 fiscal year, there was a complicated marginal rate structure. There is now a simplified structure, with employees paying a 10% rate of contribution on earnings from a floor, currently the value of the flat pension, up to a "ceiling" of £485 per week (Euros 825). Thereafter there is no marginal contribution liability on employees. For employers, contributions are payable above the value of the income tax allowance (currently £81 per week – 138 Euros) at a rate of 12.2%. There is no ceiling on contributions by employers, unlike employees. Although these contribution rates look high, it should be borne in mind that they also finance some other benefits (such as Incapacity Benefit and a small contribution to the costs of running public health care), that there is a low rate of contribution below the "floor" and a ceiling on the employee' contribution, and that most contributors pay the lower, contracted–out, rate.

Table 4.1. Expenditure on pensioners, and pensions

Category		Total cost 1998 values	As % of GDP	Criteria
Public pension Benefits	Total	£52 billion	6.1	
Basic Pension	Flat rate, Contributory	£32 billion	3.8	NI contributions for 90% of working life
SERPS	Earnings–related, Contributory	£4 billion	0.4	NI contributions, Contracted in
Other non-contributory pensions & Disability	War pensions and Widows'ensions Attendance allowance; non–contributory	£7 billion	0.8	Eligibility by contingency
Means–tested Benefits	Income Support and housing benefits; non contributory	£9 billion	1.1	Eligibility by Income level
Tax reliefs to Private pensions	Total	£13 billion	1.5	
Occupational Pensions (company-provided)	Tax relief on contributions; tax free lump sum component to benefits	£9.5 billion	1.1	Approved contracted–out schemes; ceiling on relief as % of earnings
Personal Pensions, and AVCs	DSS contributions to PP and value of tax reliefs on saving in PPs and AVCs	£3 billion	0.4	Approved contracted– out schemes; ceiling on tax reliefs as % of earnings
Total		£64 billion	7.6	

Sources: HMSO (1998a, 1998b)

Individuals who are contracted–out of SERPS, into an occupational pension or a personal Pension, pay a lower rate of contribution. The total contribution rate is reduced by just over 4%, split slightly in favour of the employer's contribution. The majority of people therefore pay the "contracted out" rate of National Insurance contribution. Self–employed people, who are only eligible for the basic state pension (the flat component) pay £6.35 a week as a flat contribution (Euros 10.8).

Public pension benefits: eligibility and levels. The basic flat pension is set in 1998 at £64.70 weekly (Euro 110) for a single person and £103.40 (Euro 175.8) for a couple. Rates of Income Support (the means–tested benefit) for pensioners are somewhat higher: for example the 1998 rate for a couple is £109.35 (Euro 185.6), and nationals of the country are usually entitled to this benefit (as well as support for rents, interest on mortgages, and local housing–based taxes, where there are no other courses of income).

Eligibility for the basic pension currently requires 44 years of contributions or credits for a man and 39 years for a woman. Since years out of the labour force usually earn credits, however, and an individual with no other sources of income will normally be eligible for Income Support, the binding lower constraint is normally the Income Support level. Furthermore, as described previously, the government has now firmly stated that it intends to implement an explicit minimum income guarantee, based on Income Support, which will be, so far as possible, indexed to earnings. Note that the contributory pension (and thus, also, the contribution "floor" and "ceiling") are indexed to prices, so that the "wedge" between the guaranteed "floor" and the basic flat pension will grow over time.

The formula for calculating SERPS (the state earnings–related pension) has changed frequently over time, as described in Section 2.2, and is highly complex. Accrual rates are different for each cohort that retires. The most generous treatment will be for those retiring in 1998–99, who will have a pension paid on an average of only 20 years earnings at an accrual rate of 1.25 per annum. The accrual factor is intended to go down year by year to 2027–28, when it reaches 0.51 per annum. So a person retiring with a SERPS pension calculated on 40 years average earnings in 2027–28 (having contributed for a much longer period) may have a lower final replacement rate, despite having contributed to the SERPS scheme for twice as long. Furthermore, SERPS pensions depend on differential indexation arrangements for different parts of the calculation, and on the real value of the contribution "floor" (which is deducted in the calculation. A simple answer to the question of how the UK government has found it easy to cut back SERPS benefits with impunity is that few people understand how entitlements are calculated, and those that do, often disagree with each other as to exactly what is the relevant calculation. Some stylised replacement rates are given in Table 4.2, with a brief description of the methodology and assumptions that I used to calculate them.

Table 4.2. Prospective Replacement Rates in the Public Pension Programme

	Single man	Married man	Single woman
Man and woman both aged 60 in 1998			
1st decile of earnings	0.53	0.73	0.60
Median earnings	0.47	0.59	0.48
9th decile of earnings	0.26	0.32	0.37
Man and woman both aged 40 in 1998			
1st decile of earnings	0.42	0.57	0.47
Median earnings	0.35	0.43	0.38
9th decile of earnings	0.21	0.25	0.30
Man and woman both aged 20 in 1998			
1st decile of earnings	0.41	0.51	0.43
Median earnings	0.37	0.43	0.42
9th decile of earnings	0.16	0.20	0.24

Notes:

Own calculations. The replacement rates are of basic pension plus SERPS entitlement divided by lifetime average earnings net of contributions *of a contributor at that point of the earnings distribution.* It is assumed that individuals are entitled to a full basic pension, and that their earnings rise in line with average earnings and are always at the assumed percentile of the (sex-specific) earnings distribution. Data on earnings are taken from the 1997 *New Earnings Survey* (uprated to allow for earnings growth to 1998). Entitlement to any additional income–tested benefits at the lowest decile are ignored.

Four features affect the trajectory of replacement rates over time: (i) the fall in the value of the flat pension relative to earnings (which are assumed to grow 1½% faster than prices each year, based on UK historical trends); (ii) the fall in the ceiling on SERPS entitlements, which is linked to the value of the flat pension; (iii) the reduction in SERPS accrual rates over time, especially prior to 2011; and (iv) the equalisation of state pension ages for men and women between 2010 and 2020.

The impact of the proposed replacement of the SERPS by the Second State Pension is unclear. It seems likely to raise the replacement ratios of those at the lower end of the earnings distribution (here, the first decile) whilst leaving returns at the median and above unchanged. The fullest impact, depending on the treatment of the first pillar of the pension scheme, may be felt amongst the middle age group discussed here.

Redistribution in the public programme. It is apparent from the preceding discussion that the public pension programme in the UK is highly redistributive, both across and between generations, and between men and women. These redistributive features arise from the flat component to benefits and the ceilings, the declining accrual rates over time, and the favourable treatment of periods out of paid employment and of spouses. The replacement rates in Table 4.2 reveal the progressivity from high earners to low earners, and from (single) men to women. Over time there is a general downward trend in replacement rates, but the differential trajectories of accrual rates, indexation assumptions and the "ceiling" on benefits give a complex picture.

It should however be noted that the majority of high earners are "contracted out" of the state scheme, and therefore do not accrue rights to SERPS. This is not surprising, because the redistribution from high earners to low earners within a generation, and from later generations to earlier generations, encourages relative "losers" to contract–out of the system; an incentive that is heightened by the size of the contracted–out rebate which adopts a fairly conservative assumption as to prospective investment returns in the private sector. Thus these stylised replacement rates are not necessarily representative of individuals, and a full analysis requires us to include private pension entitlements, which will be described in Section 2.3.

Work tests, retirement rules and other incentives to retire early. Although the rules governing public pension entitlements and the scheme of contracting–out are relatively complex in UK, the operation of retirement rules and work tests are more straightforward. As mentioned in Sect. 4.1, there is no work test on continued employment after receiving the state pension since 1989, and no scope for early receipt of the public pension before pensionable age of 65 for men, and 60 for women. However, as Fig. 4.1 illustrates, labour force participation rates have been declining for many years in the UK, especially for men, and are projected to continue to fall for men in the future.

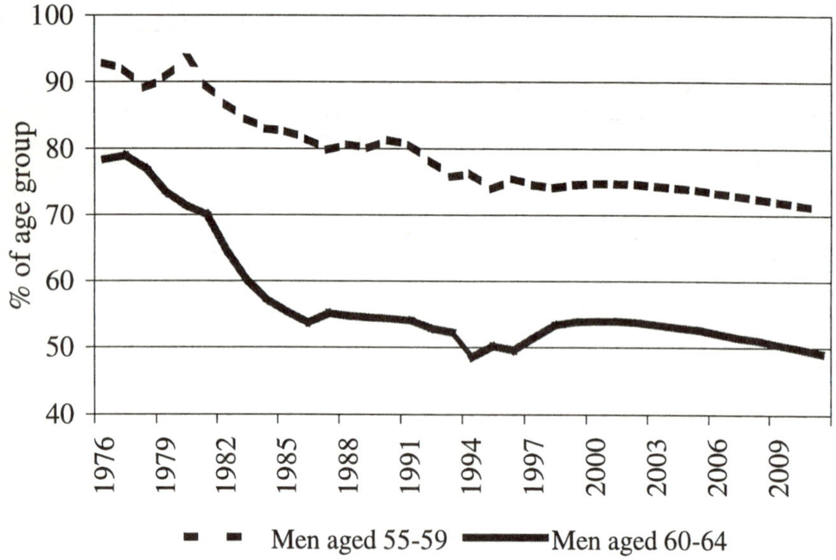

Figure. 4.1.a. Labour Force Participation of Men in GB 1976–2011

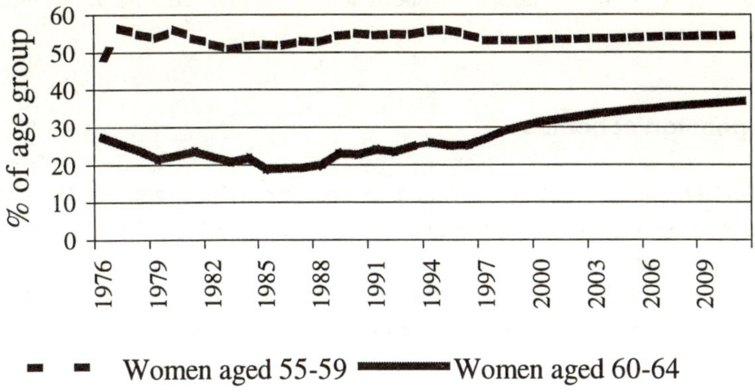

Figure 4.1.b Labour Force Participation of Women in GB 1976–2011

Source: Labour Market Trends (1998). The graphs are based on successive *Labour Force Surveys*. Points beyond 1993 are projections. Until 1983, GB labour force definitions are used; from 1984 on, ILO definitions are used.

There are two main reasons for this decline. First, individuals in private pensions can usually choose to retire somewhat earlier than state pension age. Normal retirement rules in occupational pension plans typically allow individuals to retire in their early 60s, having accumulated, say, 40 years of labour market experience, or by making additional voluntary contributions (AVCs) to their pension plan. Many schemes have also offered normal early retirement schemes on reduced, but actuarially favourable terms. In addition, during the severe recession of the early 1980s, and the privatisation process in the late–1980s, additional early retirement "windows" were commonly used to downsize the workforce by many companies and by the privatised utilities in particular. Finally, individuals who have opted to buy a Personal Pension have greater flexibility of effective retirement date, since annuitisation can take place between ages 50 and 75 and phased withdrawals from the accumulated fund are also possible.

A second "route" to early retirement in the UK has been through the use of disability benefits; not just ill health early retirement offered by private pension plans, but also by the use of public benefits, notably contributory Invalidity Benefit (IVB; now Incapacity Benefit). For individuals who had not worked for some time and who could get doctor's certification of permanent disability, retirement through IVB offered an attractive "route" to retirement in the recession of the early 1980s and throughout the longer process of decline of the primary and manufacturing sectors over the last two decades. This incentive arose because, while IVB was payable at the same rate as the flat public pension, and could be received for up to five years after state pension age, before the individual reverted to the standard retirement pension, it was payable tax free whereas the standard pension was taxable. This disparity in tax treatment has now been ended with the replacement of IVB by Incapacity Benefit and a tougher regime for regulating disability claims.

4.2.3
Private pension schemes

Occupational (company) pensions. As mentioned in previous sections, the UK has an extensive scheme of private pensions, covering a majority of the workforce and integrated into the public system by the device of *contracting–out*. For those retiring in the immediate future, company (occupational) pensions are the most substantial component of retirement income, although Personal Pensions and the new "stakeholder" pensions should figure more in the future. Occupational pension plans are typically company–provided, unlike the Netherlands where such plans operate on an industrial or sectoral basis. There are problems of portability associated with moving job, and job movers thereby tend to incur costs in terms of pension entitlements. This is because "defined benefit" plans generally calculate pension rights on final earnings and, assuming final earnings rise with age, a job mover with rights to two pensions will generally lose out relative to someone who never moves. However, these costs are not as severe as the United States, since the indexation of accumulated pension rights has been steadily made more generous in the UK (for further details, see Disney *et al*, 1994; Blake, 1995; and Disney and Whitehouse, 1996).

Occupational pension plans in the UK are *fully–funded*. Unlike the "book reserve" system of Germany, the funds are kept at "arms length" from the other assets of companies and are supervised by a board of trustees which should also be independent of the company. Many funds are managed externally by specialist financial firms. Funds are typically invested predominantly in equities, with a growing international component. These issues are discussed in much greater detail in Disney *et al* (1994), Blake (1995) and Davis (1995).

4.2.4
Sources of income of pensioners

It will be apparent that a focus only on replacement rates arising from public pensions, as in Table 4.2, gives a misleading description of pensioner incomes in the UK, when account is taken of all sources of income, including private pensions, other investment income and continued employment of family members. Figure 4.1 uses data from an analysis of households in the UK Retirement Survey in 1988–89 to examine this issue. The impact of the flat component of the public programme is clearly apparent in the declining share of public benefits (which might also include means–tested benefits and invalidity benefits) as we move from the lowest quintile (1) to highest quintile (5) of the income distribution. For the lowest quintile of couples, for example, public benefits make up over 80% of income; for the highest quintile, less than 20% of income.

Over time, the share of the household income of pensioners arising from private sources has increased. This arises from both the growth of occupational pension rights among successive generations of employees and the recent performance of the equity market. Even so, it will be observed that investment income is preponderantly received by the highest quintile, and that public pension benefits will remain important for the lowest half of the income distribution, especially as reforms increasingly concentrate public resources on the poorest. A consequence is that pensioner incomes have become increasingly unequal, with those with private resources faring considerably better than those without (Johnson and Stears, 1995).

To get an idea of how these total incomes affect replacement ratios in practice, we can turn to the evidence from the UK Retirement Survey on the relative incomes of those above pension age and those below pension age. Figure 4.2 presents "replacement ratios" of household heads aged in their late 60s relative to those in their late 50s, for each quintile of each income distribution, for married couples and single people separately. The ratios are artificial, in the sense that we

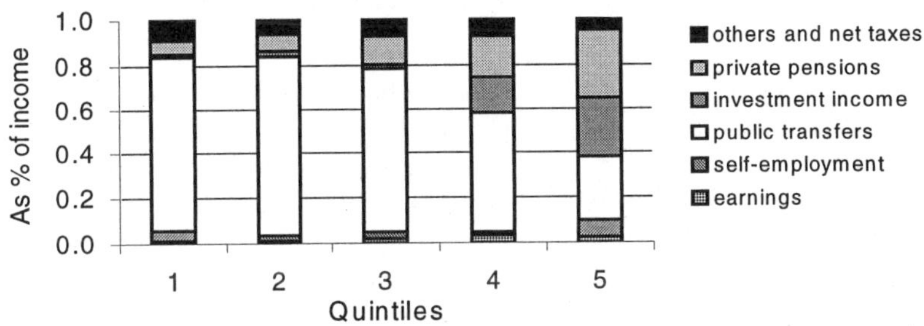

Figure 4.2 Composition of income of singles aged 65–70 by quintiles

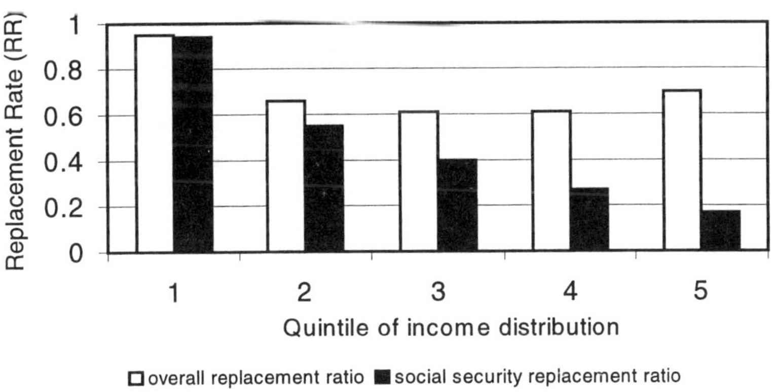

Figure 4.3a Relative incomes before and after reaching pension age: married couples

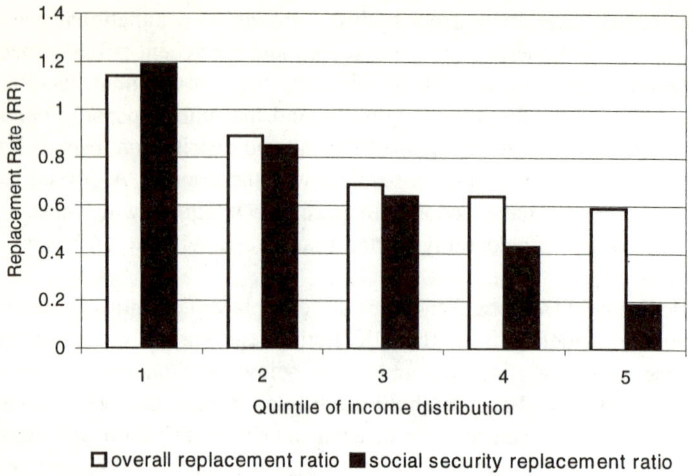

Figure 4.3b Relative incomes before and after reaching pension age: single people

are comparing different people, not the same "cohort" as they age. The incomes are net of contributions, and not all people are actually employed in their 50s – this explains why, at the lowest quintile, reaching state pension age may actually increase income, boosting the ratio above 100%. Conversely, a minority of couples continue to have some income from work even after the head of household reaches 65 (or 60, in the case of a woman) and so ratios rise for the top quintile of couples. The clearest feature of Figure 4.3 is that the share of "social security" (state pensions and other benefits) and thus the social security replacement ratio declines as we move up the income distribution, while the overall replacement ratio declines more slowly, and indeed rises for high income couples. This indicates how the flat benefit in the UK public pension programme and the existence of private pensions have very different impacts on retirement income across the income distribution. It also illustrates that, with a high degree of inactivity pre–pension age, reaching pension age can actually boost income for some low income households.

4.2.5 Personal saving and pension saving

How much saving is done through private pension plans? Employers usually contribute more than employees to occupational pension funds, but the rate of contribution will vary according to the performance of the pension fund. It is therefore hard to estimate what effective share of personal saving takes the form of contributions to occupational pensions, although it will probably be around 30-

40% of the total. In contrast, levels of personal saving through Personal Pensions are not large, reflecting the age composition of Personal Pension optants, who are typically much younger. Contracted–out rebates paid into Personal Pensions are about £2 billion, with employees and employers contributing a further £4 billion (7 billion Euros). This is only about 5% of total personal saving. Over 50% of individuals with Personal Pension plans (the fraction varies according to the source of the figures) do not make any additional contributions over and above the rebate paid into their account by the government.

Fig. 4.4 shows the trajectory of personal savings rates over time. There appears to have been a slow upward trend in personal saving, with a sharp dip during the inflationary period of the mid–1970s and the consumption boom of the mid to late–1980s. It is tempting to link the rise in the personal saving rate to the growing funded component of UK pensions and the associated decline in the generosity of public unfunded pensions. But many other factors have been at work, including major changes in the tax treatment of savings and the development of a variety of tax privileged vehicles. It is of some pertinence that, since 1997, the Labour Government has somewhat restricted tax reliefs given to occupational pensions. So far, these changes have had little impact either on contribution rates to these schemes or to personal saving because the value of funds has continued to increase in line with asset values.

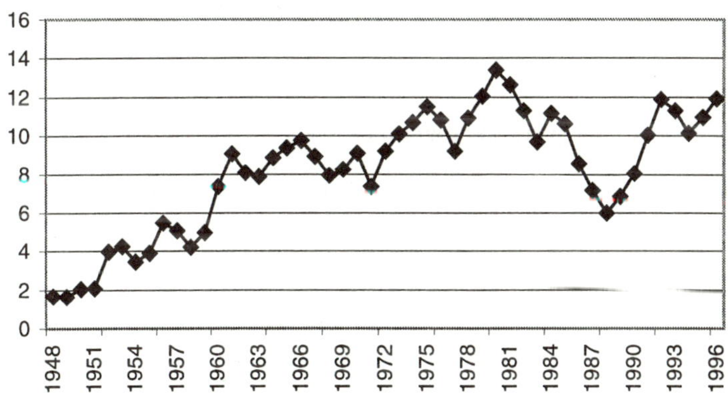

Figure 4.4 UK Personal Saving Rate (%), 1948–1996

The development of private pension plans had led to a considerable deepening of the capital market in the UK, especially the stock market holdings of occupational pension plans, which current total around 60% of UK Gross Domestic Product in value. Since holding of equity in UK companies dominates most pension portfolios, these funds have been an important source of investment funds in the UK. Nevertheless, there are not the close links between financial institutions on the one hand and production and service industries on the other that are observed in some countries. Typically pension plans had preferred an "arm's length" approach to company performance, raising some criticisms of excessive passivity of financial institutions which have substantial shareholdings in poorly performing companies.

In the context of the labour market, the lower rate of effective payroll tax in the UK relative to some other European countries has probably encouraged employment growth in the UK, although some economists would assert that the lack of transparency between benefits and contributions in a redistributive scheme of predominantly flat benefits such as the UK means that workers treat contributions as an explicit "tax", not as a vehicle for future benefits. In the case of private pension plans, companies have in the past used the offer of pensions as an explicit inducement to recruit and retain more productive workers. With greater emphasis on "flexibility" and job turnover, and reduced government intervention in setting pay rates since the late 1970s, however, employers have become increasingly interested in individualised pension accounts or defined contribution plans, in which the pre–commitment of the employer, both in paying contributions to the plan, and in protecting workers against investment risk, is considerably less, rather than providing the more traditional defined benefit plan (Disney, 1995).

4.3 Future Prospects for the UK Pension Scheme

Table 4.3 presents the Government Actuary's forecasts for the future costs of the UK contributory public pension programme.

Table 4.3 Future costs of public pension benefits, current legislation as at 1995

	Financial year starting					
	2000	2010	2020	2030	2040	2050
Support Ratio of Workers/Pensioners (without equal retirement ages)	3.3 (3.3)	3.1 (3.1)	3.3 (2.7)	2.7 (2.1)	2.4 (2.0)	2.5 (2.0)
Basic State Pension (£ billion) (Euros)	32.4 (55.1)	36.5 (62.0)	38.2 (65.0)	45.5 (77.2)	48.3 (82.1)	45.9 (78.1)
SERPS (£ billion) (Euros)	4.6 (7.8)	9.1 (15.5)	11.8 (20.1)	13.0 (22.2)	11.1 (18.8)	10.8 (18.3)
Total state pension cost (£ billion) (Euros)	37.0 (62.9)	45.6 (77.5,	50.0 (85.1)	58.5 (99.4)	59.4 (100.9)	56.7 (96.4)
Cost as percentage of GDP (%)	4.4	4.9	4.8	5.1	4.7	4.1
Required National Insurance contribution rate (%)	17.7	17.4	16.8	17.2	15.8	14.0

Note: HMSO (1995), values updated to 1997–98 fiscal year prices (Euro values in parentheses). The contribution rate is **not** a fraction of earnings but is calculated as a percentage of *eligible* earnings between the "floor" and the "ceiling" (see text). The contribution also pays for some other benefits, which are assumed broadly constant as a share of GDP in these projections.

It will be noticed that the projected joint contribution rate is almost stationary over time despite the decline in the support ratio. There are four reasons for this: (i) the continued decline in the value of the flat pension; (ii) the steady cutback in the generosity of SERPS benefits; (iii) the increased contracting–out into private plans, which in effect transfers the costs of paying pensions "upfront" from future pension payments to current reductions in contribution receipts and (iv) the equalisation of pension age for men and women.

There are various *caveats* to this optimistic scenario. First, successive official forecasts have almost all underpredicted the increase in the number of retirement pensioners; presumably by understating the growth in longevity. Second, these calculations do not take account of the costs of means–tested benefits and, in particular, they are calculated prior to the proposed introduction of a Minimum Income Guarantee and the more generous treatment of low income earners through the replacement of SERPS by the new Second State Pension. The final cost all depends on the success or otherwise of the new "stakeholder pension". Nevertheless, compared to other European countries, it is clear that the UK does not have a serious fiscal burden of financing public pensions.

4.4 Public Attitudes to Pension Reform

In the light of steady cutbacks in social security, is there any evidence that the British public yearn for a return to greater public generosity in social security provision? For a number of years, the British Social Attitudes Survey (BSAS) has studied British attitudes to many issues, including the level of public spending. There is evidence from the BSAS that the British public are broadly supportive of higher public spending, even when the questions on spending are conditioned on general explanations that higher public spending will require some degree of higher taxation. When asked to prioritise at least two areas of public spending, however, education and health, rather than social security, tend to be the first priorities of most surveyed individuals (Figure 4.5). Indeed, over the last decade, during which, as we have seen, public spending on pensions has been cut back, it is education, rather than social security, which has assumed greater priority among respondents.

Brook, Hall and Preston (1997) survey this evidence, and also tabulate, for the 1995 BSAS, the auxiliary question which asks *which* components of social security would be a priority, were social security spending to be increased. As Figure 4.6 suggests, the evidence shows that spending on the elderly is the top priority, but that there is little difference between that category and the disabled (where benefits have also been cut back) and poor working parents (where benefit generosity has, if anything, increased in recent years). Only spending on the unemployed and single mothers, who have been more clearly scapegoated in the popular press, earn less popular approval. Brook *et al* show, by a statistical analysis, that support for higher spending on retired people is positively and significantly associated with the age of the respondent, with readership of tabloid newspapers, and by manual workers, and negatively related to whether the individual reported that they voted Conservative. The positive and negative associations are almost certainly associated with the proximity of receipt and relative generosity (to the individual) of the flat pension benefit. Even so, and despite cutbacks, support for higher public spending on public pensions is low on the list of public priorities.

Questionnaires have not focused explicitly on the complexity of the pension scheme in the UK, although this would now seem to be an issue to address. Few people understand how the components of the social security scheme work, other than the idea of a "basic" flat pension. Most people are aware of the existence of private pension arrangements through the media, financial institutions such as banks, and from relatives and friends. The difficulty for individuals in establishing *which* private pension arrangement is best for them has led to accusations of misleading advertising and "mis–selling" (as mentioned previously), particularly concerning the introduction of Personal Pensions, when a number of people were persuaded to leave existing occupational pension schemes in order to purchase such individual accounts. The UK's Financial Services Authority is now overseeing a process of compensating "losers" from this process and the 1998 proposed legislation makes public understanding of private arrangements a priority, by threatening to withdraw approval from schemes which misrepresent their relative attraction.

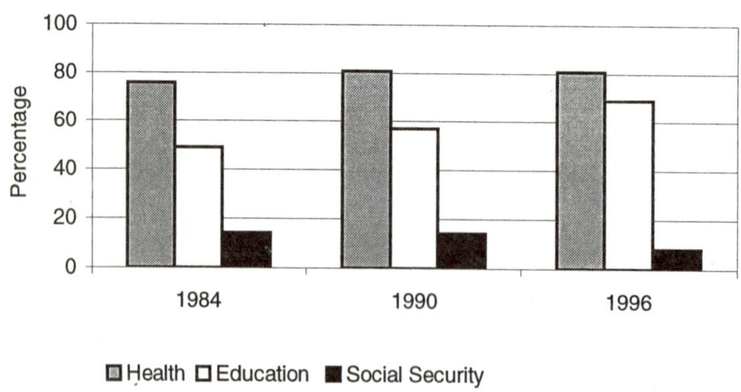

Figure 4.5. Support for additional public spending in Britain First and second priority

Source: British Social Attitudes Survey (various years)

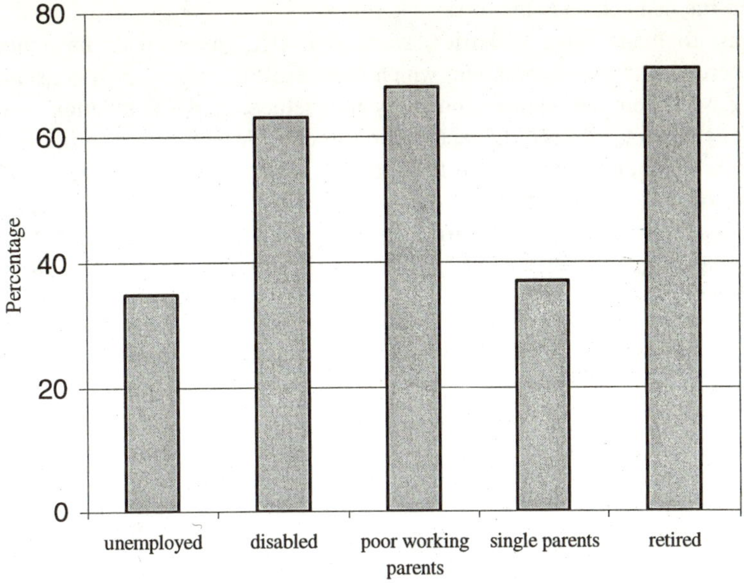

Figure 4.6. Support for additional social security spending 1995

Source: Brook, Hall and Preston (1996), Figure 4.3

4.5 A Summing Up

The UK system has moved a long distance since 1946 but, in some respects, some of Beveridge's design remain in place. The first pillar, or tier, still provides a flat contributory pension, although for people with low lifetime incomes, it is the trajectory of the new Minimum Income Guarantee that will determine their future living standards. Second pillar provision has become mandatory, unlike Beveridge's original scheme, but the experiment in the mid–1970s with Bismarckian income replacement has now largely ended – mandatory provision will, in the future, take the form largely of private, funded, provision, whether through traditional company pension plans or through group or individual provided retirement saving vehicles.

However, it will be noted that there has been no "clean break" privatisation of the second pillar: reform has proceeded by extending the range of private options in the hope that individuals will switch voluntarily to the funded, private sector. Inevitably this accumulation of pension options has produced an overly complex pension system in which incentives are far from transparent and in which there is a strong likelihood of further, piecemeal, attempts at reform. On the plus side, however, the "creeping privatisation" of the system has guaranteed that there should be no financial crisis in the forseeable future.

In contrast to many other countries, successive UK governments have not resisted tinkering with the programme, which as a result is in an almost constant state of flux, with complex choices, not fully understood by the population, and the scope for "pension mis–selling" and other scandals. A period of stability and rationalisation is required, perhaps in the form of a move to generic individual "pension accounts", to which employees, employers and (for low earners, perhaps) the government contribute. However, the presence of a variety of private and public interest groups render this at best a long run goal (see Weaver, 1998, and the discussion thereof).

References

Blake, D.: Pension Schemes and Pension Funds in the United Kingdom. Clarendon Press: Oxford (1995)

Brook, L., Hall, J., Preston, I.: What drives support for higher public spending? Institute for Fiscal Studies Working Paper W97/16, London: (1997)

Davis. E.P.: Pension Funds: Retirement–Income Security and Capital Markets. An International Perspective, Oxford University Press (1995)

Department of Social Security: Partnership in Pensions: A New Contract for Welfare. Cm 4179, Her Majesty's Stationery Office (1998)

Dilnot, A., Disney, R., Johnson, P., Whitehouse, E. Pension Policy in Britain: An Economic Analysis., London: Institute for Fiscal Studies (1994)

Disney, R.: Occupational pension schemes: prospects and reforms in the UK.Fiscal Studies, 16, August, 19–39 (1995)

Disney, R.: Can we Afford to Grow Older? A Perspective on the Economics of Aging. Cambridge: MIT Press. (1996)

Disney, R., Johnson, P.: The United Kingdom: A working system of minimum pensions? In: H. Siebert (ed) Redesigning Social Security, Institut für Weltwirtschaft an der Universität Kiel. Tübingen: Mohr Siebeck. (1998)

Disney, R., Whitehouse, E.: What are occupational pension plan entitlements worth in Britain? 63, May, Economica, 213–238 (1996)

Government Actuary National Insurance Fund: Long Term Financial Estimates (Third Quinquennial Review), HMSO (1995)

HMSO (1998a) Inland Revenue Statistics, London: 1997

HMSO (1998b) The Government's Expenditure Plans., 1998–99: Social Security Departmental Report, London.

Johnson, P., Stears, G.: Pensioner income inequality Fiscal Studies. 16, November, 69–94. (1995)

Weaver, R. K.: The politics of pensions: Lessons from abroad. in: Arnold, R.D., Graetz, M.J., Munnell, A.H.: Framing the Social Security Debate: Values, Politics and Economics. Brookings Institution Press, for National Academy of Social Insurance, Washington D.C. (1998)

5 United States: Support in Retirement: Where We Are and Where We Are Going

by David A. Wise

Social Security is the backbone of retirement support for a large fraction of Americans. Many retirees have virtually no personal saving other than home equity and only about half receive employer–provided pension benefits. The image of the three–legged stool has long been used to represent saving for retirement: one leg is social security, a second leg is employer–provided pension benefits, and a third leg is personal saving. The image is hardly apt today. The third leg is largely missing. The second is far from the ground. And now the remaining Social Security leg, which is holding up the stool, is under financial pressure. Thus many think it is important to strengthen this Social Security leg before it reaches the breaking point. What kind of mending and how much mending is needed to keep the stool standing into the future is the now the subject of substantial public debate.

Strengthening the social security leg, however is not the only way to keep the stool standing. Lengthening the other two legs can also help. Indeed, to understand the implications of proposed reinforcement of the first leg, it is important to understand how the other two legs are changing. Strengthening the second and third legs can change the degree of dependency on the first leg and can thus affect the repairs that leg requires. Retirement saving is moving from a system largely dominated by employer–provided plans, with little employee involvement, to personal retirement plans controlled by individuals.[1] These plans are not only changing the way Americans save for retirement; they are increasing the saving of young Americans and will have a substantial effect on the wealth of the future elderly.[2] Thus while this paper concentrates on Social Security in the United States, attention is also given to the other legs of the three–legged stool. I begin with an overview of the Social Security system and then discuss the current and changing aspects of the other means of retirement support. I then present a short discussion of demographic and other changes that have created financial pressure on the Social Security system and have motivated reform proposals. Finally, I describe current reform proposals.

---

[1] See Poterba, Venti, and Wise [1998]

[2] See for example Poterba, Venti, and Wise [1996]

5.1
Overview of the United States Social Security System

Perhaps the most important proximate catalyst for the United States Social Security system was the great depression of the 1930s. The Social Security Act of 1935, which also created the Aid to Dependent Children program, became the core of Franklin D. Roosevelt's New Deal and was the beginning of the Unites States welfare system. At first, only workers in commerce and industry (excluding railway) under age 65 were covered, and benefits were only for retirees over age 65. Now essentially all workers, except some State and Local Government employees, are covered. Overtime benefits were made available at age 62 and benefits were given to certain dependents and survivors, and by 1960, benefits were available to disabled workers of all ages.

The current benefit provisions–explained below–were adopted in 1977. Benefits were increased substantially in the 1970s, including unintended double–indexing of benefits. Faced with financial insolvency, the system was reformed in 1983. This legislation included a phased increase in the normal retirement age from 65 to 67, which would be attained for persons reaching age 62 in 2022. Taxation of some portion of benefits was also part of the legislation. This legislation also reduced the incentive to retire by increasing over time the increment to benefits (called the "delayed retirement credit") for persons who worked past the normal retirement age. This phased increase will eventually reach 8 percent per year.

Funding is provided by a 12.4 percent earnings tax–paid half by employees and half by employers. Tax receipts are placed in the Social Security Trust Fund. The system is essentially pay–as–you–go, although the Trust Fund now receives more in taxes than is paid out in benefits. The Social Security Administration projects that the Trust Fund will be exhausted by about 3030. An important feature of the system is that the Trust Fund is part of the unified federal budget. In fact the current federal "surplus" is accounted for almost entirely by the Trust Fund surplus. Unlike the German system, an important feature of the United States benefit structure is redistribution, as explained below.

5.2
Social Security and Other Forms of Retirement Support

The weight of retirement is supported disproportionately by the Social Security leg of the three–legged. Many families approaching retirement age have virtually no assets other than the value of promised future Social Security benefits. The median Social Security wealth of retired households with heads 65 to 69 was about $100,000 (102,000 EUR) in 1991. The median of the next most important asset, home equity, was only about $50,000 (51,000 EUR). The median of financial assets other than personal retirement accounts was only $7,400 (7,548 EUR). Including personal retirement accounts, the median of financial assets was $14,000 (14,280 EUR). The median of employer–provided pension wealth was only $16,000 (16,320 EUR). Only about one–half of persons in this age group were receiving pension benefits.[3] How home equity should be viewed is unclear. In principle, housing equity could be used to support other consumption needs as persons age, but substantial evidence suggests that older persons tend not to reduce housing equity as they age.[4] At the macro level, Social Security benefits in 1996 amounted to 4.635 of GDP, while public and private employer pension benefits amounted to 4.63% of GDP.

Table 5.1.b Median level of assets by lifetime income decile and by asset category, HRS (in USD)

Income Decile	Financial	Pers. Retirem.	IRA	401(k)	Trad. Pension	Defined Contrib.	Defined Benefit
	Asset Category						
1st	0	0	0	0	0	0	0
2nd	70	0	0	0	0	0	0
3rd	8	0	0	0	0	0	0
4th	2000	0	0	0	0	0	0
5th	3000	0	0	0	4000	0	0
6th	7000	1500	0	0	14035	0	0
7th	9500	5000	1700	0	33793	0	0
8th	17000	12000	5000	0	40808	0	1497
9th	25000	25000	12000	0	58000	0	3083
10th	36500	40000	21000	0	83259	0	22690

3 Based on data from the Survey of Income and Program Participation. See Poterba, Venti, and Wise [1994].

4 See for example Venti and Wise [1989, 1990].

Table 5.1.b Median level of assets by lifetime income decile and by asset category, HRS (in USD)

	Asset Category							
Income Decile	PY Pension Income	Vehicles	Business Equity	Other Real Estate	Home Equity	SS Wealth	Total Wealth Excl. SS	Total Wealth Incl. SS
1st	0	300	0	0	0	0	5000	33006
2nd	0	1700	0	0	8000	54754	34429	85448
3rd	0	3000	0	0	19000	75335	52803	125759
4th	0	5000	0	0	23000	88692	82620	168878
5th	0	6000	0	0	29000	101234	105166	203084
6th	0	8000	0	0	39000	108619	144188	261072
7th	0	10000	0	0	50000	117764	189832	312037
8th	0	10000	0	0	60000	119950	221692	349549
9th	0	12000	0	0	70000	137673	305536	453265
10th	0	15000	0	3000	77000	175542	387609	577107

Table 5.1 shows the median assets of families approaching retirement – with head 51 to 61 – in 1992. (Half of families have assets below the median and half above the median.) The unique feature of these data grouping by lifetime earnings decile.[5] Families with the lowest 10 percent of earnings over their lifetimes are in the 1st decile, those with the next lowest 10 percent of earnings are in the 2nd decile, and so forth. Families with the highest 10 percent are in the 10th decile. Families in the 2nd decile have about $55,000 in Social Security wealth, a small amount in home equity, and little else.[6] The same is true for families up through the 5th decile, although home equity is larger. The zeros indicate that at least half of families have no assets in the indicated category. The median of traditional pension (employer–provided) assets is zero or close to zero for the first five lifetime earnings deciles. Only with earnings in the 7th decile do employer–provided pensions and personal saving begin to be important components of wealth for most families nearing retirement age. The means of assets, which in some cases are very different from the medians, are shown in Table 5.2.

5 See Venti and Wise [forthcoming]

6 Social Security wealth is the present discounted value of future Social Security benefits, accounting for life expectancy, and discounting benefits according to the Social Security Administration intermediate assumption.

Table 5.2.a Mean level of assets by lifetime income decile and by asset category, HRS (in USD)

	Asset Category						
Income Decile	Financial	Pers. Retirem.	IRA	401(k)	Trad. Pension	Defined Contrib.	Defined Benefit
1st	20566	5628	3730	1898	12382	20	8224
2nd	16369	4337	3683	654	19285	2008	8563
3rd	18635	6266	4325	1941	22301	2498	11436
4th	31871	10185	6843	3341	32603	4431	17089
5th	34245	10340	8035	2305	38107	3461	18821
6th	36988	16000	11219	4781	55383	5137	28614
7th	50339	28291	18904	93860	79646	8886	37574
8th	56837	40531	24528	16003	91843	14193	50684
9th	112356	65461	393914	26070	132369	22498	73454
10th	88420	76454	52706	23748	145626	18185	93074

Table 5.2.b Mean level of assets by lifetime income decile and by asset category, HRS (in USD)

	Asset Category							
Income Decile	PY Pension Income	Vehicles	Business Equity	Other Real Estate	Home Equity	SS Wealth	Total Wealth Excl. SS	Total Wealth Incl. SS
1st	4138	3353	85	19213	17842	16494	79069	95563
2nd	8713	4291	2884	12884	32488	49665	92538	142203
3rd	8368	7022	5107	20548	33129	67962	113009	180971
4th	11083	8519	23140	39257	38941	82951	184515	267466
5th	15825	11155	42628	38350	44342	95980	219166	315146
6th	21633	12691	28716	54481	53143	108749	257402	366151
7th	33206	18694	45793	45940	65596	116674	334298	450972
8th	26966	15700	27982	55894	73628	119172	362413	481586
9th	36416	16142	78164	57611	91297	135626	553400	689026
10th	34367	19698	55817	80771	98326	172476	565112	737588

A large proportion of financial assets in particular are held by small fraction of households. Thus the mean is much larger than the assets of the typical household, which is better measured by the median. Notice also that because more than half the households in the lowest decile have no Social Security the median is zero; the mean, however, is \$16,494 (16,824 EUR).

In short, Americans are at once living longer and leaving work at younger ages, spending more time in retirement. Yet, most Americans have saved little. Indeed, living longer and working less has been accompanied by declining personal saving. Indeed, the U.S. personal saving rate has declined substantially since the 1970s, as shown in shown in Figure 5.1. But the rapid rise in personal retirement saving is likely to assume an increasing share of the weight of retirement support and perhaps help to balance the three–legged stool. I discuss in the next section the key features of the U.S. Social Security system. Then I describe the expansion of personal retirement saving which will have an enormous effect on how future generations of retirees are supported.

5.2.1
The U.S. Social Security System

A key feature of the Social Security system (Old Age and Survivors Insurance–OASI) is redistribution: relative to earnings, the benefits of low–income persons are higher than the benefits of high–income persons. Thus the system is not income insurance, although it is close to that for low–wage earners. As mentioned above, the system is funded by a 12.4 percent earnings tax–paid half by employees and half by employers. The tax is paid on covered earnings (earnings up to the Social Security "earnings limit"). Covered earnings have increased substantially over time, even in real dollars: in 1994 dollars, for example, the 1951 limit was $30,549 (31,160 EUR) and the 1994 limit was $60,600 (61,200). (See Figure 5.2.) Benefits are also based on covered earnings. Persons qualify for benefits by working 35 quarters in covered employment. Social Security benefit payments are indexed to the Consumer Price Index, and thus provide a real annuity.

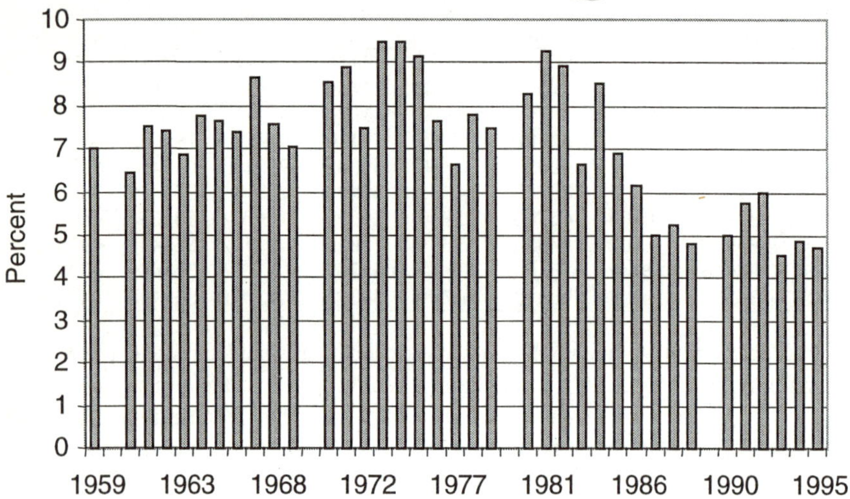

Fig. 5.1. U.S. Personal Saving

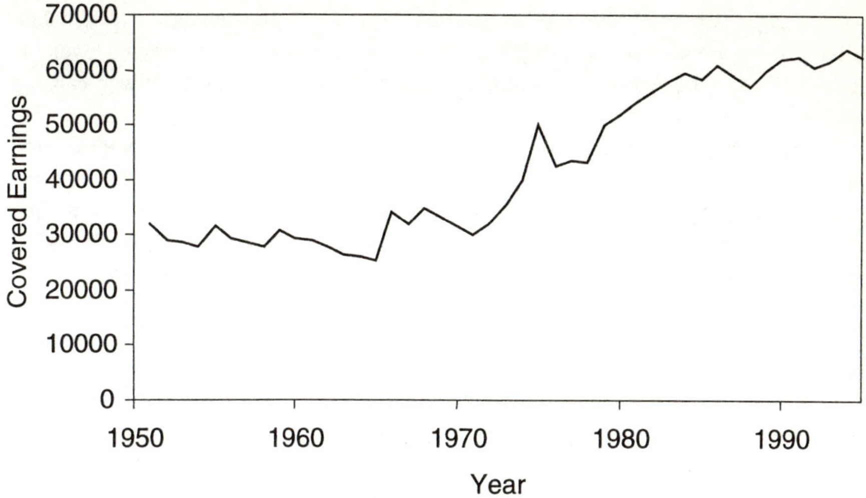

Fig. 5.2. Covered Earnings: 1995 "$s"

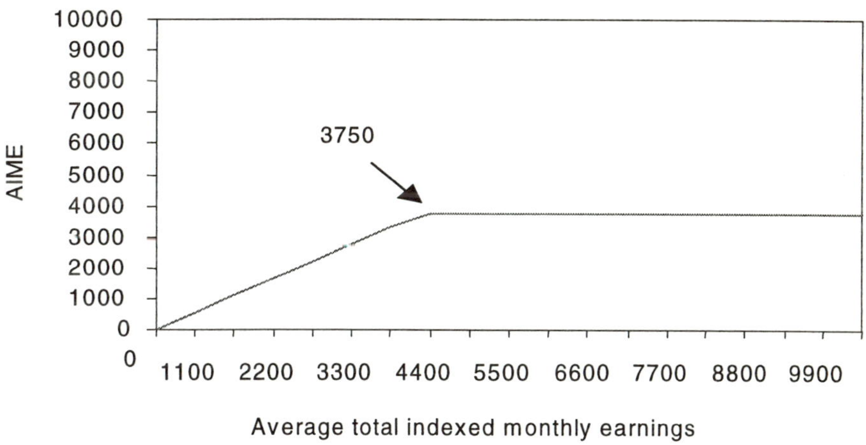

Fig. 5.3. AIME vs Total Earnings

The first step in determining benefits is calculation of Average Indexed Monthly Earnings (AIME), based on the 35 years in which a person had the highest earnings. (Covered earnings in each of these years are converted to constant dollars using a national wage index.)[7] An important feature of averaging over the highest 35 earning years is that higher earning years can replace lower earning years.

For illustration, consider the AIME calculated in 1995, assuming that covered earnings for the prior 35 years are used to calculate the AIME. Consider first the relationship between total earnings and the AIME, for simplicity assuming that indexed earnings are the same for each of the past 35 years. Over these 35 years, the average of covered earnings was $45,000 (45,900 EUR). Thus, for the illustration, I assume that the maximum AIME is $45,000/12 = $3,750 (3,825 EUR). Based on these assumptions, AIME is plotted against total (indexed) earnings in Figure 5.3. Keep in mind that an annual income of $45,000 is well above median annual earnings.

The second step is to determine the Primary Insurance Amount (PIA), the benefits available at the normal retirement age. The PIA is based on the AIME, but in such a way that the ratio of the PIA to the AIME falls with the AIME–which introduces redistribution into the system.[8]. The formula is illustrated in Figure 5.4, which shows the relationship between the PIA and the AIME (with the maximum AIME taken to be $3,750).

---

[7] Past earnings are converted to constant dollars of the year the person reaches age 60. So if a person turns age 60 in 1999, for example, past earnings are put in 1999 dollars. Earnings after age 60 are not indexed, but enter the averaging as nominal dollars.

[8] In 1995, for example, the PIA was given by: 90% of the first $426 or less of AIME, +32% of any AIME between $426 and $2,567, + 15% of AIME exceeding $2567.

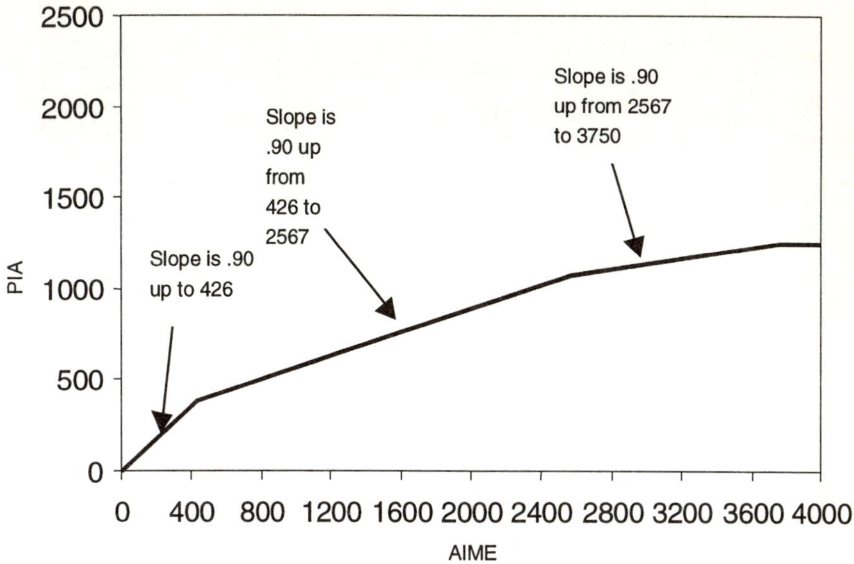

Fig 5.4. Pia versus AIME

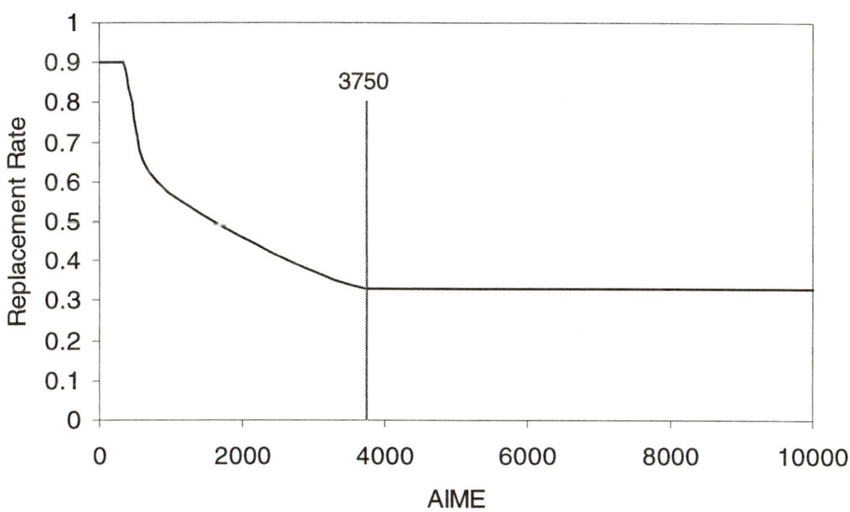

Fig 5.5. SS AIME Replacement Rate

The proportion of AIME replaced by social security benefits is shown in Figure 5.5. For the lowest wage earners, the "AIME replacement rate" is 90 %. It declines

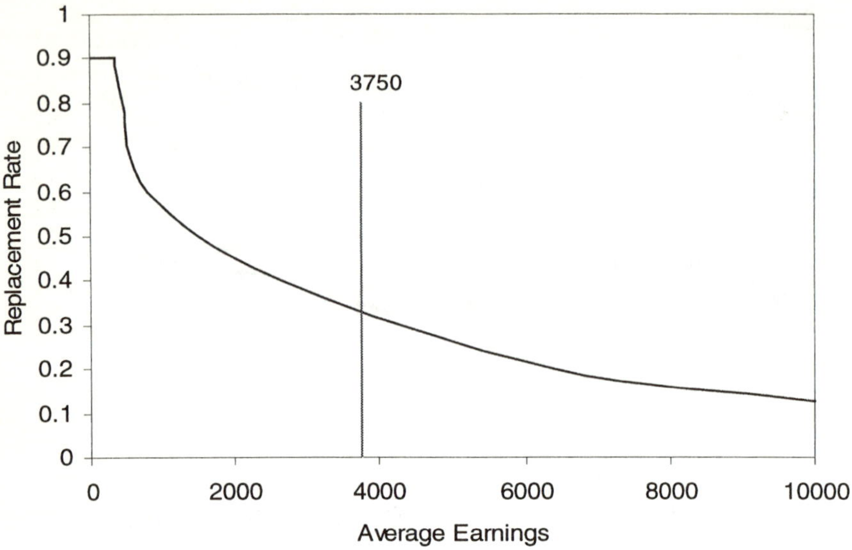

Fig 5.6. SS Earnings Replacement Rate

to 33% for those with AIME greater than $3,750. The proportion of total earnings–as opposed to covered earnings–replaced by Social Security benefits is shown in Figure 5.6. For the lowest wage earners, this "earnings replacement rate" is again 90%. But it declines to about 12% for persons with incomes of $10,000 (10,200 EUR) per month. The reason that the earnings replacement rate is lower than the AIME replacement rate for high wage earners is of course that covered earnings are capped at $3,750 (3,825 EUR) . The median of individual earnings in 1995 was about $18,500 (18,870 EUR), which would suggest an earnings replacement rate of about 45 percent at the median. This "progressivity" in the replacement rate is thus due both to the limit on covered earnings as well as the redistributive benefit formula for covered earnings.

There are additional features of the system which also affect the actual earnings replacement rate. Up to 85% of Social Security benefits are taxed, for recipients with sufficiently high incomes. For others a smaller proportion of benefits is taxed. If the sum of other income and one–half of SS benefits is less than $32,000 ((32,640 EUR), Social Security benefits are not taxed. But all of wage earnings are taxed. Thus the effective earnings replacement rate is higher than the rate shown in Figure 5.6.

The base PIA assumes retirement at the normal retirement age, which is currently 65. Benefits can be taken beginning at age 62, the early retirement age. Benefits are reduced by 5/9 of one percent for each month that benefit receipt precedes age 65, and thus taken at age 62 are 80 percent of normal retirement age benefits. The reduction is intended to leave lifetime benefits unchanged, whether they begin at 65 or at some age between 62 and 65. The receipt of benefits can also be delayed beyond are 65. In this case benefits are increased 5 percent for each year benefit receipt is delayed. An "actuarially fare increase"–leaving lifetime benefits unchanged–would be about 8 percent. Thus, unlike the actuarial decrease between 65 an 62, after 65 benefits are not increased enough to offset the fewer years of benefit receipt. At age 69, for example, the loss in Social Security benefits from working an additional year offsets approximately half of wage earnings. This provides a substantial incentive to leave the labor force at 65. The retirement incentive effects of the United States system and the much larger incentive effects inherent in the social security systems in ten other countries, including Germany, are explained in Gruber and Wise [1999].

Social Security provisions provide an additional incentive to limit work. Benefits are subject to an "earnings test" until the recipient reaches age 70. If a recipient earns more than the earnings test limit, SS benefits are reduced for each additional dollar of earnings. In 1995, the earnings limit was $8280 (8,446 EUR) for persons between 62 and 65, and $12,500 (12,750 EUR) for persons between 65 and 70.[9] For persons between 62 and 65 benefits are reduced $1 for each $2 of earnings; for workers between 62 and 65 benefits are reduced $1 for every $3 or earnings.[10]

Family benefits depend on family status. The spouse of a beneficiary receives 50 percent of the beneficiary's PIA, beginning at age 62.[11] In addition, each dependent child is eligible for 50 percent of the PIA, but the total family benefit is limited to about 175 percent of the PIA. Surviving spouses typically receive 100 percent the PIA.

5.2.2 Related Public Programs

Two other programs interact to some extent with the Social Security program. The first is Disability Insurance, which provides benefits for employees who are unable to work. Social Security benefits taken before the normal retirement age are reduced by 5/9 of one percent per month. But persons who qualify for disability insurance benefits receive full benefits with no reduction. The interaction between disability and Social Security benefits is much less pronounced than in Germany, although there is a small decline in the proportion of persons receiving disability benefits at age 62, when Social Security benefits are first available.

---

[9] The limits are increased each year with average earnings.

[10] The earnings limit for persons between 65 and 69 will be increased gradually to $30,000 (30,600 EUR) by 2002, based on 1996 legislation. Earnings above the earnings limit, although taxed when the work occurs, do entitle the person to higher benefits later.

[11] A spouse could receive benefits based on her labor market earnings, but can only receive the larger of this amount and 50 percent of her spouses benefit. Spousal benefits can begin before age 62 if there is a dependent child in the household.

The second program which may interact with Social Security, is the Supplemental Security Income program, which provides benefits to low income elderly and some disabled persons. Supplemental Security Income benefits are based on income at a point in time, rather than lifetime income. Fewer than 4 percent of Social Security beneficiaries age 65 and older also receive Supplemental Security Income. But over two–thirds of those receiving Supplemental Security Income benefits receive Social Security benefits. Thus Supplemental Security Income serves as an alternative to Social Security for low income elderly, and as a supplement for those with very low Social Security benefits.

5.2.3 Employer–Provided Pensions

About one–half of current employees and retirees are covered by employer-provided pensions. As shown in Table 5.1, fewer than half of persons with the low lifetime earnings are covered and even for those with higher lifetime earnings, employer–provided pension assets are typically much lower than social security assets. There are two types of traditional employer plans. The most prevalent used to be the defined benefit (DB) plan, with benefits determined by years of employment and salary–usually in the last years of employment. The second type is the defined contribution (DC) plan, with benefits determined by contributions placed in an employee's individual account, together with the market rate of return on these contributions. Traditional DC plans were often supplemental to DB plans put could also be the only employer plan. Over time the number of persons covered by these DC plans has increased, while the number covered by DB plans has decreased. Beginning in the early 1980s, individual 401(k) plans were introduced and grew rapidly thereafter. Because they are like traditional employer–provided DC plans in some respects, they are often included in the count of DC plans. The expansion of these and other individual retirement saving plans in discussed in the next section. Figure 5.7 shows the number of persons covered by DB, by 401(k) and by DC + 401(k) plans from 1975 to 1994, the latest year for which data are available. After 401(k) plans were introduced, they accounted for most of the growth in DC + 401(k) plans.

An important feature of the typical DB plan is the incentive for early retirement implicit in typical plan provisions. These incentives are discussed in detail in Kotlikoff and Wise [1989] and the effects are evaluated in Stock and Wise [1990 and 1996], and in Lumsdaine, Stock, and Wise [1990, 1992, 1994, 1997]. Like Social Security benefits after the age of 65, the incentive to retire arises because the increase in future benefits when a person works an additional year is typically not large enough to offset the receipt of benefits for one fewer years. Such incentives in employer–provided DB plans, however, often begin at the early retirement age, which in many plans is age 55. Because of these incentives, a large fraction of persons covered by DB plans retire before the Social Security early retirement age of 62.

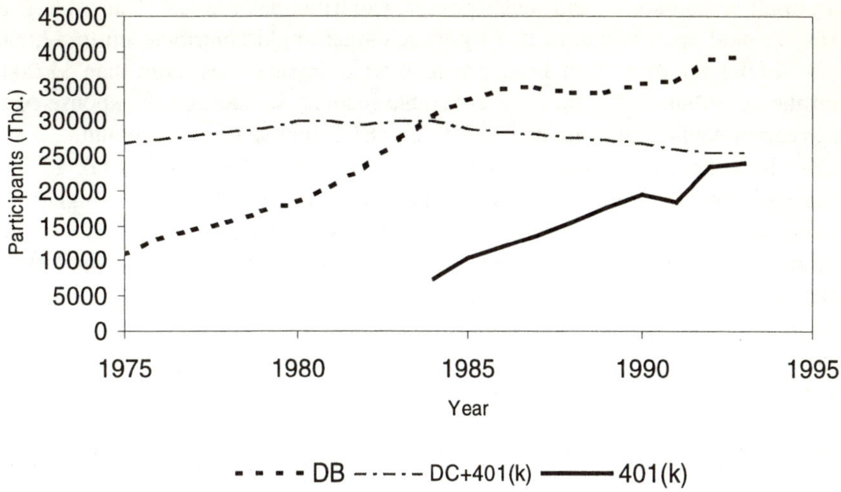

Fig 5.7. Employer Plan Participants

Both Social Security and employer–provided DB plans determine benefits on a defined benefit basis. But there is an important difference: Social Security benefits are based on lifetime earnings indexed to age 60–that is, benefits are based approximately on lifetime earnings in retirement–age dollars. And, Social Security benefits are indexed to the Consumer Price Index. Employer–provided DB benefits, on the other hand, are based on current earnings, typically the final earnings in a firm. Thus if a person leaves the firm at age 35, benefits at age 65, for example, are based on earnings 30 years ago. With earnings inflation, these benefits are not worth much. Thus a key source of risk associated with employer–provided DB plans is job change, which now in the United States is very prevalent. In addition, employer–provided DB plan benefits are not indexed and thus do not keep up with inflation, although ex post increases in benefits are sometimes made on an ad hoc basis.

Finally, many employer–provided DB plans incorporate "Social Security offsets" so that benefits are reduced to some extent depending on the amount of Social Security benefits. This is one of the reasons that employer–provided pension benefits are often small.

5.2.4 Personal Retirement Saving

The most dramatic change in saving for retirement in the United States is rapidly expanding participation in personal retirement plans: IRAs, 401(k)s, and Keoghs. Both 401(k)s and IRAs are relatively recent innovations. Individual Retirement Accounts (IRAs) became popular after 1982 when they were made available to all wage earners and their spouses. Contributions are tax–deductible and taxes are paid upon withdrawal. Any wage earner could contribute up to $2,000 (2,040 EUR) per year to an IRA, provided wage income was more than $2,000, with the contribution deducted from taxable income. In addition the spouse of a wage earner could contribute up to $250 (255 EUR) per year to an account.

The Keogh plan is intended for the self–employed. This plan has tax advantages equivalent to those of an IRA, but the contribution limits are much higher.

Employer sponsored personal saving plans were established in 1978 under section 401(k) of the Internal Revenue Code, but were not widely used until 1982 (after the IRS issued clarifying regulations in 1981). These accounts are available only to employees of firms that offer a 401(k) plan. Like IRAs, deposits in 401(k) accounts are tax–deductible and the return on the contributions accrues tax free. Taxes are paid upon withdrawal. Prior to 1987 the employee annual contribution limit was $30,000 (30,600 EUR). The Tax Reform Act of 1986 reduced the limit to $7,000 (9,140 EUR) beginning in 1987 and instituted indexation for inflation in subsequent years. The contribution limit is $10,000 (10,200 EUR) for the 1998 tax year. There are several additional features of 401(k)s that employers may choose to adopt. Employers can "match" employee contributions. About 60 percent of contributions are matched at rates above 10 percent, 26 percent above 100 percent. Some plans permit pre–retirement "hardship withdrawals" in certain circumstances, although such withdrawals are usually subject to a penalty tax. Some employees can also borrow funds from their 401(k) accounts.

The Taxpayer Relief Act of 1997 reversed the 1986 IRA retrenchment by expanding the availability of "front–loaded" IRAs and by creating a new "back-loaded" IRA known as the "Roth IRA." Over the next decade the income limit for deductibility of the existing IRA will increase, and the deduction available to a non–working spouse was increased from $250 to $2,000 (255 to 2,040 EUR). thus increasing the combined deduction for a family with a non–working spouse from $2,250 to $4,000 (2,295 to 4,080 EUR). Contributions to the new back–loaded Roth IRA are not deductible, but no tax is paid upon withdrawal (if the funds are held for at least five years and if the recipient is over age 59 ½). Like the front-loaded IRA, the investment return accrues tax free. Contribution limits are the same as for the "front–loaded" IRA. But the Roth IRA contribution limit is after tax, instead of before tax. Thus potential accumulation of retirement saving is much higher under the Roth IRA. In addition, the income limit for contributions is much higher under the Roth than under the older IRA.

Portability is an important feature of all of these plans. Unlike traditional DB pension plans–in which benefits are substantially reduced by job change, as shown in Kotlikoff and Wise [1989]–the value of these plans is not affected by job change, as long as contributions continue to be made. This is obviously the case for IRAs and Keogh plans which are managed entirely by individuals. The 401(k) plans are also essentially portable. If an employee leaves the firm the plan assets can remain in the existing plan and continue to accrue returns, or they can be

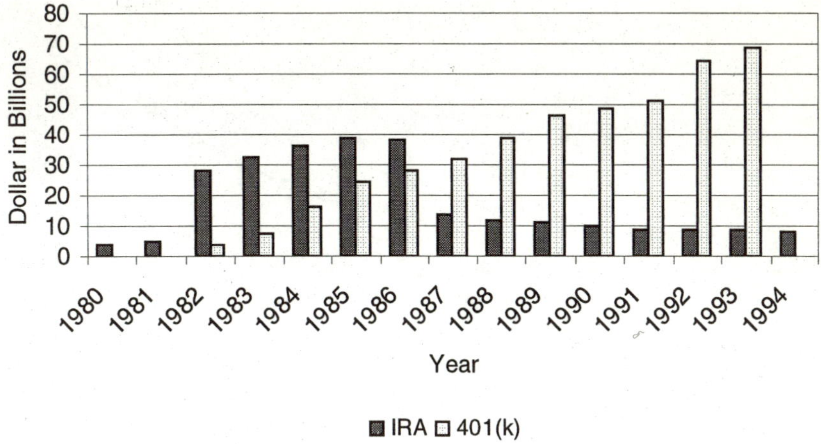

Fig 5.8. IRA and 401(k) Contributions

"rolled" over into an IRA, or they can be rolled over into a 401(k) with a new employer. The investment of assets in IRA and Keogh plans is virtually unconstrained, the employee can invest the assets in bonds, mutual funds, or individual equities. The investment of 401(k) assets is typically made from a menu of money market, bond, and equity mutual funds which varies among employers. In practice, about two–thirds of assets in these accounts are held in equity mutual funds or in the stock of the firm. The proportion held in equities tends to increase with income and to decline with age. (See Poterba and Wise [1999] for more discussion of asset allocation.) In short, the assets in these accounts are owned and controlled by the individual and are not subject to appropriation by government or private parties.

The trend in total contributions to 401(k) and IRA accounts is shown in Figure 5.8. IRA contributions increased from less than $5 billion to almost $30 billion as soon as they became available to all wage earners in 1982. Thereafter annual contributions increased to almost $40 billion by 1986. Contributions fell sharply after the 1986 legislation and by 1990 were under $10 billion. On the other hand, 401(k) contributions grew continuously from close to zero in the early 1980s to almost $70 billion by 1993. Annual contributions to 401(k) plans probably exceed $100 billion today. Indeed, there was no change in the growth of 401(k) contributions when IRA contributions plummeted after the 1986 legislation. (For further discussion of these plans and, in particular their saving effects, see Poterba, Venti, and Wise [1994a, 1994b, 1995,1996, 1998a, 1998b].)

The relationship between personal and total retirement saving is shown in Figure 5.9, which is taken from Venti and Wise [1997]. Retirement saving is defined as the sum of employer contributions to defined benefit and defined contribution pension plans, and individual contributions to IRAs, Keogh, and 401(k) plans.

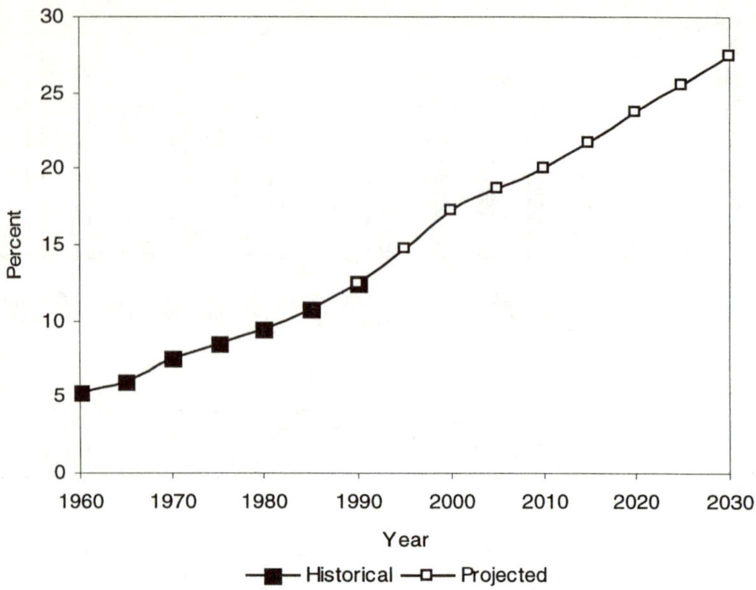

Fig 5.9. IRA and 401(k) Contributions

Total contributions to each of these plans is shown in the figure. Retirement saving in Figure 5.9 does not include any accruing benefits in the Social Security system, and it also excludes (for lack of data) any saving for retirement that is done outside these retirement plans.

Total retirement saving increased sharply until 1986 and fell substantially thereafter, following the pattern of IRA contributions. In spite of the increase in the number of conventional employer–provided defined contribution pension plans and in the number of employees covered by them, total contributions to these plans remained almost constant over the entire period. There was a large drop in contributions to defined benefit pension plans, reflecting increases in the value of pension funds invested in the stock market and thus lower required additional contributions to meet projected benefit entitlements, as is discussed in Bernheim and Shoven [1988]. In addition, various legislative changes reduced allowable contributions to these plans. The reduction is much greater than can be attributed to the fall in defined benefit coverage. In the early 1990s contributions to these defined benefit plans increased rather sharply, even though the number of employees covered by such plans declined.

The key feature of the data is the enormous increase in the proportion of retirement saving through personal retirement saving plans. By 1990, IRAs, 401(k)s, and Keogh plans together accounted for almost 56 percent of total retirement saving. Counting defined contribution pension plans, by 1990 over 80 percent of retirement saving (compared with 41 percent in 1980) was in "individual" accounts. Thus personal retirement saving has rapidly become an important component of the future financial support of the elderly.

In the mid–1990s, at least one spouse in over 50% of families is eligible for a 401(k) plan and about 70% of those eligible contribute. What does the future hold? The most recent data show no slackening in the growth of 401(k) plans. Personal retirement saving plans have not only changed the way people save for retirement, but are likely to substantially increase wealth at retirement.

5.2.5 What Does the Future Hold?

For persons who retire three decades from now, wealth in the from of personal retirement saving is likely to be greater than Social Security wealth. Together with James Poterba and Steven Venti, I have made projections of the 401(k) assets of future retirees. (See Poterba, Venti, and Wise [1998].) We have made projections for the cohort retiring in 1925 and the cohort retiring in 1935. These projections depend on estimates of future participation and contributions. For comparison, we have also made projections based on universal participation in 401(k) plans.

For each of the projections, we assume three different rates of return: the average rate of return on corporate bonds since 1926 (6%), the average rate of return on the S&P 500 over the same period (12.7%), and the rate of return assuming that a person is invested half in bonds and half in the S&P 500.

The results for these three projections are reported in Table 5.4, in 1992 dollars. For comparison, the 1992 assets of retirees now approaching retirement are shown in Table 5.3. In particular, the mean of Social Security wealth is about $104,000 (106,080 EUR). Remember that 401(k) assets are accumulated tax free; taxes would be paid when funds are withdrawn. The tax on Social Security benefits depends on income, with zero to 85 percent of benefits taxed at the income tax ratc.

Table 5.3 Median and Mean 1992 Assets of HRS Respondents, by Asset Category (in USD)

Asset Category	Total Wealth	Total Retirement Excl SS	Employer Pension Assets	Total Personal Retirement	Non-Retirement Financial	401(k) Assets	Social Security Wealth
Median	284229	44010	15913	3200	13000	0	106808
Mean	415833	112677	82212	30465	54724	10808	103392

Source: Poterba, Venti, and Wise [1998]

Table 5.4 Projected Mean 401(k) Assets by Cohort, and Rate of Return (in USD)

	Bond	50/50	S&P 500
Cohort: 65 in 2025	50111	91620	181567
Cohort: 65 in 2035	66765	125534	256056
Universal Coverage	109435	211445	443005

Source: Poterba, Venti, and Wise [1998]

The projections show that the cohort retiring in 2025 will have 401(k) assets at retirement ranging from $50,111 to $181,567 (51,113 to 185,198 EUR) depending on the rate of return. These levels are very large relative to average Social Security wealth of $104,000 and are much larger than the HRS respondent mean 401(k) balance of $10,808 (11,024 EUR) in 1992, when the respondents were 51 to 61. The means for the cohort retiring in 2035 range from $66,765 to $256,056 (68,100 to 261,177 EUR). Universal coverage would yield mean 401(k) balances at age 65

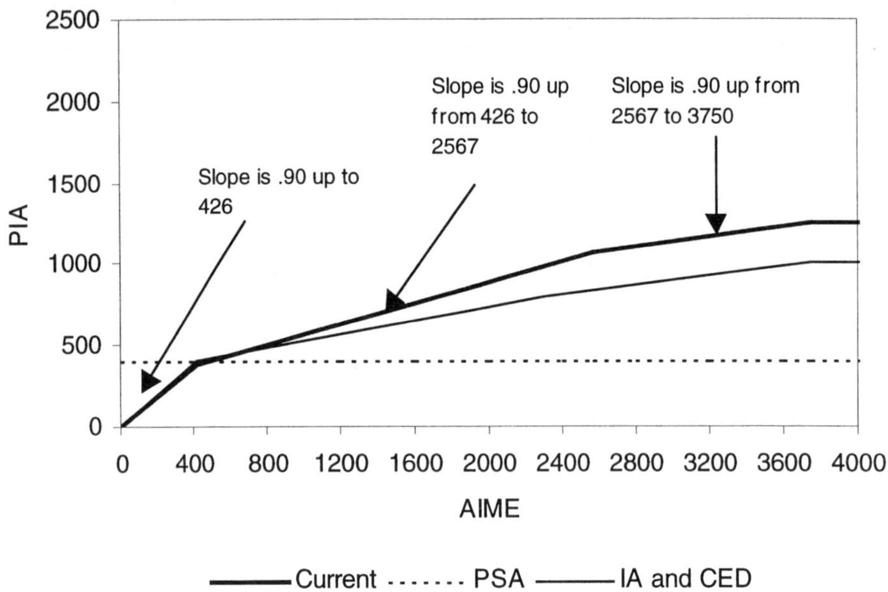

Fig 5.10. PIA versus AIME

ranging from $109,439 to $480,798 (111,628 to 490,414 EUR), depending on the rate of return.

It is clear that personal retirement saving will surely be an important source of retirement support of future retirees. The decisions to open 401(k) plans, which are the basis for the projections have largely been made already. Projections including IRA contributions would be substantially larger than those for 401(k) assets alone. With the expected further expansion of IRA contributions, personal retirement plan accumulations are likely to be even greater. Indeed, we believe that updated projections for 401(k) assets would be substantially greater than those shown above.

5.2.6 Public Perception

There is perhaps no good way to judge reliably how the public views the Social Security system and how perceptions of that program are affected by changes in other components of retirement support. There is evidence, however, that the public lacks confidence that the Social Security system will be able to deliver promised future benefits. Figure 5.10 is taken from Shoven [1999] and shows that a large fraction of respondents are not confident about the future of the program. The figure gives the percent of respondents in public opinion polls reporting that they are "not too confident" or "not at all confident" about the future of Social Security. At least some judgements about reform proposals seem to be based on the worry that fundamental changes in the system might erode public support for the pay–as–you–go system. But surveys such as this one suggest that without reform confidence may also erode.

5.3 Future Developments

Like most developed countries, the United States population is aging rapidly. In the United States now there are about 2 people 65 and over for every 10 people in the "working age" population. By 2030 there will be almost 4 people 65 and over for every 10 in the working age group. The aging of the American population is due primarily to the high birth rates between the years 1946 and 1964, the baby boom generation. But increasing life expectancy also contributes to population aging. Indeed the life expectancy of women now 65 is almost 3 years longer than it was just three decades ago. For men life expectancy at 65 is almost 2 years longer than it was three decades ago.

Although Americans are living longer, they are leaving the labor force a younger and younger ages. In 1960, over 81 percent of men 60 to 64 were in the labor force. Now only about 53 percent are still working. Over 34 percent of men age 65 to 70 were working in 1960, but now only 17 percent. This trend is common to other industrialized countries as well, as shown in Gruber and Wise [1999]. Indeed decline in the labor force participation of men has been much greater European countries than in the United States. The decline in the labor force participation of older workers magnifies the financial imbalance faced by Social Security due to population aging, and reduces national production–thereby making it more difficult to support retirees.

In addition, as explained above, most Americans now retired have saved very little and the personal saving rate is low and apparently declining. But as discussed above, the rapid rise in personal retirement saving may change that trend.

There is a third trend that interacts with the first three. Increasing medical cost is likely to make living longer, working less, and saving little even less sustainable. Nearly 14 percent of national income in the United States is spent on medical care, one and one–half to twice as much as in most other developed countries. Projections suggest spending of over 25 percent of GDP by 2030 (see Figure 5.11). A small part of the projected increase comes from population aging; the cost for persons 85 and older is approximately 12 times as high as the average cost for persons 19 to 64, for example. But for any given age, the costs are rising rapidly. The Medicare Trust Fund (the public program providing health care for persons 65 and over) is projected to go broke in the next few years and to run very large deficits thereafter. It is in this context, that a great deal of attention is now being given to Social Security reform.

5.4 Social Security Reform

Social Security reform proposals in the United States can be placed in two categories: incremental reform and fundamental reform. Incremental proposals do not change the basic structure of the current system, but address the financial imbalance of the system by some combination of increased taxes, reduced benefits, and increased retirement age. Fundamental reform includes various proposals that would change the basic structure of the system. The current proposals of this type involve at least some pre–funding of the system, through the creation of personal accounts. I will discuss incremental reform proposals first and then proposals for fundamental reform.

5.4.1 Incremental Reform

It is helpful to keep in mind that the United States pay–as–you–go system means essentially that Social Security taxes collected today from current employees are used to pay benefits today to current retirees. As explained in the introduction to this volume, the relationship can be represented by

$$\text{Labor rate} \cdot \text{wage rate} \cdot \text{tax rate} = \text{Retirees} \cdot \text{Benefit}$$

where the left side gives receipts and the right side give benefits ("benefit" is the average benefit per retiree). If receipts are to match benefits, the tax rate is given by

$$\text{Tax rate} = \frac{\text{Retirees}}{\text{Labor force}} \cdot \frac{\text{Benefit}}{\text{Wage rate}}$$

$$= \text{Dependency Ratio} \cdot \text{Replacement Rate}$$

The dependency ratio is the number of retirees to persons in the labor force and the replacement rate is the ratio of benefits to the wage.

Two trends increase the dependency ration. One is population aging, and increasing life expectancy, which increases the number of persons over any given older age. The other is the decline in the retirement age, which reduces the number of persons in the labor force and increases the number of retirees, given any age structure of the population. Both trends have been at work in the United States. The result has been a progressive increase in the dependency ratio. The dependency ratio can be reduced by increasing the retirement age, taking population aging as a given.

The increase in the dependency ratio could be counter–balanced by a decrease in the replacement rate, keeping the tax rate constant. There are two way to do this: One is to reduce benefits and the other is to increase the wage rate. (Through productivity growth, wage rates are likely to increase over time. In the foreseeable future, however, productivity growth will not be large enough to offset the increase in the dependency ratio.)

Incremental reform proposals include measures to reduce the dependency ratio and measures to reduce the replacement rate, as well as increases in the tax rate. To reduce the dependency ratio, the proposals typically include an increase in the normal retirement age, and in some cases the early retirement age as well. It is important to recognize that the increasing the retirement age is equivalent to a reduction in benefits. In fact, the greatest reduction in benefits comes from a delay in the receipt of benefits.

For example, to reduce the dependency ratio, Henry Aaron[12] proposes that the planned increase in the normal retirement age to 67 be accelerated to 2012 and thereafter be indexed to increases in life expectancy. He also would gradually increase the early retirement age from 62 to 64. To reduce benefits further, Aaron proposes several changes: (1) Benefits would not be fully indexed to the Con-

[12] See Alvin Hansen Lecture, Harvard University, April 27, 1998.

sumer Price index, as they are now, but would be increased ½ percent less than the CPI increase. (2) All benefits in excess of employee contributions would be fully taxed, implying that approximately 85 percent of benefits are taxed.[13] (3) The AIME would be based on the highest 38 instead of the highest 35 years of covered earnings. This would necessarily reduce the AIME, since the additional earnings will be no greater than the lowest of the earnings in the 35 years now used. Aaron also proposes an immediate increase of 0.2 percent in the tax rate paid by both employees and employees–a total increase of 0.4 percent in total.

The 1994–95 Social Security Advisory Commission made three alternative proposals. One, called the "Maintain Benefits" plan proposes changes similar the those suggested by Aaron. It does not in fact maintain benefits, but cuts benefits by raising the income tax on benefits and by increasing the number of years used to calculate the AIME. In addition, the proposal raises the payroll tax rate by 1.6 percent, but not until 2045.[14]

In fact, not all Social Security taxes are paid directly to beneficiaries as the formula above suggests. Instead, tax revenues are deposited in the Social Security Trust Fund and benefits are paid out the Trust Fund. Fund balances are invested in U.S. Treasury Bills and in principle earn the Treasury Bill rate of return. Currently the increase in the trust fund–resulting from the deposit of revenues and the return on the balance–exceeds the amount of benefits paid out. But current projections indicate that by the year 2029 the Trust Fund balance will be exhausted and the fund will begin to run deficits. Although the Trust Fund may facilitate accounting, it has no fundamental economic meaning. Social Security tax receipts are part of the overall Federal budget. Thus if receipts exceed benefits, as they do now, the excess is counted as part of the budget surplus. Indeed the current "budget surplus" in the United States is accounted for almost entirely by the surplus in the Trust Fund. When benefits begin to exceed receipts, the shortfall must be made up out of general revenues. In principle, the Trust Fund would begin to sell Treasury Bills that have been set aside for this purpose. But the macro economic consequences of the Social Security deficit would be the same regardless of the Trust Fund.

This more complete representation of the U.S. pay–as–you–go system motivates an additional incremental reform proposal. In addition to proposals to in-

[13] This proposal treats Social Security retirement benefits on an income tax basis, unlike employer–provided and individual retirement saving plans which are taxed on a consumption tax basis, and thus taxes both the contribution as well as the implicit return on the contribution. Now, income tax is paid on the employee contribution but not on the employer contribution. Thus the goal is to tax the "return" on the employee contribution, plus the contribution as well as the return on the employer contribution. It has been estimated that taxing 85 percent of benefits would approximate an actual income tax treatment. Now only couples with incomes above $44,000 and single persons with incomes above $34,000 pay taxes on 85 percent of benefits.

[14] Even though Medicare is in worse financial shape than Social Security, this plan also proposes diverting some funds from the Health Insurance Trust Fund for Medicare to the OASDI Trust Fund, beginning in 2010.

crease the Social Security tax rate, to reduce benefits, and to increase the retirement age, an additional suggestion to forestall the bankruptcy of the Trust Fund is to invest Trust Fund balances in equities, which historically have had a much higher rate of return than Treasury Bills. Both the Aaron proposal and the Advisory Council's "Maintain Benefits" proposal suggest that some of the Trust Fund be invested in the private equity market– Aaron proposes that 40 percent be invested in stocks and the Maintain Benefits proponents suggest that up to 40 percent be invested in private stocks and bonds. Indeed President Clinton has recently proposed that some portion of the Trust Fund be invested in equities.

Such proposals will likely have little affect on overall saving for retirement. Because most Treasury Bills sold by the Trust Fund will be purchased by private pension funds, assets will be re–allocated but not increased. In addition, there is considerable concern that investment in equities will lead to politically–motivated investment decisions and analysts have raised important concerns about this potential danger. For example, Alan Greenspan, the Chairman of the Federal Reserve Board, has been a prominent critique of investment of the Trust Fund assets in the equity market.

5.4.2 Fundamental Reform: Individual Accounts, Pre–Funding, and Market Investment

There have been several proposals for pre–funding of Social Security–typically partial–through the introduction of personal Social Security accounts, similar to personal IRA accounts. There have been two related reasons for these proposals. One is that the rate of return on these accounts would be much larger than the implicit rate of return on contributions to a pay–as–you–go system (which is the rate of growth of the tax base, that is, the rate of growth of GDP, which in turn is the product of the growth in the labor force times the real increase in the wage rate–productivity growth). For example, the Social Security administration now assumes a long–run GDP growth rate of 1.1 percent (although over the past four decades the grow rate has been 3.1 percent). On the other hand, the average real rate of return on equities since 1926 has been about 9 percent. This suggests that in the long run the system could be funded with a lower tax rate if personal accounts were invested in private financial markets. This is the reasoning that motivates the analysis of personal accounts by Feldstein and Samwick [1996, 1997] for example.

The second reason that personal accounts have been suggested is to increase the personal saving rate in the United States, which as explained above is extremely low. A strictly pay–as–you–go system involves no saving, unlike private employer–provided or individual retirement saving plans, for example, are funded by saving today to pay for future retirement benefits. (Discussion of Social Security personal accounts typically refer to contributions to fund the personal account component, as well as taxes to fund the pay–as–you–go component, as tax rates.

There is a difference, however. The personal component is used to fund an account like an IRA or a 401(k) account. Perhaps the a personal account contribution is better thought of as forced saving, if it is mandatory, or personal saving if it is not. On the other hand, the pay–as–you–go tax conforms more closely to a typical tax: it can be used to support a social program broader than the personal account component.

Complete transition to a funded PRA system is unlikely, however. Perhaps the most politically realistic proposals in the United States involve a combination of the pay–as–you–go defined benefit system together with a personal account component. Several proposals–the "Individual Accounts" (IA) plan of the Social Security Advisory Council, the Committee for Economic Development (CED) plan, and the "Personal Security Account" (PSA) plan of the Social Security Advisory Council–suggest a rather similar structure but differ in the details.

All of these proposals begin by reducing benefits under the current system. First, both the IA and the CED plans maintain the PIA of the lowest wage earners but reduce the PIA–and thus benefits–of all persons with higher earnings. Referring to Figure 5.12, the conversion of 90 percent of earnings to the PIA for low wage earners is maintained, but 32 percent rate lowered to 22.4 percent and the 15 percent rate to 10.5 percent. The effect on the PIA is shown in the figure. Second, both plans reduce benefits by increasing the number of years used to calculate the PIA, by increasing the retirement age, and by increasing the tax on benefits. Both plans increase the retirement age–to 70 in the CED and to 67 with indexing to life expectancy thereafter in the IA plan. Both tax 85 percent of Social Security benefits. (Thus attempting to tax on an income tax basis.) Both also reduce benefits of one–earner families by reducing spouse benefits from 50 percent to one–third of the primary earners PIA.

To offset the reduction in the defined benefit component (tier one) both plans propose mandatory individual accounts. The CED proposes 3.0 percent of earnings be placed in the personal account and the IA proposes 1.6 percent.

The third proposal with elements similar to the above two is the PSA plan of the Social Security Advisory Council. This plan also begins by reducing benefits under the current system. The first tier benefits are set at a flat $410 for single retirees and $615 for married couples for those with 35 years of earnings. These flat rates would be indexed to real wage earnings in the future. For comparison, the PIA under this more extreme reduction in the PIA for all but the lowest wage earners in also shown in Figure 5.12 for single retirees. The normal retirement age would also be increased and the early retirement age would also be increased gradually from 62 to 65. This proposal, however, by taxing benefits on a consumption tax basis, reduces the tax on benefits–50 percent of benefits are taxed.

Under the PSA proposal 5 percent of earnings would be placed in the PSA. The tax rate to support the tier one benefits would be set at 8.92 percent. (Thus the total payroll "tax rate" is increased by 1.52 percentage points–from 12.4 to 13.92 percent. In is perhaps more accurate to say that the payroll tax rate is reduced from 12.4 to 8.92 percent, and a mandatory 5 percent contribution to the PSA is insti-

tuted.) Like the other two–tier proposals, this one would be phased in over time, with gradual adoption of the PSAs.
Sylvester Schieber and John Shoven (see Schieber and Shoven [1999] and Shoven [1998 and 1999]) have suggested a variant of the PSA plan. They propose lowering the current payroll tax rate to 9.9 percent and introduces a mandatory 5 percent contribution to an individual account. In addition, they set the flat tier one benefit at $450 (459 EUR) instead of $410 (418 EUR).

Feldstein and Samwick (1998) have also proposed a two–tier system, which takes advantage of the current budget surplus to adopt personal accounts. Then when benefits are taken, part of the gains from the personal account are offset by a reduction in the tier–one (current system) benefits. Their proposal is to guarantee benefits at least equal to those under the current system. Individuals would contribute 2 percent of earnings–up to the Social Security limit–to a personal account. The contribution is treated as a "cashable" income tax credit. (If the contribution is greater than the tax bill, the excess is received as a tax refund from the Internal Revenue Service.) The contributions are invested in the private market. The benefits from the personal account would be in the form of an indexed life annuity, like the current Social Security benefits. But for every dollar of tier two benefits, tier one benefits would be reduced by 75 cents. Thus the concept is that no one would receive lower benefits under this two–tier system.

5.5 Summary

The United States Social Security system is facing a future financial crisis. Several incremental and several fundamental reform proposals have been made. Most of these proposals include components intended to reduce the cost of the system. Perhaps the most important proposed cost–cutting measure is the increase in the normal (and in some cases the earl) retirement age. More fundamental proposals for reform include both cost–cutting measures and the introduction of some form of personal Social Security retirement account. In spite of the intensive public and private discussion of reform, the prospects for change in the near term seem dim. President Clinton has recently proposed that a large portion of the "budget surplus" tax dollars be allocated to the Social Security Trust Fund, which is equivalent to an increase in the Social Security payroll tax. Ironically, the curious suggestion is to allocate a significant part of the future "surplus," which now is due almost entirely to the "surplus" in the Social Security Trust Fund, back to the Trust Fund. The proposal includes no measures to reduce the cost of the system. Thus political posturing may doom much needed reform. If this is so, the problem will only get worse while the politicians terry and proclaim.

In the meantime, the most important change in prospective support in retirement will come from the rapid spread of personal retirement saving in the form of

401(k) accounts, IRAs, and other retirement accounts controlled by individuals. In a real sense, the personal control of retirement saving is progressing rapidly, perhaps more quickly than any resolution of the debate about Social Security personal accounts. Universal 401(k) coverage would indeed look much like a Social Security system with personal accounts.

References

Bernheim, D., Shoven, J.: Pension Funding and Saving, in: Bodie, Z., Shoven, S., Wise, D. A.: Pensions in the U.S. Economy, NBER – University of Chicago Press: Chicago, 1988, 85–111. Reprinted in: O'Brien Hylton, M.: Cases and Materials on Employee Benefits Law, West Publishing Company, forthcoming.

Feldstein, M., Samwick, A.: Social Security and Marginal Tax Rates. National Tax Journal, Vol. 45(1), 1–22, 1992.

Feldstein, M., Samwick, A.: The Economics of Prefunding Social Security and Medicare Benefits. In: Bernanke, B., Rotemberg, J.: NBER Macroeconomics Annual 1997, MIT Press, 1997.

Feldstein, M., Samwick, A.: The Transition Path in Privatizing Social Security. In: Feldstein, M.: Privatizing Social Security. Chicago: University of Chicago Press, 1998.

Feldstein, M., Samwick, A.: Potential Effects of Two Percent Personal Retirement Accounts. Tax Notes, May 4, 1998, 615–620.

Gruber, J., Wise, D. A.: Social Security and Retirement Around the World: Introduction and Summary.in: Gruber, J.,Wise, D. A.: Social Security and Retirement Around the World. Chicago: University of Chicago Press, 1999.

Kotlikoff, L., Wise, D. A.: The Wage Carrot and the Pension Stick. W.E. Upjohn Institute for Employment Research, 1989.

Lumsdaine, R., Stock, J., Wise, D. A.: Efficient Windows and Labor Force Reduction. Journal of Public Economics 43, 1990: 131–159.

Lumsdaine, R., Stock, J., Wise, D. A.: Three Models of Retirement: Computational Complexity Versus Predictive Validity. In: Topics in the Economics of Aging. Chicago: University of Chicago Press, 1992.

Lumsdaine, R., Stock, J.H., Wise, D. A. : Pension Plan Provisions and Retirement: Men & Women, Medicare, and Models. In: Studies in the Economics of Aging. Chicago:University of Chicago Press, 1994.

Lumsdaine, R., Stock, J., Wise, D. A.: Retirement Incentives: The Interaction Between Employer–Provided Pension Plans, Social Security, and Retiree Health Benefits. in: Hurd, M., Yashiro, N.: The Economic Effects of Aging in the United States and Japan. Chicago: University of Chicago Press, 1997.

Poterba, J., Wise, D. A.: Personal Retirement Accounts and Personal Choice. in: Wise, D. A. Personal Saving Personal Choice. Hoover Institution Press, forthcoming 1999.

Poterba, J., Venti, S., Wise, D. A.: 401(k) Plans and Tax–Deferred Saving. In: Wise, D. A.: Studies in the Economics of Aging. Chicago: University of Chicago Press, 1994.

Poterba, J., Venti, S., Wise, D. A.: Targeted Retirement Saving and the Net Worth of Elderly Americans, American Economic Review 84:2, May 1994.

Poterba, J., Venti, S., Wise, D. A.: Do 401(k) Contributions Crowd Out Other Personal Saving? Journal of Public Economics 58: 1–32,1995.

Poterba, J., Venti, S., Wise, D. A.: How Retirement Saving Programs Increase Saving. Journal of Economic Perspectives, Fall 1996.

Poterba, J., Venti, S., Wise, D. A.: Implications of Rising Personal Retirement Saving. In: Wise, D. A.: Frontiers in the Economics of Aging. Chicago: University of Chicago Press, 1998.

Poterba, J., Venti, S., Wise, D. A.: Personal Retirement Saving Programs and Asset Accumulation: Reconciling the Evidence, in: Wise, D. A.: Frontiers in the Economics of Aging. Chicago: University of Chicago Press, 1998.

Schieber, S.J., Shoven, J.B., The Real Deal: The History and Future of Social Security. New Haven: Yale University Press, 1999.

Shoven, J.B.: Social Security Reform: Two Tiers Are Better Than One. Alvin Hansen Symposium on Public Policy. Harvard University 1998.

Shoven, J.B.: Personal Choice and Social Security, in: D. Wise: Personal Saving, Personal Choice. Hoover Institution Press, forthcoming.

Stock, J., Wise, D. A.: The Pension Inducement to Retire: An Option Value Analysis, in: Wise, D. A.: Issues in the Economics of Aging. Chicago: University of Chicago Press, 1990.

Stock, J., Wise, D. A.: Why are Retirement Rates so High at Age 65?, in: Wise, D. A.: Advances in the Economics of Aging. Chicago: University of Chicago Press, 1996.

Venti, S., Wise, D. A.: Aging, Moving, and Housing Wealth. In: Economics of Aging. University of Chicago Press, 1989.

Venti, S., Wise, D. A.: But They Don't Want to Reduce Housing Equity. In: Issues in the Economics of Aging. University of Chicago Press, 1990.

Venti, S., Wise, D. A.: The Wealth of Cohorts: Retirement Saving and the Changing Assets of Older Americans, in: Schieber, S., Shoven, S.: Public Policy Toward Pensions. MIT Press, 1997.

Venti, S., Wise, D. A.: Choice, Chance and Wealth Dispersion at Retirement, in: Ogura, S., Tachibanaki, T., Wise, D. A.: Aging in the United States and Japan. University of Chicago Press, 1999.

6 Chile's Pension Revolution Coming of Age

by Klaus Schmidt-Hebbel

6.1 A Brief History: From Public Pay–As–You–Go to Private Fully–Funded Pensions

Chile started in 1924 a mandatory pension system organized around private and state–managed social–security institutions (SSIs) for particular groups of workers.[1] Originally designed as fully–funded pension schemes, pension reserves were depleted over the years as a result of restrictive investment policies and low returns, unsustainable contribution–to–benefit ratios, and use of reserves to finance other benefits including health services, family allowances, and subsidized mortgage loans provided to some contributors. Heterogeneity of pension regimes, contributions and benefits, inter and intra–generational redistribution, and efficiency among SSIs was large, reflecting differences among participating groups in their political weight in securing special benefits provided by ad–hoc laws or administrative/budgetary decisions granted by the executive.

In 1952 a significant pension reform took place, replacing the nominal FF system by an explicit adoption of PAYG and defined–benefit pension schemes administered by existing SSIs. Other changes involved separation of health and pension programs, major increases in contribution rates, and explicit adoption of defined–benefit formulas based on high replacement of pre–retirement wages and differential mandatory retirement ages for men and women. In the absence of hard budget constraints imposed on the SSIs, the political system was vulnerable to major lobbying efforts by organized labor to raise pension benefits beyond contributions. Indeed this occurred during the next decades, when SSI deficits were covered by government transfers.

The reform of 1952 was also unsuccessful in reducing the disparity in pension contributions and benefits across SSIs, across cohorts within any given SSI, or across individuals within any given cohort. Chile's PAYG system was bad at

---

[1] Excellent accounts of the history of Chile's pension system and the 1980 pension reform can be found in Wallich (1983) and Diamond and Valdés-Prieto (1994).

reaching the old–age poor but very effective in benefiting massively the first cohorts of pensioners and those that benefited from subsidized credit programs financed by early pension surpluses – mostly middle–class contributors. High and variable inflation exacerbated the effects that frequent changes in pension contributions and benefits had on worker uncertainty about their future pension benefits. Blatant inefficiency in SSI management – reflected in high administrative costs and bad customer service – were added to the structural problems of Chile's old PAYG system.

This dismal view of Chile's PAYG system – beset by large inequities, inefficiences, and rising fiscal and macroeconomic costs – led to various reform proposals made in the 1960s and 1970s, i.e., during democratic governments. However, Chile's actual pension reform took place only in 1979–1980, designed and implemented by a group of economists headed by Labor Minister José Piñera under the military government of Pinochet. The reform's underlying diagnose was broadly in line with the previous reform proposals. However the reform departed from the preceding proposals by implementing a system comprising full funding of the main pension pillar, full privatization of pension services, full separation between the redistributive and old–age saving functions, and devolution of all relevant pension decisions to individual participants. In fact, Chile's new pension system implies a revolutionary departure not only from the country's history but also from all mandatory pension schemes existing in the world in 1980. Moreover Chile's pension reform has been the most radical of all pension reforms adopted worldwide since the 1980s.

The reform took place in two stages. In the first stage (in 1979) the existing PAYG system was overhauled by adopting uniform indexation mechanisms for all pensions and, most important, by substituting minimum retirement ages (60 for women and 65 for men) for lower retirement ages and generous retirement rules based on years of work. The latter change reduced dramatically the government's implicit PAYG debt, without changing the fundamentals of the existing system but reducing dramatically the cost of any subsequent systemic reform.

Stage 2 came in 1980 with the adoption of a radically different pension system, to be started in May 1981. The new pension law (DL 3500) implemented a gradual transition from the preceding "one–pillar" to a new "three–pillar" pension system [2] (Table 6.1). Clear separation of the redistributive and old–age saving functions of the pension system was accomplished by completely delinking the first and second pension pillars.

---

[2] Here we use the World Bank terminology introduced by the now classical Old-Age Crisis report (World Bank 1994), whose proposed three-pillar structure was very much modeled on the Chilean reform of 1981.

6.2 The Pillars

6.2.1 Main Features of the Pension Pillars and their Interactions

First pillar. The first pillar is comprised by two means–tested government transfer programs targeted at the old–age poor, designed as complements to the second pillar. First, the elderly poor that have not participated in any pension system are entitled to a means–tested assistance pension, at approximately US$ 56 per month or 12% of the average taxable monthly income in 1998. Second, participants in the second–pillar pension system are benefited by an option or minimum–pension guarantee, that is a government–financed supplement to their pension savings at retirement in order to achieve a minimum pension level, at approximately US$ 126 per month or 26% of the average taxable monthly income in 1998. Second–pillar participants are not entitled to receive only the minimum pension, not on top of the assistance pension.

Complete separation on the financing side of the first pension pillar from the second pillar is ensured as both government assistance programs are financed by general government revenue – not by worker contributions. However the minimum pension guarantee implies a potentially important disincentive effect (a 100% implicit tax on voluntary saving returns in excess of mandatory pension saving), at least for those income groups that are close to the eligible minimum pension level. 65–year old men and 60–year old women are entitled to the minimum pension supplement if they have contributed continuously to any pension system for at least 20 years and if they have not any other income in excess of the minimum pension level. In Chile, however, government identification of non–pension wealth of contributors claiming a minimum pension at retirement is probably not very effective. Hence the disincentive effect is lessened, at the cost of raising substantially the fiscal cost of the minimum pension guarantee, as discussed in section 6.3.

Table 6.1. Chile's Old and New Pension Systems

Old System (1924 – 1981; gradual extinction after 1981)	
One Pillar	PAYG defined–benefit system managed by state SSIs with heterogeneous costs and benefits
New System (Gradual transition since 1981)	
Three Pillars	
First Pillar (Old–Age Re–Distribution and Insurance)	Assistance pension for non–participating old–age poor, means tested Minimum pension guarantee for participating old–age poor, means tested
Second Pillar (Old-Age Saving and Insurance)	Defined contributions Individual pension accounts Private industry of pension fund managers and insurance companies Strong government regulation and supervision Government guarantees on pension fund assets and rates of return
Third Pillar (Voluntary Old–Age Saving)	Tax incentives on complementary voluntary saving for old age

Second pillar. The new and dominant second pillar embodies a radical departure from the previous one–pillar system. The new defined–contribution scheme is based on participant contributions to pension funds invested in financial assets. Second–pillar participants hold individual pension accounts that register their contributions and pension fund returns net of management fees paid to pension fund management companies, termed AFPs (the acronym for "Administradora de Fondos de Pensiones" or pension fund management company). AFPs are private providers of pension services during the active life of pension system participants. They are specialized financial companies that are separate legal entities from the pension funds they manage. AFP participants belong to three groups: contributing workers, non–contributing workers, and pensioners under the phased-withdrawal pension option. AFPs provide the following services to participants: collection of contributions, pension fund investment, record keeping, and information provision. Participants are entitled – and forced – to choose one among all AFPs at an individual level – neither their unions nor their employers are allowed to negotiate on their behalf. Participants are currently entitled to switch AFP every 5 months.

Retirement age is generally 65 for men and 60 for women but each participant is entitled to bring forward retirement (if she has accumulated sufficient pension savings to finance a benchmark pension level) or postpone retirement (if she decides to continue working). At retirement the worker has access to her full cumulative pension savings and faces two choices. Her first option is a phased pension capital withdrawal for a pre–determined number of years (at a rate of return formula defined by law), choosing among AFPs that provide this post-retirement service on a fee basis. The second option involves buying a pension annuity from an insurance company. Survival risk associated to the first option is capped by retaining the option of accessing to the government minimum pension once the retirement pension capital is exhausted.

Third pillar. The system's third pillar is comprised by tax incentives provided to two types of voluntary savings beyond mandatory retirement savings. The first category is voluntary additional contributions deposited jointly with the mandatory contribution. This additional retirement saving benefits from the same tax treatment of mandatory contributions, that is, income tax exemption on both principal and returns but pension benefits are treated as any other form of taxable income. The second category is voluntary additional contributions to a separate, second individual account at the AFP of the first choice; here the principal is not tax exempt but returns are. Funds can be withdrawn at any time from the second account; therefore this is a general saving incentive, not specific to retirement savings albeit managed by an AFP. There are additional tax incentives on specific savings instruments in Chile but they are totally unrelated to retirement savings.

Regulation, government guarantees, and supervision. Pension funds, the AFP industry, and pension annuities paid by insurance companies are heavily regulated and tightly supervised by specialized government agencies. Pension fund investment by AFPs is strongly regulated by portfolio ceilings imposed on specific asset classes, specific issuers, companies related by ownership to the corresponding AFP, and investment by an individual AFP in a specific company. Investment of reserves for pension annuities by life insurance companies are subject to similar portfolio regulations.

AFPs and life insurance companies are subject to regulations on minimum capital (debt–equity ratios) and pension fund reserves. AFPs are required to hold a guarantee fund on 1% of pension fund assets to finance any difference between their managed pension fund's annual real rate of return and the larger of 2% and 0.5 times the industry average pension fund return. If replenishment of the guarantee fund in case of required withdrawal by the AFP is not achieved within 15 days, the AFP license is revoked and the pension fund is sold to other AFPs or a new market entrant. If the AFP guarantee fund is depleted an ultimate government minimum–return guarantee is triggered, covering any return shortfall by government revenue. The AFP guarantee fund has been used only twice by AFPs due to shortfalls in their pension fund returns and the ultimate government guarantee has never been used since 1981.

A second government guarantee is on pension annuities managed by life insurance companies. The government guarantees 100% percent of the annuity up to the level of the minimum pension and 75% above that level. This guarantee has been exercised once, when a life insurance company went bankrupt in 1984. Strong supervision of the AFP and life insurance industries is exercised by the Superintendency of AFPs and the Superintendency of Securities and Insurances. Both institutions monitor closely financial performance and compliance of regulations of all firms and are also actively involved in administrative and legal changes of the existing regulatory and supervisory framework. In fact, regulation of the privately managed pension industry has evolved significantly since the initial law of 1980 – at any point in time at least one pension industry reform proposal is considered by Congress.

Systemic transition. Instead of mandating a discrete shift by all active contributors from the existing state–run PAYG scheme to the new privately–managed FF system, the reform allowed for a long, gradual, and partly endogenous transition. A half–century long transition has two advantages: it is easier to implement administratively and it allows to spread out over 50 or more years the fiscal costs of the reform.

PAYG pensioners in 1980 remained in the old system. Active contributors to PAYG were allowed to choose among staying in the old system or switching to the new scheme. Their affiliation to the new system was strongly encouraged by a significant decline in pension contributions (from an average close to 20% of taxable income under PAYG to a flat 10% under FF, subject to a monthly wage ceiling currently at ca. US$ 1,900. The 10% reduction in pension contribution rates was added to take–home pay, hence providing a massive incentive for most contributors. Shifting to the new system was also encouraged by government information and AFP marketing campaigns (that emphasized, in addition to the gains in take–home wages, the expected increase in pension fund returns in comparison to PAYG returns).

New labor market entrants are forced to participate in the new FF system – a feature that implies that the old PAYG system is extinguished after the last active participant in the PAYG system passes away at some point after the year 2025.

Unsurprisingly most young and middle–aged PAYG contributors switched to the new system. At December 1982 – only 19 months after the reform start – 36% of the Chile's employed had shifted to the FF system, and only half that figure, 19% of total employment, remained in the PAYG system (Fig. 6.1). At the end of 1997, 61% of the employed were active contributors to the FF system and only 5% were remaining in the old PAYG (mostly workers close to retirement). Therefore coverage of total employment (as measured by active contributors) has increased significantly after the pension reform, from 51% in 1980 to 66% in 1997.

Pension system coverage, contributions, and benefits. Pension system coverage by the PAYG system of old–age population aged 55 and above stood at 68% in 1980, before the reform start. This figure increased to a peak of 75% in 1985, falling gradually afterwards to attain 69% in 1997. Pension system coverage by the new FF system increases gradually over time, attaining 21% in 1997. While

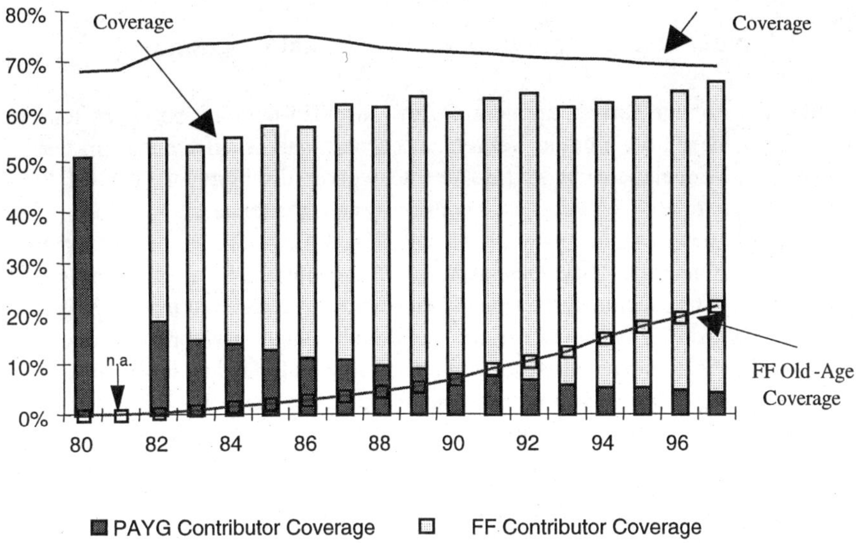

Fig. 6.1. Pension System Coverage of Active and Passive Population, 1980–1997 (percentage)

Notes: Employment coverage is defined as the ratio of active contributors to PAYG (or to FF) to total employment. Old–age coverage is defined as the ratio of PAYG (or FF) pensioners to the population of age 55 and above.

Source: PrimAmérica (1999), INP (various issues), INE (variouss issues), and Central Bank of Chile.

the figures of old–age coverage by the old and new system are not directly comparable[3], they suggest a significant increase of total pension coverage of the elderly since the start of the new system.

Total contributions to the new system (old system) attained 3.3% (0.5%) of GDP in 1997, implying an aggregate 3.8% pension contributions in Chile. Due to the gradual transition, most pensions are still paid out by the old system (by an amount equivalent to 2.6% of GDP) while the new system is paying benefits to a much smaller number of people (equivalent to 0.9% of GDP). Individual pensions averaged 39% of current average taxable income under the old pension system and 45% of current taxable income under the new system in 1997.[4,5] Note that the pension benefit paid by the new system is a weighted average of the benefits that accrue in lieu of contributions to the old and new pension systems.

---

[3] This figure is over-estimated by referring to PAYG pensions, not pensioners. Some people receive more than one PAYG pension and some PAYG pensioners are below age 55.

[4] All pension figures are aggregates or averages for old-age, disability, and survivor pensions due to lack of disaggregated data.

[5] The pension to taxable income ratios reflect pension benefits paid to current pensioners relative to incomes of current workers and hence are not replacement ratios.

6.2.2 Interaction of Pension System with other Social Programs

As mentioned above early retirement is freely decided by contributors as long as they have achieved a minimum retirement capital. This is different from earlier access to individual pension savings due to worker disability or survival by a spouse or close relative of a deceased pension system participant.

In fact, the new pension system is closely linked to two other social programs: disability insurance and survivors insurance. Contributions to all three programs are mandatory for pension system participants and are made on a monthly basis to their selected AFP. Contribution rates on disability and survivors insurance are market determined for benefits determined by law and stand at 0.5% of taxable income in 1997 (Table 6.2). As in the case of standard pensions, the government guarantees a minimum pension level to beneficiaries of disbility and survival pensions. The two latter insurance programs are kept separate from the pension system other than their joint management by AFPs. AFPs reinsure both disability and survivor insurances with insurance companies.

Health insurance is kept separate from the pension system in all its dimensions – mandatory contributions, management, and provision of health benefits. A (mostly richer) 30.3% of the labor force contributes 7% of taxable income to a privately–managed system of private health provision. The remaining part of the labor force are either not covered at all (and hence may qualify to minimum social health services provided by the public system) or contribute voluntarily to private health programs. Unemployment benefits are also kept separate from pension benefits. The current program of unemployment benefits is a means–tested targeted program that provides small and temporary contingent benefits to a small share of the labor force. In addition employment legislation requires employers to pay a severance payment of 1 month per working year up to 11 years. Congress is currently discussing a government–proposed unemployment insurance program that would require workers and employers to share contributions toward unemployment savings deposited in individual accounts at AFPs, that could be used during unemployment spells or otherwise be added to pension savings at retirement.

6.2.3 Microeconomic Features of the Second Pillar

This sub–section focuses on microeconomic features of the private pension system, including the structure and costs of the AFP industry, the composition of the average pension fund portfolio and its rate of return, the structure of commissions charged by AFPs to their customers, and the AFP cost structure.

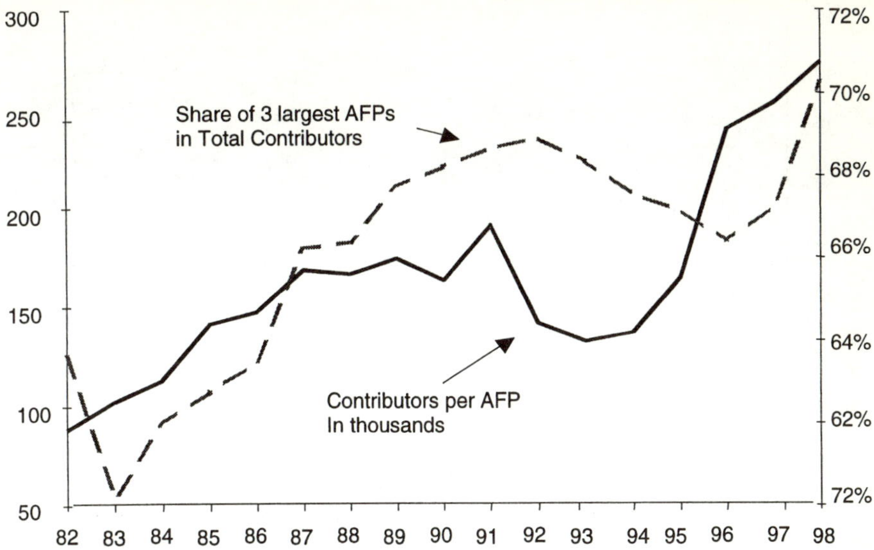

Fig. 6.2. Scale of Concentration of AFP Industry, 1982–1998
Source: PRIMAMERICA (1999)

AFP operational scale and market concentration. The pension fund industry started with 12 AFPs in 1981, a number that increased to a peak of 21 companies in 1993–1994, then falling again – through mergers, acquisitions, and closures – back to 12 AFPs in 1998. The average scale of operation trebled from 88,000 active contributors per AFP in 1982 to 274,000 in 1998 (Fig. 6.2). Some years ago economies of scale had been estimated to be reaped up to 60,000 active contributors (Diamond and Valdés Prieto 1994) but market participants estimate them today at a much larger number. Average pension fund assets managed by each AFP have increased from US$ 51 million in 1982 to US$ 2.4 billion in 1998.
However, average figures are misleading because AFP industry concentration is large and rising. The share of the three largest AFPs is 70.3% by affiliates and 60.7% by managed pension fund assets in 1998. Rates of return on AFPs' own capital – not to be confused with the rates of return on pension funds managed by AFPs or on pension assets held in individual accounts, analyzed below – became positive and very high after being negative during the first three years of startup of the system, when the scale of operation was low and marketing costs were high. Very high returns of 39–48% in real terms on AFPs' own capital reaped during 1989–1991 prompted a massive entry into the industry and a substantial reduction in subsequent returns – together with industry consolidation – down to 11.1% in real terms in 1997.

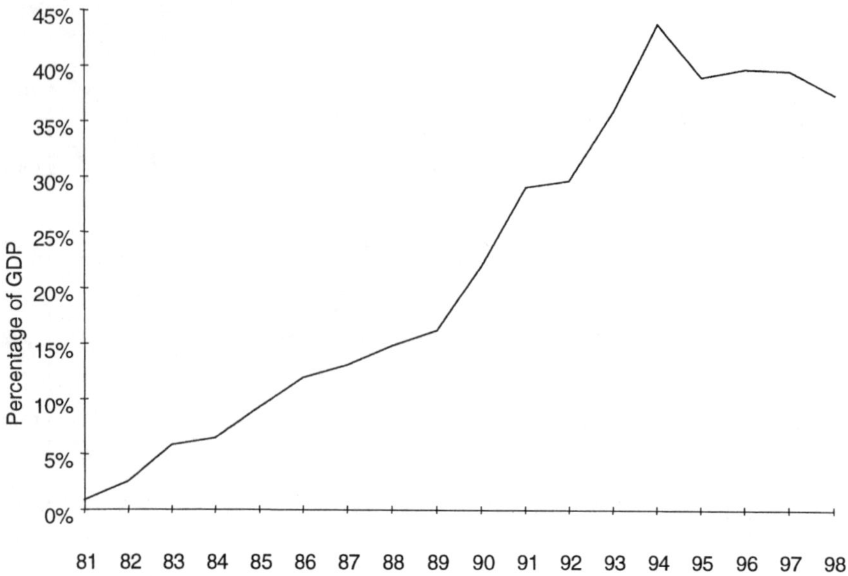

Fig. 6.3. Pension Funds Assets/ GDP, 1981–1998 (percentage)
Source: Central Bank of Chile and SAFP (various issues).

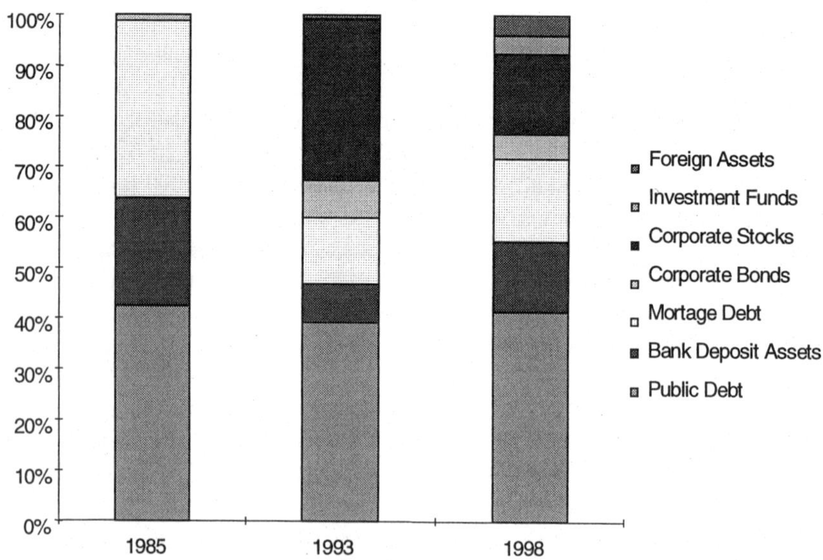

Fig. 6.4. Pension Funds Portfolio Composition (percentage of total assets)

Source: Central Bank of Chile and SAFP (various issues).

Pension fund assets and portfolio investment. Total pension fund assets managed by AFPs rose rapidly in the early 1980s with the large increase in new contributors and high initial rates of return on pension funds. Total assets attained a peak of US$ 30.5 b. in 1997 and, as a share of GDP, a peak of 43.8% in 1997 (Fig. 6.3). While the number of contributors is still rising, their outstanding aver age pension wealth has been stagnating during the last 3–4 years as a result of low pension fund returns.

Portfolio investment by AFPs has been heavily regulated by investment instruments although regulations have been gradually liberalized over the last 18 years. Until the mid–1980s investment was mostly restricted to government bonds, bank deposits, and mortgage debt. Investment in stocks has been allowed since 1986 and investment abroad is only allowed since 1993 (Fig. 6.4). All investment categories are limited by portfolio share ceilings that are gradually revised upward over time. For instance, in early 1999 the ceiling on investment abroad was raised from 12 to 16%, of which the share invested in variable-income assets was increased from 6% to 8%. As of end–1998 the average pension fund portfolio is still largely concentrated in government paper (i.e., central bank debt, at 41.4%), bank deposits (14.1%), and mortgage debt (16.3%). Assets invested abroad add up to only 3.9% of aggregate pension assets but this share is growing rapidly since late 1997 as a result of the decline in domestic–market as compared to international–market rates of return.

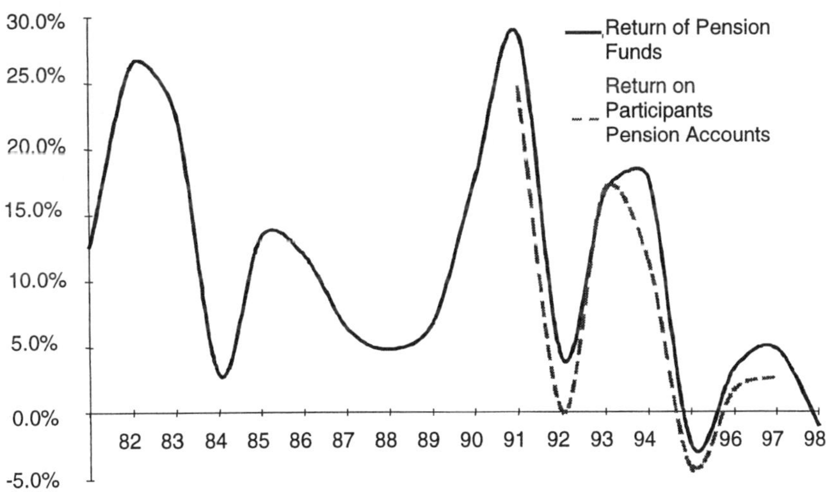

Fig. 6.5. Rates of Return of Pension Funds and Individual Pensional Accounts (percentage), 1982–1998

Source: PRIMAMERICA (1999) and Central Bank of Chile.

Returns on pension funds and individual accounts. Pension fund returns in real terms were high but volatile from 1981 through 1994 – a reflection of Chile's high but volatile investment opportunities (Fig. 6.5).
From 1995 through 1998, however, pension fund returns have been barely positive on average, with two years recording negative real returns. Stagnating yields since the mid–1990s reflect both a stagnating domestic stock market and, in 1998, high short–term interest rates and a steep growth reduction in the aftermath of the international financial crisis. The start of the new pension system is likely to have contributed to the high asset yields observed during 1981–1995. This is one important reason why it is unlikely that the high average annual real rate of return of pension funds, at 13.8% during 1981–1994 (or 11.0% during 1981–1998) could be sustained into the future.

Real rates of return on individuals' pension accounts stand significantly below pension fund returns as a result of relatively high commissions paid by contributors to AFPs. Over the 1991–97 period for which data is available, individual accounts yielded on average 8.3%, a figure that is 1.9% lower – due to commissions – than the return on pension funds.

Structure of commissions paid by contributors. AFPs are currently entitled to charge a fixed and a variable commission (Table 6.2). The fixed commission has declined by some 80% since 1981. The variable gross commission – levied as a percentage of wages – comprises payment of insurance premia on disability and survivor insurance, as well as the variable net commission paid to AFPs to cover their costs and profits. Insurance premia have declined from 1.9% to 0.5% of taxable income during the last decade. However the residual net commission – the sum of AFP costs and profits – has risen from 1.7% to 2.4% of taxable in come during the last decade. [6] The total net commission paid to the AFP – the sum of fixed and variable net commissions – has risen slightly, from 2.2% of taxable income in 1988 to 2.5% in 1997.

[6] A third commission was charged on the outstanding pension savings account until 1987, when it was abolished.

Table 6.2. Commissions paid by Contributors to AFPs, 1981–1997 (percentages of taxable income)

	Fixed commission (1)	Variable gross commission (2)	Insurance premia (3)	Variable net commission (4) (4)=(2)-(3)	Commission on balance (5)	Total net commission (6) (6)=(1)+(4) +(5)
1982	0.79%	2.66%	N/A.	N/A.	0.17%	N/A.
1983	1.01%	3.60%	N/A.	N/A.	0.43%	N/A.
1984	0.92%	3.58%	N/A.	N/A.	0.60%	N/A.
1985	0.72%	3.57%	N/A.	N/A.	0.59%	N/A.
1986	0.53%	3.40%	N/A.	N/A.	0.63%	N/A.
1987	0.48%	3.39%	N/A.	N/A.	0.52%	N/A.
1988	0.49%	3.56%	1.89%	1.67%	0.0%	2.16%
1989	0.31%	3.25%	1.76%	1.49%	0.0%	1.80%
1990	0.22%	2.99%	1.47%	1.52%	0.0%	1.74%
1991	0.16%	2.97%	1.05%	1.92%	0.0%	2.08%
1992	0.13%	2.93%	0.70%	2.23%	0.0%	2.36%
1993	0.09%	2.95%	0.71%	2.24%	0.0%	2.33%
1994	0.08%	2.92%	0.64%	2.28%	0.0%	2.36%
1995	0.07%	3.04%	0.52%	2.52%	0.0%	2.58%
1996	0.09%	2.90%	0.51%	2.39%	0.0%	2.48%
1997	0.08%	2.90%	0.53%	2.37%	0.0%	2.45%

Note: The commission on pension savings balance was eliminated in 1988. All figures are ratios to the average taxable income of the pension system. Insurance premia are calculated considering the total cost of insurance and the total income of AFP contributors.

Source: PRIMAMERICA (1999) and author's calculations.

AFP cost structure. A quick review of the AFP industry cost structure reveals the large share of marketing costs in AFP total revenue, growing from 10% in 1988 to 34% in 1997 (Fig. 6.6). AFPs devote a large effort to raise their market share by hiring salespeople that often lure contributors away from competing AFPs by offering side payments or even changing individuals' affiliation without their prior knowledge. A 1997 administrative ruling by the AFP Superintendency has made more difficult these practices, implying a significant drop in salespeople and marketing costs of AFPs during 1998, which have been partly passed on to consumers in the form of lower variable commissions.

6.2.4 Fiscal and Macroeconomic Effects of Pension Reform

Significant fiscal and macroeconomic effects could be expected from Chile's pension reform. This sub–section starts by evaluating the reform's fiscal consequences and putting the pension reform in the overall context of macroeconomic stabilization and structural reform. The latter comparison enables next to approach the more difficult task of isolating the quantitative contribution of pension reform to Chile's improvements in factor market efficiency, overall factor productivity growth, saving, investment, and aggregate growth.[7 8]

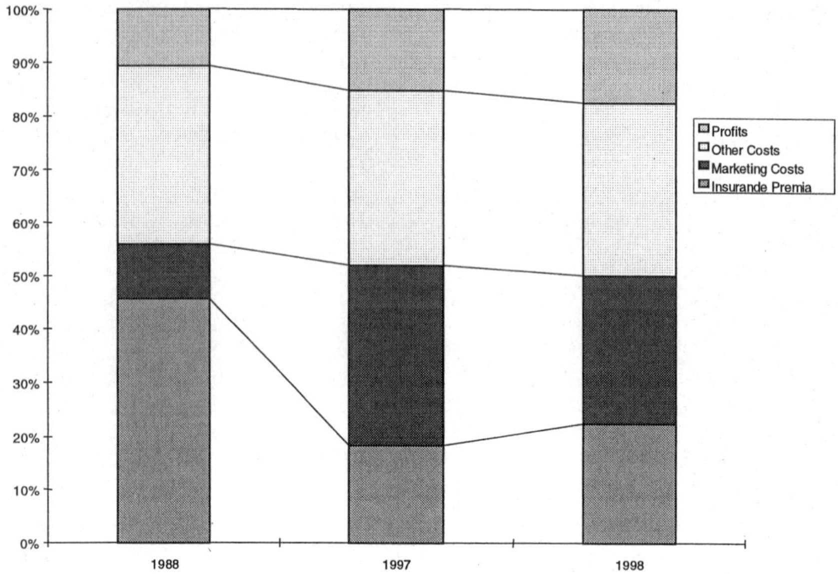

Figure 6.6 Cost Structure of AFPs (percentage of total costs)

Source: PRIMAMERICA (1999) and Superintendence of AFPs

Pension Reform and Public Defict. When active contributors switch from PAYG to FF the government incurs suffers a loss in PAYG contributions, having to finance two types of pension benefits: ongoing pension payments to PAYG pensioners and payments of future PAYG pension benefits in lieu of past contributions to PAYG made by switching contributors. Any reforming government faces the theoretical option of making immediately explicit its total implicit PAYG debt by paying it off, simply by issuing checks to both PAYG pensioners and switching workers for their total pension wealth at the time of the reform. For budgetary reasons – finance ministers dislike explicit government deficits even if they arise from amortization of implicit debt – the Chilean reformers (as well as all subsequent reformers in other countries) did not follow this option. Instead they decided to spread out the fiscal cost of the transition (that is, the making explicit

[7] Simulations of transitional (steady-state) growth effects of pension reform in representative economies are reported for the exogenous (endogenous) growth case in Arrau and SchmidtHebbel (1991) (Corsetti and Schmidt-Hebbel 1997).

[8] The measurement of the contribution of pension reform to Chile's takeoff is based on regression results for private saving, private investment, and productivity growth in Chile, reported in Schmidt-Hebbel (1998 a,b).

of the implicit cost), roughly in tandem with the systemic transition of changes in affiliation from PAYG to FF.

Therefore the fiscal cost of pension reform is reflected in two pension deficit components. One is the so–called "operational deficit", arising from paying out pensions to current and future PAYG pensioners. The second is the so–called "recognition–bond deficit", due to the payment of past (pre–switching) PAYG pension benefits that accrue to FF pensioners at retirement. Every previous PAYG contributor is issued a government promise at switching to FF, called recognition bond, that matures at her retirement. At that date the government hands out a check to the pensioner that approximately reflects the present value of her historical PAYG contributions.[9] [10]

The operational pension deficit rose rapidly after the reform start – reflecting the stampede of PAYG contributors to FF – toward a peak of 3.8% of GDP in 1984 (Fig. 6.2). Its slow subsequent decline is a function of the average life span and age distribution of PAYG pensioners, standing at 1.6% of GDP in 1997 and estimated to converge to zero around the year 2020. In the absence of FF pensioners at the start of the new system, the recognition–bond deficit starts at zero in May 1981 and increases gradually over time, attaining 0.8% of GDP in 1997. Its convergence toward zero is estimated to take place after 2030.

Therefore the total pension reform deficit relative to GDP attains a maximum of 4.1% in 1984 – but its constant domestic–currency value is still rising. In 1997 the total pension reform deficit attained was US$ 1.9 b. or 2.5% of that year's GDP.

In 1979, before the 1981 pension reform, the government started a massive improvement in fiscal policy by attaining a significant and systematic general-government surplus. Excepting the recession period 1982–1986, the total government surplus has averaged 1.8 % of GDP between 1979 and 1997. The non-pension surplus – the sum of the overall surplus plus the pension reform deficit – attains a high average 5.4% of GDP from 1987 to 1997 (see Fig. 6.7). The latter figure is the economically more relevant one because the pension deficit is simply equivalent to the fiscal effort in paying off the implicit PAYG debt.

How large is the total implicit PAYG debt that is made explicit by pension reform? Arrau (1991) estimates that the first–stage PAYG reform of 1979, that raised substantially retirement ages of the old PAYG system, cut the government's implicit PAYG debt by half. Estimates for the remaining PAYG debt in

[9] Although the PAYG regime was a defined-benefit system, calculation of the recognition bond was based on an estimate -- often done roughly due to the lack of systematic records on past PAYG contributions -- of the present value of PAYG contributions, at the date of switching. From that date through retirement the outstanding recognition bond earns a real rate of return (after adjustment of principal to inflation) of 4% per annum.

[10] Note that instead of handing out a check at retirement, the government could have chosen an even more gradual reform transition deficit by making pension payments to future pensioners. This alternative would have extended the length of the transition deficit – possibly by some 20 years – in a way exactly consistent with the demographics of the reform transition generations.

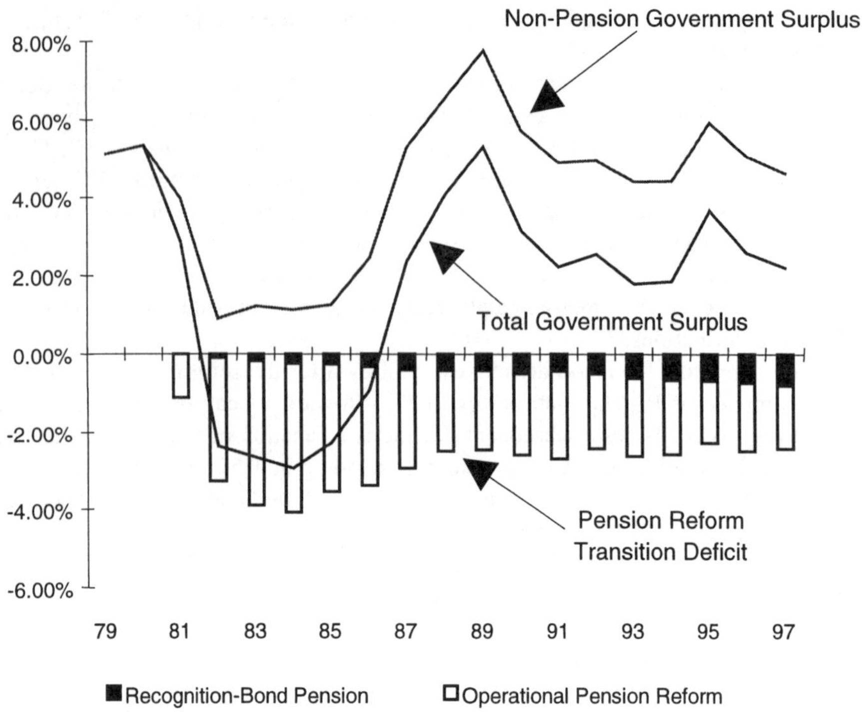

Figure 6.7 Government Non-Pension and Government Pension Reform Transition Deficit, 1979-1997 (percentage GDP)

Source: DIPRES (1997), INP (various issues) and Central Bank of Chile

1980, shortly before the second–stage reform, point toward an implicit debt of 85% of GDP. A conceptually different estimate is for the present value of reform transition deficits, estimated at 126% of GDP (Arrau 1991). These figures are higher than those of many other developing or transition countries that have either implemented or considered reforming their PAYG pension systems but is significantly lower of similar estimates made for OECD countries.[11]

[11] Comparisons of implicit PAYG debt estimates for various countries can be found in Arrau and Schmidt-Hebbel (1994) and Schmidt-Hebbel (1998a).

A critical issue for assessing the macroeconomic effects of pension reform transitions is to identify how the pension deficit is financed. [12]

Some authors argue credibly that the Chilean government started in the late 1970s to prepare actively for the pension reform transition deficit by showing large surpluses – for the first time in recent economic history (Diamond and Valdés 1994). However, unless one refers to a counter–factual lab experiment that holds constant other factors affecting government balances, it is impossible to learn from ex–post government accounts in which way a particular government program or reform has been financed in any real–world economy. Fungibility of financial resources does not allow to infer any causal relation from the changes in pension transition deficits and the non–pension transition fiscal position.

Such an attempt is particularly futile in Chile's experience of the early 1980s as public finances had to absorb the most intense shocks – completely unrelated to pension reform – that hit Chile during the last decades. Among them were a major terms–of–trade loss, complete cut–off from voluntary foreign lending, a deep recession, and a huge banking crisis. For instance, asserting that pension reform was financed by non–pension surpluses before and after 1981 is equivalent to saying that changes in all other non–pension revenue and expenditure categories – including the costs of the 1982–85 banking crisis estimated at a cumulative 41.1% of GDP (Marshall and Schmidt–Hebbel 1994) – were accommodated residually by the available mix of tax resources, debt issuance, and inflation taxation. This illustrates that it does not make much sense to single out a particular financing source of Chile's reform transition deficit. While Chile's pension reform was supported by an improvement in the fiscal position some years before the reform start it is not possible to identify the precise financing mix of this reform or any other structural change or shock affecting Chile's public finances thereafter.

Macro stabilization and structural reform. More than two decades of systematic stabilization and structural reform efforts are reflected by country's improved fiscal and monetary stance (Table 6.3). Non–financial public–sector surpluses were attained early on (in the late 1970s), reversed in sign during the early 1980s due to the financial crisis and deep recession, and were again corrected in the

[12] If the reform deficit is offset by raising the non-pension surplus, reform transition generations bear the cost of paying off the implicit PAYG, benefiting post-transition generations by freeing them from servicing the old PAYG debt. The corresponding intergenerational transfer to future cohorts raises long-term income, saving, and capital levels – as in the case of any other contractionary fiscal policy that improves the net asset position of the government (Diamond 1965, Auerbach and Kotlikoff 1987). Alternatively, if the reform deficit is financed by issuing government debt or reducing government assets (by selling international reserves or public enterprises) the implicit PAYG debt is simply swapped for issuing another public net liability. Without a first-order change in the public sector's net asset position, there are only second-order intergenerational transfer and long-term macro effects due to differences in PAYG and FF rates of return.

mid–1980s. Since 1975 Chile has pursued a very gradualist anti–inflation program, bringing inflation down from some 1000% in 1973 to 4.7% in 1998.

Chile has adopted a broad and deep program of structural reform since the mid–1970s. An international index of structural reform progress (Lora 1997, Schmidt–Hebbel 1998b) shows for Chile an improvement in policy reforms from an index value of 8.4 for the 1960s–early 1970s to 62.0 in the 1990s. How much did pension reform contribute to the 54–point improvement? If pension reform acts by improving financial and labor market policies – as argued below – one should focus on the improvement observed in the two latter sub–indexes that are part of the overall reform index. Research by Schmidt–Hebbel (1998a) suggests that the relative contribution of pension reform to the progress in the overall index of Chilean policies has been in the range from 5% to 20%.

Capital markets. Banking and capital markets have developed rapidly and diversified broadly in Chile since the start of domestic financial liberalization and capital–market reforms in 1974–75. Capital–market deepening is reflected by the substantial increase in broad financial liabilities measured by M3 (from 16% of GDP in 1961–74 to 37% in the 1990s) and in stock market capitalization (from 28% in 1980–81 to 92% in the 1990s). Capital–market liberalization helped developing new financial instruments and industries, including insurance services, bond markets, mutual funds, and risk–rating agencies. Banking and capital-market development takes place under conditions of sound regulation and effective supervision by specialized agencies.

Private pension fund assets have increased to 35% of GDP in the 1990s and pension funds hold significant shares of Chile's equity, bank deposits, and public debt. There is little doubt that the AFP industry has helped in developing and deepening Chilean capital markets. But going beyond this general assessment is very hard. However estimating the precise contribution of the privatized and FF Chilean pension industry to the current structure and quality of financial and capital markets is tricky – it would require agreeing on an appropriate model and counterfactual which is still not available.

Table 6.3. Chile: Various Indicators, 1961–97 (percentages unless noted otherwise)

	1961–74	1975–81	1982–89	1990–97
Pension Systems and Public Finance				
Pension system contribution rate	n.a.	26.0	10.0	10.0
Pension system contributors / labor force	n.a.	n.a.	57.6	62.5
Pension transition deficit / GDP	0	0	3.0	2.5
Non–pension public deficit / GDP	6.3	-2.8	-3.3	-5.1
Macroeconomic Stabilization and Structural Reform Indicators				
Total non–financial public deficit / GDP	6.3	-2.8	0.9	-1.9
Normalized inflation ($\pi/(1+\pi)$)	29.3	43.0	16.3	11.6
Index of structural policy progress (1995=62.8)	8.4	40.5	54.5	62.0
Capital markets				
M3 / GDP	15.9	18.4	28.4	36.8
Stock market capitalization / GDP	n.a.	27.7 (2)	24.8	91.7
Private Pension Fund (AFP) Assets / GDP	0	0	9.9	34.9
Labor Markets				
Unemployment rate	6.3	13.1	13.2	7.2
Real wage growth	2.1	10.5	-0.7	4.1
Labor market informality	n.a.	43.3 (1)	43.8 (3)	40.3 (4)
Male labor force participation rate	n.a.	70.2	72.2	75.9
Saving, Investment, and Growth				
National Saving / GDP	12.5	11.4	12.1	24.8
Foreign Saving / GDP	2.6	5.6	6.2	2.4
Gross Domestic Investment / GDP	19.2	17.8	19.2	29.2
Gr. FK Investment / GDP (const. prices)	19.2	16.0	17.9	25.5
Average Productivity of Capital	33.7	34.7	35.7	41.8
TFP growth	1.2	2.0	-0.1	2.7
GDP growth	3.3	4.4	2.6	6.7

Notes: n.a.: not available. (1) 1981. (2) 1980–81. (3) 1985. (4) 1990–94. The data for 1990–97 includes projected figures for 1997.

Source: Central Bank of Chile, Lora (1997), Schmidt–Hebbel (1998 a,b), and authors' calculations.

Labor markets. Pension reform can contribute to improved labor markets by reducing the pure tax component of pension contributions. Lower labor taxes on formal–sector employment contribute to lower structural employment, less employment (and production) informality, higher informal–sector wages, and a higher overall labor supply. What does the evidence show for Chile?

After almost two decades of high unemployment, Chile has reached levels close to full employment since the early 1990s, allowing for high annual real wage growth (Table 6.3). Edwards (1997) simulates the contribution of pension reform to labor–market improvements in Chile. The author considers the extreme case when the full PAYG contribution is a pure tax on labor. In that case pension reform could have reduced structural unemployment by a range of 2.0 to 3.2% and could have raised real wages in the informal sector by a range of 4.6 to 7.7%.[13]

In regard to total employment informality, ILO data shows that since the start of pension reform, the share of informal employment has declined from 43% in the early 1980s to 40% in the early 1990s (Table 6.3). This three–percentage point decline may seem small. However it is remarkable when comparing it to the evolution of labor informality in every one of 12 other Latin American countries (all with PAYG pension systems), where on average labor informality increased from 31% to 42% during the same decade (ILO 1996, Uthoff 1994). In a separate study Loayza (1996) shows that Chile has the smallest level of production informality in Latin America in the early 1990s, at 18% of GDP, with the next country (Argentina) recording a 22% and the last one (Bolivia) with 66% of output produced in the informal economy.

Finally consider the evolution of total labor supply after pension reform in Chile. Total male labor force participation has in fact increased substantially, from 70.2% in the late 1970s to 75.9% in the 1990s.[14]

Saving. After decades of economic under–achievement, a major shift of performance took place in the late 1980s. Chile's decade–long takeoff is reflected by significant trend breaks of saving, investment, and growth rates from historical levels (cf. Table 6.1). National saving attains 25% of GDP in the 1990s, twice its average level observed during the preceding three decades. Current–price gross domestic investment reaches 29% of GDP during 1990–97, exceeding substantially its historical level. Gross fixed–capital investment (GFKI) rises by less, to 26% of GDP during 1990–97, as inventory accumulation jumps to 3% in the 1990s. TFP growth attains 2.7% per annum in the 1990s, a figure that exceeds substantially the meager 1.2% recorded in 1961–74 or the 0.9% observed in 1975–89. As a result of higher investment and TFP growth, GDP growth doubles, increasing from a modest historical level of 3.3% to a level of 6.7% in the 1990s.

---

[13] Edwards' simulations should be taken as upper-bound values of pension-reform benefits. When considering a pure-tax component of PAYG contributions less than 100%, or allowing for capital reallocation among sectors that differ in capital-intensities and for static and dynamic general-equilibrium feedback effects (as in Schmidt-Hebbel 1997a), the values are likely to be much lower than those obtained by Edwards.

[14] Male labor force participation is a better indicator of labor supply than total male plus female labor force participation because of the long-run trend increase that is observed in female participation.

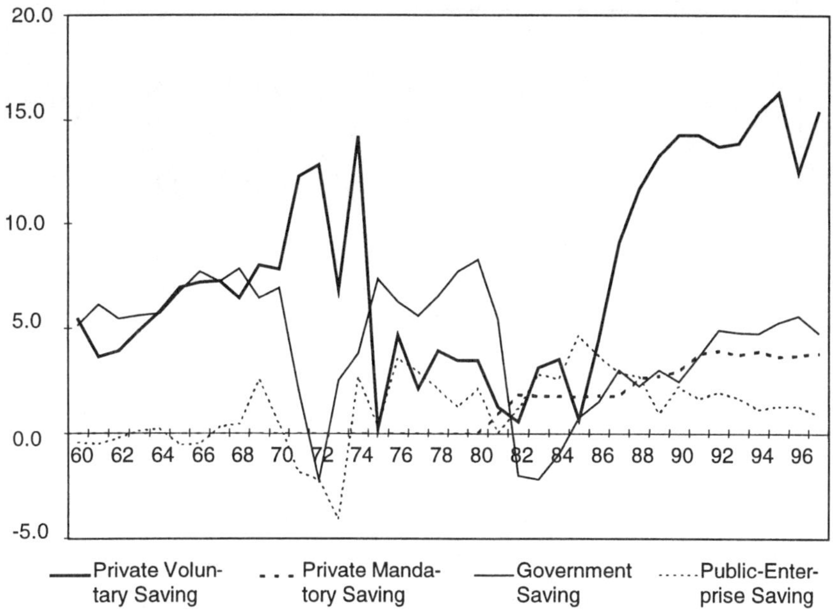

Figure 6.8 Sector Saving Rates, 1960–97 (percentage of GDP)

A major shift in the structure of national saving has taken place in Chile (Fig. 6.8). The large swings of the central government saving ratio to GDP reflects policy shifts and business–cycle effects that have characterized the last three decades, but it stabilizes in the 1990s at an average 4.5% of GDP. Public enterprise rationalization adopted since 1974 raised public enterprise saving to positive levels but subsequent privatization led to a trend decline of public enterprise saving levels. Chile's radical pension reform of 1981 led to a gradual increase in mandatory private pension saving that stands today at 3.8% of GDP. However the most radical change in any individual saving component is observed in the case of voluntary private saving. After a dozen years of sub–standard saving from 1985 through 1986, the private sector has been able to raise quickly its voluntary saving rate, from 4.5% in 1986 to an average 14.4% throughout 1990–97. There is preliminary evidence that most of this increase has taken place in the corporate sector while households are saving little more than before 1987.

Using regression results for voluntary private saving in Chile (Schmidt–Hebbel 1998a), the large increase in saving can be decomposed according to its explanatory determinants. Figure. 6.9 summarizes the decomposition of the structural rise in saving that took place between the 1961–1974 pre–reform period and the 1990–97 post–reform period, when a significant part of the reforms – including pension reform – had already taken place and saving had taken off. The results show that the doubling in the national saving rate is due to a rise in non- financial public sector saving (from 4.9% to 6.6% of GDP), the emergence of mandatory private

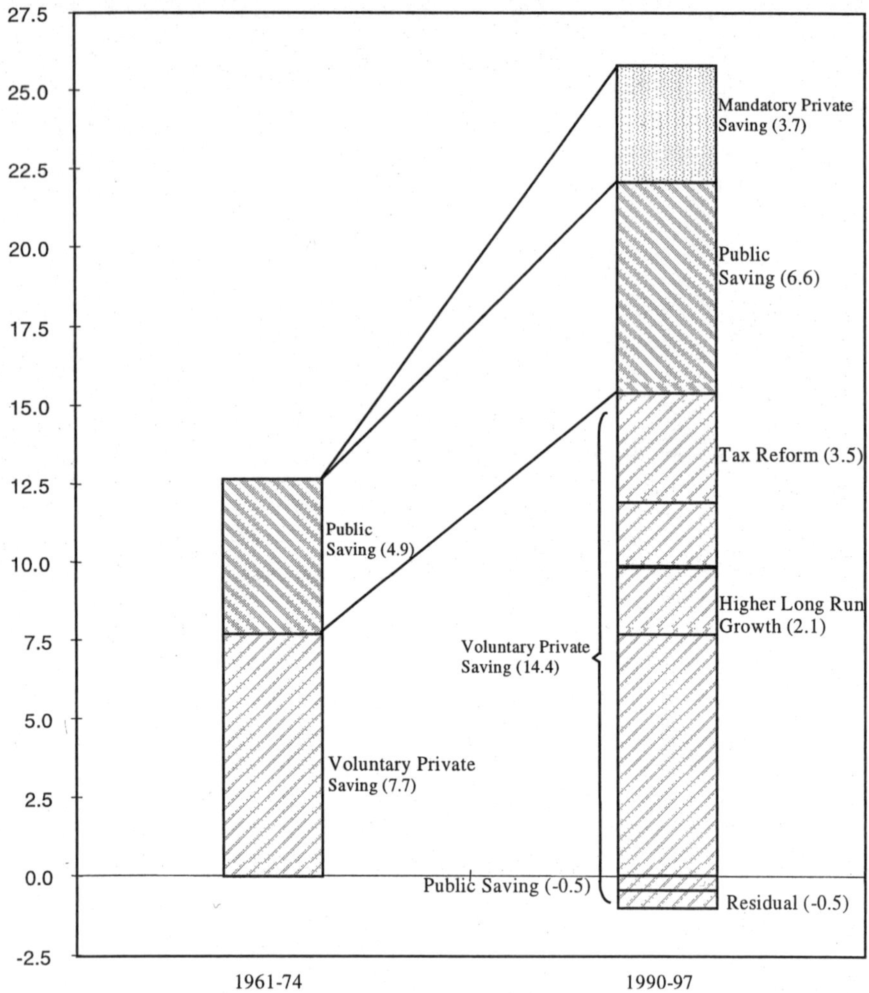

Figure 6.9 Explaining Chile's Higher National Saving (percentage of GDP)

pension saving at an average 3.7% of GDP, and a large increase in voluntary private saving (from 7.7% to 14.4% of GDP).

Fiscal adjustment as reflected by the aforementioned increase in total public saving was only partially offset by lower private saving and by a low amount (0.5% of GDP). The combined effect of overall tax reforms and saving incentives is reflected in a 3.5%–of–GDP rise in voluntary private saving. The small in crease in foreign saving contributes to a tiny 0.1%–of–GDP in private saving. More important is the effect of Chile's demographic transition, explaining 2.1% of the private sector's saving increase. Finally, the increase in trend GDP growth from the 1960s to the 1990s explains another 2.1% of Chile's private saving rise. The latter variable confirms the existence of a virtuous saving–growth cycle, widely documented in other takeoff experiences.

Now let's look at the overall contribution of pension reform to saving. This is not an easy task. First, as discussed above, there is no way to pin down how pension transitions were financed and therefore how public saving was affected by the reform. Second, it is difficult to establish the direct contribution of pension reform through overall tax reforms net of crowding out of MSAV. Table 6.4 summarizes three alternative estimates of the effects of pension reform on the rise of national saving from 1961–74 to 1990–97.

Table 6.4. Contribution of Pension Reform to the 1961–74 to 1990–97 Rise in the National Saving Ratio to GDP (percentage)

	Large effects (1)	Moder. Effects (1)	Small effects (2)
Rise in total public deficit due to pension deficit, at hypothetical proportions of 0, 25%, and 50% of pension deficit	0	-0.25*4.4= -1.1	-0.5*4.4 = -2.2
Rise in mandatory private pension saving	+3.7	+3.7	+3.7
Increase in voluntary private saving due to:	+1.8	+1.2	-0.3
(i) Crowding in by lower total public deficit at regression coefficients	0	0.26*1.1 =0.3	0.34*2.2 = 0.7
(ii) Crowding in by overall 1980s tax reforms at regression coefficients and hypothetical participation of pension reform in overall 1980s tax reforms	0.5*3.5 = 1.8	0.25*3.5 = 0.9	0.5*5.3= 2.7
(iii) 100% crowding out by mandatory pension saving	0	0	-1.0 * 3.7= -3.7
Rise in national saving explained by pension reform	+5.5	+3.8	+1.2
Total rise in national saving rate	+12.2	+12.2	+12.2

Note: (1) Based on equation (1a), Appendix, Schmidt–Hebbel (1998a). (2) Based on equation (1b), Appendix, Schmidt–Hebbel (1998a).

The two main features determining that determine the effects of pension reform on national saving are how transition deficits are financed and how the private sector reacts to mandatory pension saving. For the first dimension we assume fiscal–contraction financing of pension reform at 100%, 75%, and 50% in columns 1, 2, and 3, respectively. For the second we assume moderate net crowding in at 50% and 25%, and moderate net crowding out at -27% (= (2.7 – 3.7)/3.7) of mandatory pension saving, in columns 1–3, respectively.

The results of this simple calculation suggest that national saving has increased in response to pension reform by a range of 1.2% to 5.5% of GDP. The mid–point contribution of 3.8% is equivalent to 31% of Chile's national saving rise. The remaining 69% is due to other measures of fiscal adjustment, tax reform, and various structural changes.

Investment and productivity. A major shift in the structure of gross domestic investment at constant prices has taken place in Chile. The ratio of gross fixed capital investment (GFKI) by the central government to GDP fell significantly after 1974, with little further variations or structural breaks. Public enterprise GFKI shows a trend decline reflecting the decreasing share of public enterprises in GDP, as a result of large–scale privatization. Inventory accumulation is highly erratic and close to zero up to 1983 and stabilizes at a couple of percentage points of GDP afterwards. As in the case of saving, private GFKI shows a massive structural break.

Using regression results for private GFKI in Chile (Schmidt–Hebbel 1998), the large increase in the latter is decomposed according to its explanatory determinants. Applying a procedure similar to the one used in explaining the contribution of pension reform to saving allows to estimate a range for its contribution to

Table 6.5. Contribution of Pension Reform to 1961–74 to 1990–97 Increase in Private GFK Investment Rate, Average Productivity of Capital (APK), and TFP Growth Rates

Variable	Total Rise	Rise attributed to Pension Reform		
		Large effects	Mod. Effects	Small effects
Private Investment Rate	13.0			
Due to rise in strucpol	7.2			
Due to pension reform		1.5	0.9	0.4
APK	8.1			
Due to rise in strucpol	5.7			
Due to pension reform		1.2	0.7	0.3
TFP Growth Rate	1.5			
Due to rise in strucpol	1.8			
Due to pension reform		0.4	0.2	0.1

Source: Author's calculations.

higher private GFKI (Table 6.5).

Overall improvements in structural policies explain 7.2% of the 13.0% rise in the latter, of which we estimate a contribution of pension reform in the range from 0.4% to 1.5%. For the mid–point case of 0.9% of GDP, this is equivalent to a small contribution (9%) of pension reform to the overall rise in the private GFKI rate. Finally use is made of regressions for average productivity of capital (APK) and growth in total factor productivity (TFP) in order to identify the contribution of overall structural policy improvements and pension reform to the observed increase in both measures of productivity (Table 6.5). [15] For the mid–point estimates of the contribution of pension reform, the latter explains 0.7 point of the total 5.7-point increase in APK and 0.2% of the 1.5% rise in the TFP growth rate.

Overall contribution of pension reform to growth takeoff. Now let's put together the preceding estimates in order to infer about the possible contribution of pension reform to Chile's 3.4% increase in GDP growth observed between the 1960s and the 1990s. Using a simple growth model, it is straightforward to decompose the growth increase by the contribution of the higher investment (or saving) rate, the higher average product of capital, and the increase in TFP growth.

The contribution of pension reform to growth through the three mentioned variables is estimated to range from 0.4 to 1.4 percentage points (Table 6.6). The increase in growth attributed to pension reform in Table 6.6 implies that pension reform may have contributed from 12% to 41% to Chile's 3.4 percentage point increase in GDP growth, with a mid–point estimate of 26% or 0.9 percentage points of growth increase. Contributing by a quarter to a country's growth takeoff implies a large payoff to Chile's radical pension reform. [16]

---

[15] TFP is measured residually by a standard Solow growth equation, also reported in Schmidt-Hebbel (1998a).

[16] Holzmann (1997) estimates an even larger range of estimated values for the contribution of pension reform to higher growth, at a range of 1.0 to 2.9 percentage points.

Table 6.6. Contribution of Pension Reform to 1961–74 to 1990–97 Increase in GDP Growth

Variable	Total Rise	Rise attributed to Pension Reform		
		Large effects	Mod. Effects	Small effects
National Saving Rate	13.0			
due to pension reform		5.5	3.7	1.2
Average Product of Capital	8.1			
due to pension reform		1.2	0.7	0.3
TFP Growth Rate	1.5			
due to pension reform		0.4	0.2	0.1
GDP growth	3.4			
due to pension reform (share of total GDP growth gain)		1.4 (41%)	0.9 (26%)	0.4 (12%)
through higher saving		0.8	0.5	0.2
through higher APK		0.1	0.1	0
through higher TFP growth		0.4	0.2	0.1
growth–saving feedback		0.1	0.1	0.1
due to other reforms and structural changes (share of total GDP growth gain)		2.0 (59%)	2.5 (74%)	3.0 (88%)

Note: calculations are based on a standard Solow Cobb–Douglas growth model with a 40% capital share.

Source: Author's calculations.

6.3 Current Shortcomings of Chile's Pension System and Reform Options

Chile's three–pillar pension system does not face fundamental fiscal, financial, and macroeconomic problems. With a mostly fully funded and privately managed pension system, Chile's ongoing demographic transition toward a much older population structure during the next decades will be smoothly absorbed by the pension system. In fact, by reforming early on, Chile has defused any "ticking pension time bomb" – there is no old–age crisis in Chile's future (World Bank 1994). The reason is that an ageing population – and Chile's population will undoubtedly age as demographic maturity is attained in the next 3 to 5 decades – will not put increasing pressures on its pension system because people's pension benefits will reflect the country's return on its net savings and not past promises made by a PAYG transfer system that can not be honored. Another advantage of the reformed system is that its decentralized design – combining private management and individual pension accounts – makes it more robust to pressures or outright assault from the political system.

Having solved the major traditional problems of state–managed PAYG systems does not warrant avoiding secondary shortcomings and problems of its own. In fact, Chile's private pension pillar faces a number of problems in the microeconomic realm of its regulatory incentives industrial organization. Some shortcomings have been solved by various administrative and legal changes undertaken after 1980. However a significant number of issues remains to be addressed. These issues are very much in the public domain and are currently discussed by industry participants, regulatory authorities, academic specialists, the Superintendency of AFPs, and the media. [17] The Chilean Congress is currently considering various reform proposals. In the following some of these issues are briefly described and some solutions are mentioned.

Excessive investment restrictions. Continuing liberalization of excessive investment restrictions (tight ceilings on asset classes) is required to insure getting closer to the risk–return frontier. However a balance has to be struck between avoiding excessive risk–taking by AFP management of pension funds and achieving better risk–adjusted returns. One obvious measure that requires prompt implementation is a substantial liberalization of the low current ceiling on foreign assets (and its sub–ceiling on foreign variable–income assets), currently at 16% (8%). While this ceiling is still not binding for any individual pension fund, it will become so in the near future as AFPs continue their ongoing strategy of portfolio shifts toward foreign equity holdings.

Excessive restrictions on portfolio diversification and consumer choice. Contributors are currently forced to concentrate their pension savings in one account managed by the particular AFP of their choice – but AFPs tend to replicate each other's portfolio (see below). Therefore no significant portfolio differentiation is available to contributors. This lack of choice is particularly acute for those contributors that are close to retirement and therefore are more averse to bear return risk. [18] Addressing this problem faced by older workers, a reform project is considered by Congress that would offer contributors up to 10 years below retirement age and pensioners an option to open a second pension account (with the same AFP of their first account) specialized on fixed–income assets. However this would

[17] Recent studies on pension system problems and solutions include Gemines (1999), Iglesias (1999), and Superintendency of Pension Fund Administrators (1999).

[18] For instance, the number of people that retired under the AFP system declined by 6% in 1998 as compared to 1997, postponing retirement because of negative returns on their pension accounts.

not be enough for addressing different risk–return preferences within cohorts of younger workers. To address the latter need, more choice of different portfolios should be offered to all contributors, possibly a choice among 2 or 3 different pension funds offered by different AFPs. This also would allow AFPs to specialize in different types of portfolios.

Excessive switching of AFPs. Enticed by side payments from AFP sales agents instead of differences in risk–adjusted returns or services, contributors switch affiliation at an excessive rate. A number of 120,000 monthly changes in affiliation were recorded in 1997 – a figure that is disproportionately high in comparison to the average stock of ca. 3 million contributors in 1997. After the administrative changes adopted by the AFP Superintendency in November 1997 that were mentioned above, switching fell substantially to ca. 50,000 per month, al figure that is still high. The consequence of excessive switching is high marketing costs and excessively high commissions, as discussed in section 6.3.
One way to reduce excessive switching (and hence excessive marketing costs) further – other than imposing more severe administrative barriers that could reduce the industry's level of competition – is to introduce a new commission structure, discussed below.

Inefficient commission structure. The structure of commissions appears to be inefficient in two dimensions: the individual commission structure and non-differentiation of commissions among contributors.

The individual commission structure is biased toward the variable commission and against the fixed commission, in comparison to the cost structure of AFPs (Diamond and Valdés 1994). This has two implications: redistribution from higher to lower–income contributors and excessive marketing efforts by AFPs in capturing high–income contributors. It also does not seem efficient to rule out commission charges on outstanding balances (as done worldwide by private pension funds and mutual funds) because investment management costs are at last partly proportional to the size of the funds. However there are two problems in substituting variable commissions on outstanding pension savings balances for commissions on wages: pension savings balances of young contributors are low and a constant rate of variable commission charged on outstanding pension savings balances implies increasing contributions over active life. This tradeoff has inhibited a revision of the commission structure to date.

The current pension law forbids both charging different commissions to different contributors and collective negotiations of AFP commissions by groups of workers or their representatives (employers or unions). This legal restriction is costly. First it avoids reaping economies of scale in marketing and contracting costs. Second it leads to a rigid commission structure that cannot reflect cost differences among contributors. Third it leads to excessive contributor switching of AFPs as the latter are not able to induce consumer loyalty through permanence discounts. Finally it leads to higher commissions. Hence a reform that allows for a flexible commission structure is urgently required and is currently considered by Congress.

Rate–of–return guarantee. The floor guarantee on pension fund returns is perceived as a major cause of the excessive herding of AFPs regarding their investment strategies, leading to almost identical pension fund portfolios. Reduction of outright elimination of this guarantee (as in Peru's privately–managed FF pension pillar) would provide an incentive to AFPs to specialize better in investment strategies, therefore enhancing consumer choice.

AFP sharing in pension fund returns. The AFP's current participation in the investment risk of their portfolio choice is asymmetric and non–linear, ocurring on the negative side when their rate–of–return guarantee is called upon. When returns on their managed pension funds are high relative to a benchmark level, they have to be accumulated as excess reserves to complement their rate–of-return guarantee. This provides little direct incentive to improve AFP investment policies. A better way would be to allow for more extensive sharing of AFPs in the investment risk.

Ballooning costs of the government's minimum–pension guarantee. The government's minimum pension guarantee has both incentive and fiscal costs. Indeed, one problem of this guarantee is that it provides a potentially strong disincentive to voluntary saving, as discussed in section 6.1. On the fiscal side, according to a recent study (Gemines 1999), the cost of the minimum pension guarantee will balloon in the future. Solutions to address this dual incentive and fiscal problem comprise better targeting and means testing of the guarantee and/or gradually reducing the value of the government guaranteed minimum pension relative to the economy's average wage level.

Insufficient coverage. As discussed above, two thirds of Chilean employed were covered by the pension system in 1997, most of them by the new FF system. While this fraction is substantially higher than before the pension reform, this still leaves out one third of total employment, mostly comprised by dependent workers in the informal economy and independent workers and entrepreneurs. Many of them are poor and have little resources and face weak incentives for contributing to the formal pension system. The rigid commission structure does not allow to reflect possibly larger administrative costs of these groups. In addition many of the poorer non–contributors will be eligible to assistance pensions. Therefore for both equity and efficiency reasons a government incentive to AFP affiliation by independent and informal workers should be evaluated.

6.4 Conclusions

This paper has taken stock of the accomplishments and shortcomings of the Chilean pension revolution started in 1981. Its general conclusion is that radical substitution of a new pension system anchored on a dominant fully–funded and privately–managed second pillar – complemented by a limited distributive first pillar – is paying off. Capital and labor markets operate more efficiently. National saving, TFP growth, and aggregate growth have increased substantially and significantly. But the largely privately–managed and strictly regulated fully–funded pension system also shows some flaws regarding its microeconomic incentives and performance that were analyzed here. Addressing these shortcomings in the future would allow further improvements in the way the Chilean pension system provides old–age security to its population.

References

Arrau, P. (1991): La Reforma Previsional Chilena y su Financiamiento durante la Transición, *Colección Estudios CIEPLAN* 32: 5–44.

Arrau, P. and K. Schmidt–Hebbel (1993): Macroeconomic and Intergenerational Welfare Effects of a Transition from Pay–as–you–go to Fully Funded Pensions, *manuscript*, The World Bank, Washington, D.C.

Arrau, P. and K. Schmidt–Hebbel (1994): Pension Systems and Reforms: Country Experiences and Research Issues, *Revista de Análisis Económico* 9 (1): 3–20.

Auerbach, A. and L.J. Kotlikoff (1987): *Dynamic Fiscal Policy*. Cambridge University Press.

Corsetti, G. and K. Schmidt–Hebbel (1997): Pension Reform and Growth, in S. Valdés–Prieto (editor): *The Economics of Pensions: Principles, Policies, and International Experience*, Cambridge University Press.

Diamond, P. (1965): National Debt in a Neoclassical Growth Model, *American Economic Review* 55 (5): 1126–50.

Diamond, P. and S. Valdés–Prieto (1994): Social Security Reforms, in B. Bosworth, R. Dornbusch, and R. Labán (editors): *The Chilean Economy: Policy Lessons and Challenges*, The Brookings Institution.

Edwards, S. (1997): Chile: Radical Change Towards a Funded Pension System, *manuscript*, prepared for presentation at the Kiel Week Conference, June.

Feldstein, M. (1974): Social Security, Induced Retirement, and Aggregate Capital Accumulation, *Journal of Political Economy* 82: 905–26.

Feldstein, M. (1977): Social Security and Private Savings: International Evidence in an Extended Life–Cycle Model, in M. Feldstein and R. Inman (editors): *The Economics of Public Services,* Macmillan.

Feldstein, M. (1995): Social Security and Saving: New Time Series Evidence, *NBER Working Paper* 5054.

Feldstein, M. (1996): The Missing Piece in Policy Analysis: Social Security Reform, *American Economic Review* 86 (2): 1–14

Gemines Consultores (1999): AFPs: Evolución, Reesttructuración y Perspectivas, *manuscript*, Santiago, January.

Holzmann, R. (1997): On the Economic Benefits and Fiscal Requirements of Moving from Unfunded to Funded Pensions, *AICGS Research Report* 4, American Institute of Contemporary German Studies, The Johns Hopkins University.

Iglesias, A. (1999) La Reforma a las Pensiones, manuscript in progress, Santiago.

ILO (1996): *América Latina y el Caribe: Panorama Laboral '95*, No. 2.

Loayza, N. (1996): The Economics of the Informal Sector: A Simple Model and Some Empirical Evidence from Latin America, *manuscript, Policy Research Department*, The World Bank, Washington, DC, January.

Lora, E. (1997): Una Década de Reformas Estructurales en América Latina: Qué se ha Reformado y Cómo Medirlo, *manuscript*, Inter–American Development Bank, Washington, D.C., March.

Marshall, J. y K. Schmidt–Hebbel (1994): Chile: Fiscal Adjustment and Successful Performance, in W. Easterly, C.A. Rodriguez, and K. Schmidt–Hebbel (eds.): *Public Sector Deficits and Macroeconomic Performance*. Oxford University Press, Oxford.

PrimAmérica Consultores (1999): Sistema de AFP en Chile: Antecedentes Estadísticos, *manuscript*, Santiago.

Schmidt–Hebbel, K. (1998a): Does Pension Reform really spur Productivity, Saving, and Growth?, *Central Bank of Chile Working Papers* 33, March.

Schmidt–Hebbel, K. (1998b): Chile's Takeoff: Facts, Challenges, Lessons, *Central Bank of Chile Working Papers* 34, March.

Schmidt–Hebbel, K. (1997a): Pension reform, Informal Markets, and Long–Term Income and

Welfare, *EDI – The World Bank manuscript*, Washington, D.C., October.
Schmidt–Hebbel, K. (1997b): Fiscal and Macroeconomic Effects of Colombia's Pension Reform, *Revista de Análisis Económico* 12 (2): 37–71.
Superintendency of Pension Funds Administrators (1999): *The Chilean Pension System.* Superintendency of Pension Funds Administrators, Santiago, Third Edition.
Uthoff, A. (1994): Some Features of Current Pension System Reform in Latin America, *Revista de Análisis Económico* 9 (1): 211–35.
Van den Noord P, and R. Herd, R. (1994): Estimating Pension Liabilities: A Methodological Framework, *OECD Economic Studies* 23: 131–166.
Wallich, C. (1983): Savings Mobilization through Social Security: The Experience of Chile during 1916–1977, *World Bank Working Paper* 553, The World Bank, Washington, DC.
World Bank (1994): Averting the Old Age Crisis: Policies to Protect the Old and Promote Growth. Oxford University Press, Oxford.

Abbreviations

401(k)

Paragraph 401(k) of the US income–tax law regulates company pensions, by which an employer (on behalf of the employee) sets up an individual account and (partly) makes direct payments into it. 401(k)–plans are fixed–contribution plans (see DC), which in principle resemble IRA–accounts (see IRA). However, employers can arrange better terms with the financial market institutions than a single private employee could. Larger firms often offer the employee several different 401(k)–plans to choose from, smaller firms often provide only one plan.

AFP (Administradoras de Fondos de Pensiones)

The "Administradoras de Fondos de Pensiones" are the competing Chilean pension funds that administer and put into accounts all obligatory contributions paid through the new Chilean pension system. Although private, they are subject to strict regulatory supervision, stricter than, for example, the German capital–sum life insurance .

AHV/IV (Alters–, Hinterlassenen– und Invalidenversicherung)

Old–age and survivor´s insurance *(AHV),* which covers basic insurance in Switzerland. It is designed as a pay–as–you–go system and supplemented by disability insurance *(IV).*

BV (Berufliche Vorsorge)

Occupational provision in Switzerland, regulated in the Federal Law on the Occupational Provision (BVG). The BV expands the basic insurance of the old-age and survivor´s insurance *(AHV/IV)* into a pension that is more earnings-related. This second pillar of the Swiss pension system is funded.

COR (Contracted–Out Rebate)

The "Contracted–out Rebate" is the discount on the contributions to the "National Insurance" (see NI) of Great Britain. It is granted when an employee can prove that he has sufficient private or company pension and therefore need not rely on the state's second pillar. There is however, no opting–out of the first pillar, so that these NI contributions must be paid nonetheless. The rebate (approx. 4% of net income) also serves as an incentive to switch to a private pension.

DB (Defined Benefit)

A pension insurance with fixed benefits consists of a contract in which the insurer (often the employer, who himself has a backing insurance) guarantees a fixed benefit when an employee enters retirement. The insurer must take care that these benefits can be maintained through the use of reserves and, under certain circumstances, by raising the contribution. In the end, the insurer carries the risk of financing in the face of unexpected changes in the capital markets, demography and employment. The contrasting mechanism is the fixed contribution insurance (see DC), which does not pay a fixed benefit. Most traditional company pensions are defined–benefits plans.

DC (Defined Contribution)

Pension insurance with fixed contributions consist of a contract in which the insurer (for the most part, life insurance companies or pension funds) receives a fixed, usually monthly contribution. These payments are invested in the capital market and paid out to the insured after his entering retirement. The repayment further comprises interest and compound interest minus administrative costs and profit. In contrast to defined benefit plans (see DB), participants in defined contribution plans carry the capital market risk, i.e. the risk of a lower yield than expected.
Most investment instruments in the third pillar are defined contribution plans (e.g., the traditional endowment insurance). Defined contribution plans are also becoming increasingly popular in second pillar insurance agreements, e.g. the US 401(k)–plans. DB– and DC–plans may be combined, when certain minimum guarantees are given by the insurer.

GDP (Gross Domestic Product)

The value of all goods and services that are produced domestically within a year.

GRV (Gesetzliche Rentenversicherung)

The pay–as–you–go pension system in Germany. It is a mandatory system run by the state.

IRA (Individual Retirement Accounts)

Individual retirement accounts, which under US tax–law are subsidized in a similar manner to the German capital–sum life insurance. However, these tax advantages can be realized only if money is withdrawn after an appointed year in the saver´s life. The tax conditions have changed repeatedly; recently, "alternative" models of providing tax–incentives have been put in place ("frontloaded IRA", "backloaded Roth–IRA").

Keough

Equivalent of IRA–plans, but with more favorable tax conditions, targeted to those for whom no company pension is available, i.e. mainly the group of the self-employed.

NI (National Insurance)

The "National Insurance" in Great Britain completes the basic insurance and the earnings–related Second Pillar (see SERPS) as well as some other insurance benefits. All contributions to the state insurance benefits, less the "contracting out" residual rebate (see COR), are accounted by and paid to the NI.

PAYG (Pay As You Go)

A Pension System, in which all current contributions are used to pay all current benefits units. In its pure form there is no capital reserve at all.

PPP (Purchasing Power Parity)

Absolute sums of money are avoided as much as possible. Where necessary, contributions were calculated in Euros by means of purchasing power parity. See the conversion table for the exchange rate used.

SERPS (State Earnings Related Pension System)

The state Second Pillar of the British pension system, which pays the earnings-related pension, Participation in SERPS is not mandatory if a private or company pension provision of equivalent value can be demonstrated. (see COR)

SSI (Social Security Institution)

The entities in the former Chilean public pension system, which administered the PAYG system, now replaced by the AFP (compare there). The SSIs continue to pay out pensions that result from existing liabilities of the SSI system.

List of Contributors

Börsch-Supan, Axel
Professor, Department of Macroeconomics and Public Policy, University of Mannheim,
Director of the Institute of Economics and Statistics,
Member of the Council of Advisors to the German Ministry of Economics and Technology.
Schloß L 9,7, 68163 Mannheim, Germany
Tel.: 0049-621-181-1862 , Fax.: 0049-621-181-1863
E-mail: axel@econ.uni-mannheim.de

Bovenberg, A Lans
Professor, Department of Economics, Tilburg University.
Tilburg University, P.O. Box 90153, 5000 LE Tilburg, The Netherlands
Tel.: 0031-13-4662912 , Fax.: 0031-13-4663042
E-mail: a.l.bovenberg@kub.nl

Brombacher-Steiner, Maria Verena
Deputy at the Swiss Federal Ministry for Social Affairs
Effinger Str. 33, Ch – 3003 Bern, Swiss
Tel.: 0041-31-3229046 , Fax.: 0041-31-3223735
E-mail: verena.brombacher@bsv.ch

Disney, Richard
Professor, Department of Economics, University of Nottingham,
Board of the Scientific Directors of the Institute for Fiscal Policy in London,
Advisor of the Blair government for pension policy.
University Park, Nottingham, NG7 2RD, United Kingdom
Tel.: 0044-115-951-5619 , Fax.: 0044-115-951-4159
E-mail: richard.disney@nottingham.ac.uk

Meijdam, Lex
Professor, Department of Economics, Tilburg University.
Tilburg University, P.O. Box 90153, 5000 LE Tilburg, The Netherlands
Tel.: 0031-13-4662385 , Fax.: 0031-13-4663042
E-mail:a.c.meijdam@kub.nl

Miegel, Meinhard
Director of the Institute of Economics and Society in Bonn
Ahrstraße 45, 53175 Bonn, Germany
Tel.: 0049-228-372044 , Fax.: 0049-228-375869
E-mail: iwg.bonn@t-online.de

Schmidt-Hebbel, Klaus
Senior Research Economist at the National Bank of Chile
Augstinas 1180, Santiago, Chile
Tel.: 0056-2-670-2586 , Fax.: 0056-2-670-2853
E-mail: kschmidt@condor.bcentral.cl

Wise, A. David
Professor, Department of Economics at the J.F.Kennedy School of Government of Harvard University
Director of the Research Area "Health and Retirement" at the National Bureau of Economic Research.
10580 Massachusetts Avenue, Cambridge, MA 02138, USA
Tel.: 001-617-868-3900 , Fax.: 001-617-868-2742
E-Mail: dwise@nber.org